# Regulating
# Covert
# Action

# Regulating Covert Action

**Practices, Contexts, and Policies of Covert Coercion Abroad in International and American Law**

**W. Michael Reisman**
**James E. Baker**

**Yale University Press**
**New Haven and London**

Set in Times Roman and Eras type by Composing Room of Michigan. Printed in the United States of America by Vail-Ballou Press, Binghamton, New York.

Library of Congress Cataloging-in-Publication Data

Reisman, W. Michael (William Michael), 1939–
   Regulating covert action : practices, contexts, and policies of covert coercion abroad in international and American law / W. Michael Reisman, James E. Baker.
     p.  cm.
   Includes bibliographical references and index.
   ISBN 0-300-05059-3
   1. Duress (International law)  2. Reprisals.  3. Retorsion.  4. Aggression (International law)  5. Duress (Law)—United States.  6. Intelligence service—Law and legislation—United States.
I. Baker, James E., 1960– .  II. Title.
JX4486.R45  1992
341.5′8—dc20                                     91-24639
                                                              CIP

The paper in this book meets the guidelines for permanence and durability of the Committee on Production Guidelines for Book Longevity of the Council on Library Resources.

10      9      8      7      6      5      4      3      2      1

# Contents

# Acknowledgments

The U.S. Institute of Peace invited us to undertake this study and provided an honorarium for the initial paper from which this book then developed. The authors also benefitted from the many comments of the participants at the Institute of Peace conference. In addition, we are grateful for the comments of Mahnoush H. Arsanjani, Myres S. McDougal, Andrew R. Willard, H. Bradford Westerfield, James Nendza, Robert O. Kimball, William E. Odom, and William T. Cozean. Cheryl A. DeFilippo supervised the final preparation of the manuscript.

W. Michael Reisman was a fellow at the Institute of Advanced Study in Berlin in 1990 when much of the writing was done and is grateful to the institute and its library staff for the help extended. He delivered earlier versions of parts of this manuscript in lectures at the Free University of Berlin and the University of Würzburg. The library staff at the Yale Law School and the Seeley-Mudd Collection were also very helpful.

After substantive work on the manuscript was completed, James Baker joined the Legal Adviser's Office of the Department of State. The views expressed in this book are those of the authors and not necessarily those of the Department of State or Yale University.

Extracts from the following article have been adapted and incorporated in this work: W. Reisman, *No Man's Land: International Legal Regulation of Coercive Responses to Protracted and Low Level Conflict,* 11 Hous. J. Int'l L. 317 (Spring 1989).

# Introduction

The core of this work originated as a discussion paper presented at a meeting of the Institute of Peace concerned with low-intensity warfare. That particular meeting took place several days after reports of a mysterious (and some might say providential) fire at the chemical weapons plant in Rabta, Libya, and two weeks before the revelation of Iraqi nuclear activity. Subsequent reports suggested that Colonel Qaddafi himself may have staged the fire to deflect the growing international concern about the production of chemical weapons in Libya. Meanwhile President Saddam Hussein threatened in advance Iraqi retaliation for attacks on his various nuclear, biological, and chemical activities. All these events gave an acute and painful relevance to the subject, while showing how much of it is viewed through reflecting mirrors. After Iraq invaded Kuwait, it was reported in the U.S. media that President Bush had established as a goal the removal of Saddam Hussein from power.

We were anxious to undertake this assignment not because we like the idea of covert action—we do not—but because this moment in international politics presses scholars to rethink many assumptions that have crystallized over the past forty years. These assumptions may have begun to deform our perception of and appreciation for the potential of emerging trends and to undermine the formulation of responsible proposals for this new environment.

In the initial presentation as well as in this expanded version, we have not aspired to codify a general authoritative legal rule on the lawfulness or unlawfulness of the different covert uses of international politics' strategic modalities. The available data do not support such a single answer and our basic conception of decision making does not view the formulation of a rule, were it possible, as a solution to the intellectual, legal, and moral problems presented. Rather, the focus has been on an exposition of the authoritative international and national policies that have been expressed, the ways they have been applied in practice, the contexts of past decisions, and, not without a certain diffidence, a "guesstimate" of the likely configurations in the future in which covert actions of various sorts may be contemplated.

Jurists frequently present the law in a single statement. But this conflates what happened in the past, the reasons for it, what may happen in the future, and what the jurists may want. McDougal and Lasswell have described this particular pathology as a "normative ambiguity."[1] As far as material is available, our research has sought to distinguish among events that occurred in the past, the conditioning factors that accounted for them, our estimates of likely future behavior in comparable or different environments, and our conception of normative arrangements that might better serve the common interest.

Although fundamental policy decisions concerning many types of covert action are not always clear in international law, in the United States there has been a remarkably consistent national policy in favor of maintaining a competence to conduct a wide range of covert operations. To be sure, a number of political battles have been fought over particular covert actions, but, none of them involved an absolute congressional prohibition. Rather, some restrictions were introduced. The periodic crusades initiated by the media in the United States and conducted by Congress have resulted in a shift in authority over such actions to Congress rather than a proscription. The national debate has, thus, focused not on the lawfulness of covert action but on the constitutional allocation of competence to control it. This makes it all the more important to reconsider whether and to what extent a covert competence should be maintained.

The special research problems encountered in studying this subject are formidable. A few sensational fiascoes have been well publicized and some commentators have concluded from them that all covert actions are unnecessary or counterproductive or doomed to fail, though failure is often defined in quite different ways by different writers. Successful operations, some, perhaps, spectacularly so, may remain unknown. Other reports are incomplete or themselves infected by "disinformation." There is a large, almost "voyeuristic" literature on covert operations. Some of it provides some useful data; some is part of the genre of violence-pornography. We have not tried to emulate it nor to write either an exposé or a defense of covert action, but only to sample trends in order to test normative formulas, propose certain hypotheses, infer implications, and suggest some policy guidelines for the future.

Because the international law-making and law-applying process is quite different from its domestic counterparts and some readers may not have legal training, chapters 1 and 2 present some of the structural properties of the international legal system that we think pertinent to the discussion. Covert action is part of the more general theoretical problem in international law of the propriety of unilateral action. For jurists, this is probably the most difficult feature of international law, for since Hobbes and Bodin, most scholars have assumed that law requires the centralization of coercion. Unilateral action— covert or overt—generates particularly high emotions, because many view it as the litmus test of one's commitment to international law. We are committed to international law but recognize its current structural weaknesses and see proper and lawful unilateral action as contributive and supplementary to rather than destructive of international law. Current trends, reviewed in chapters 3 to 5, would appear to confirm that our view is shared, though, as one would imagine, there are wide differences of opinion about the proper circumstances for unilateral action. Readers with background in international law may wish to go directly to chapter 3.

If one takes the view that all coercive actions, overt or covert (or a fortiori covert) are unlawful, the only intellectual problem becomes a factual one: determining whether something was done. If one takes the view that nothing is prohibited, there are, similarly, no legal issues. But if one hypothesizes that in some circumstances, it may be appropriate to use some types of covert measures, then the questions of *what, when, why, by whom, against whom,* and *with what consequences* become urgent legal, moral, and practical issues. As we show, U.S. law, with its elaborate preparations for carrying out and overseeing some types of covert operations, is based on this last hypothesis, but though the legislative infrastructure is in place, the intellectual, moral, and legal systems have yet to deal explicitly with many of the difficult questions that arise. It is not hard to understand why. Like nuclear weapons, these measures are almost "unthinkable" and certainly unpalatable. Unlike nuclear weapons, however, covert actions have been and may well be used often. Hence legal consideration is all the more urgent.

But the very consideration of such action collides with the legal principle of equality. The United States legislative authorization for covert action hardly concedes a comparable license for other governments to engage in such operations. The U.S. program is premised on a special responsibility assigned to this country in world politics that permits or requires it to do things many others may not. The lack of mutuality may find some justification in functional theories of law or public order, but it is most difficult to accommodate with more conventional legal theories or Kantian notions of morality.

# Chapter 1

## The Problem: Its
## Conceptions and Contexts

Consider the following hypothetical situations:

1. Country X is conducting "low-intensity" operations against its neighbor Y with a view toward replacing the elected government in Y with a leadership sharing its own political views and programs or its tribal composition. The operations involve guerrilla training and support, weapons supplies, and the provision of base camps as well as a large-scale disinformation campaign. X publicly denies that it is involved and claims that even if it were, whatever it may be doing remains below the threshold of "armed attack"[1] and hence precludes Y or states whose assistance it may seek from acting against X. Y and other states are considering responding in kind, but covertly.

2. Intelligence indicates that Country X is developing a substantial chemical warfare[2] production facility. On the basis of intelligence, it appears that the weapons will be used against domestic opponents and against a proximate state with which X is in dispute over an oil-rich tract and may also be sold on the international market to gain needed foreign currency. The matter has been raised in the United Nations Security Council, but X has rejected the charges and appears to be continuing its development. As X has already been subjected to a variety of economic sanctions, no additional feasible measures appear likely to secure a change. Nearby states, with whom the United States is on friendly terms, resist an overt attack on X's facility, for fear that it will arouse violent anti-American protests within their own countries. But privately they

concede that they are deeply disturbed by the plant and its implications. The United States and its allies are considering an aerial attack designed to destroy the plant before it becomes operational. But others in the United States and among its allies are recommending a covert operation in which explosives will be supplied to opponents of the X regime operating within the country, together with instructions on how to go about destroying the plant.

3. The structure of the genome has been mapped and receptor points have been identified. Information from INTERPOL, confirmed by various national intelligence services, indicates that a terrorist group is designing genetic weapons that will target the genotype of particular ethnic groups. The terrorist group is operating in a state whose central authority is ineffective. Hence local authorities can neither be informed nor mobilized for action against the group. Groups within the North Atlantic Treaty Organization (NATO) are urging a covert operation to seize the group's research and neutralize its capacity.

4. The president of Y, nominally a democracy under an extended state of siege, announces that open presidential elections will be held in three weeks. This will be the first election under Y's new constitution. Opponents of the regime are disorganized and have limited resources to mount a campaign. This opposition requests financial assistance and technical campaign advice from the clandestine service of State A.

5. Country Z is on the verge of civil war. In response, President B declares martial law and suspends civil liberties consistent with his "constitutional authority." A group within the military, known as the "Young Reformers," decides to seize power. The reformers tell contacts that if successful they will restore order and hold free and general elections. They also note that the chief of the general staff will block any military violation of civil authority. Although the reformers have given assurances to the contrary, they will likely kill the chief of staff. Country A is asked to covertly fund the reformers, furnish limited intelligence, and provide arms to the reformers.

6. Through intercepts, confirmed by "soft" information provided by friendly embassies, the United States has come to believe that Country Y is providing haven for a number of terrorists. At the same time, the United States is trying to improve relations with the government of Y. Rather than release this information to the public and create resistance among domestic constituencies to improved relations with Y, the United States decides to present its information in a secret communication, in the hope of persuading Y to change its behavior in desired ways.

We have chosen this unconventional method for commencing discussion of international law and U.S. law and policy with regard to covert actions to make clear, at the very outset, that this particular modality of international politics is not, in our view, dismissible as an epiphenomenon of the Cold War. Nor can all covert action be taken as the implausible self-justifications of lunatics with irrepressible urges to wreak mayhem, the personality types who are frequently viewed as part and parcel, if not key causes, of the Cold War. Secret unilateral actions or secret phases of unilateral actions are very common. Some of these hypothetical situations, which set key problems in sharp relief, are vintage, some current and familiar, some projections. We believe that every thoughtful reader will find some of the arguments for covert action by the United States or an ally, if not initially persuasive, then at least disturbing in terms of the potential negative consequences of inaction or public action.

The first hypothetical example could be applied mutatis mutandis to Central America or Central Asia. It might also apply in the future to an unstable Eastern Europe. In all, the utility, if not the morality of some hypothetical covert operations seems, at least initially, plausible. Certainly, the prevention of what is commonly called "terrorism" presupposes covert phases of overt action as well as classically covert actions. Many other hypothetical situations might be generated regarding criminal justice investigations, for as crime becomes increasingly transnational, so too does its investigation and apprehension. When such activities cross a border, they frequently become "covert" in the international sense.

## REACTION AND PROACTION

These hypothetical examples should also make clear that covert action can be both reactive *and* proactive. In the recent past, the general focus on covert action has concerned itself with the proper reaction to the use by an adversary or its proxy of continuous low-intensity conflict. This sort of covert activity is usually depicted as something "they" (whoever the wicked incumbents of "they" may be at the time) practice against the United States and its friends (whoever they may be at the time). Hence, for the United States, whether its motives are moral or tactical, covert action is essentially viewed as a defensive problem. But the examples show that the international and domestic legal problems and moral quandaries of covert conflict may require both reactive and proactive resolution.

## U.S. POLICY

It is no secret that the United States has made legal and administrative provision for both modes of covert action and that a number of recent presidents have publicly reserved a national capability to effect them. At a press conference on September 16, 1974, President Ford was asked:

> Under what international law do we have a right to attempt to destabilize the constitutionally elected government of another country? And, does the Soviet Union have a similar right to destabilize the government of Canada, for example, or of the United States?

Ford replied:

> I'm not going to pass judgment on whether it's permitted or authorized under international law. It's a recognized fact that historically as well as presently, such actions are taken in the best interests of the countries involved.

Seymour J. Rubin, executive director of the American Society of International Law, wrote the president to request clarification of the remark. The president responded:

> I am sure you are right in your interpretation of my views about the relevance of international law. It is my intention that the Government of the United States shall observe international law, and endeavor to promote its strengthening in all areas to which it applies.[3]

Other presidents have made comparable statements. President Reagan said, "I do believe in the right of a country, when it believes that its interests are best served, to practice covert activity."[4] Still others, for example Jimmy Carter during the abortive hostage rescue mission, have kept their intentions covert, yet their deeds indicated that their policies were consistent with those expressed by their more open or indiscreet predecessors or successors. As we will see in chapter 6, the periodic criticisms mounted by Congress with regard to covert actions have never prohibited presidents from engaging in covert actions but have usually culminated in a transfer of more control from the executive branch to Congress in these matters.

Because the internal political systems of many allies and adversaries do not require or match the openness of our own, evidence of comparable legislative oversight is harder to come by, although such oversight probably does exist.[5] Even states that do not provide for legislative oversight and do not contemplate covert action may, if exigency requires it, use alternative procedures to authorize some form of external covert action. In this sense, extant national decisions by the United States and other governments have already made these matters potentially more than hypothetical. As a result, any study of the subject, if it is to be relevant to policy appraisal and formation, must, in our view, examine international and national law and policy questions relating to the contingencies and procedures for reacting to as well as proacting through the range of strategic modalities referred to by the words *covert action*.

Putting both sides of the matter on the agenda does not mean that both must be endorsed, or endorsed without qualification, as national capacities to be cultivated and possibly used in the future. Nor does it involve assuming the burden of defending the wisdom or morality of every covert action undertaken by governments the United States generally considers "good." The fact that there have been and will be some fiascoes or that there have been and will be some peripheral costs to covert actions is no more an argument against them than it would be to welfare programs, surgery, or government itself. Certainly, we would not wish the inclusion to be viewed per se as a tacit argument for the wide use of covert operations. On the other hand, keeping one or both sides of the matter off the scholarly and policy agenda does not mean that the problem has ceased to exist. Even if one should choose to opt out of these practices, others may not. Hence the question of international lawfulness continues to be relevant. The point we would make here is only that this dimension of our subject is not a period piece, quaint or otherwise, but, like its counterpart, a continuing policy and strategic problem for responsible decision makers.

The problem may be stated briefly. In many plausible constructs of the future in which there may be widespread agreement about the legitimacy of certain objectives and, often, about their lawfulness, the costs, in terms of lives, *matériel* and social and economic disruption, to the United States, to particular target states and to non-targeted third states might be substantially less if the modality of implementation selected were in whole or in part covert. Consider, for a moment, the costs of expelling General Noriega from Panama in October, 1989, by means of an internally-initiated but externally and covertly supported coup, as opposed to the destructive economic war of attrition with the same objectives that reduced much of Panama to economic rubble before the full-scale military invasion in December finished the job.

This is not, of itself, a justification for the covert use of coercion, in Panama or elsewhere, either as a factual or a legal matter. Factually, it is not certain that the removal of certain elites and a change of vocabulary would have brought about the structural changes which may have been sought (if they were sought) in Panama. Whatever the objectives may have been, conclusions about lawfulness, while taking account of costs and benefits of different strategies, are based on a much wider range of considerations and policies. Secrecy often has benefits for the agents of action, but it is a property of actions which has substantial political costs, particularly with regard to democratic principles of sharing participation in deciding on particular actions before the fact and in reviewing and ascribing responsibility, after the fact. And, as Beitz has observed, secret actions have an evil-seductivity: Things that would not be contemplated in sunlight may be planned and implemented in the shadows.[6]

### DIFFICULTIES OF APPRAISAL

In the popular mind, the term *covert warfare* evokes images of lonely assassins stalking a particular target or of commando groups of one government infiltrating the territory of another, conducting military operations, and then departing, all without the target government, other governments, or the public in the initiating state knowing their identity and provenance.

To people with very simple notions of law, it seems easy, even ineluctable, to condemn such operations under contemporary international law. In the past, it was not always easy to do so. In part, as we will see in chapter 3, legal clarity was lost in the post-1945 period by the general blurring of the traditional distinction in international law between war and peace. Psychologically and often factually, the Cold War was not quite either. If the Cold War is actually ending, quick condemnations may be easier. But even if the general tempera-ture of international politics warms, particular bilateral relationships may still amount to small-scale Cold Wars with varying regimes approximating the post–World War II ice age.

Quick condemnation may also become more difficult because of changes in the very criteria for appraisal of lawfulness. Even assuming that covert action is nothing more than armed secret agents creeping across borders, appraising the lawfulness of even these limited activities has become more complex because of the multiplicity of versions of contemporary international law, the evolution of a number of neo–just war doctrines, and the emergence of a rather ill-defined doctrine of so-called countermeasures.

Appraisals of lawfulness are also more difficult when the full scope of covert action is taken into account. For example, many of the phases that precede the overt use of military force are properly viewed as part of covert action; some of these phases may be accomplished and some must be accomplished in covert fashion. In this broader conception of the scope of the term, questions of the lawfulness of particular phases become knotty, even if other phases seem easy to judge.

The intergovernmental assumption implicit in the popular notion of covert action ignores the fact that much covert action is now directed against the private armies[7] of national and transnational gangs and other nongovernmental entities that use military force, sometimes with territorial bases, to accomplish their ends. Conceptions of the lawfulness of covert activities that are derived from doctrines prohibiting the use of force against the territorial integrity or political independence of states are essentially inapplicable to these types of covert operations. This does not mean, again, that a legal vacuum exists or that covert operations of this sort are per se lawful, but it does mean that criteria for appraising lawfulness cannot always be derived from the familiar international texts.

## SCOPE

It should already be clear that scholars and popular commentators define the scope of the terms *covert action, covert warfare,* and *secret warfare* differently. In the popular mind, warfare evokes images of "hot war," the application of high levels of coercion by specialists in violence, accompanied by large-scale death and destruction. From the perspective of the disengaged scholar, the popular image is only one part of a complex war system in which antagonists and members of various latent war communities routinely take account of the variable of power, which all expect to be a critical factor in decision outcomes. All seek to apply or neutralize it by preparation; weapons development; prepositioning; acquisition, mobilization, and retention of allies; and negotiation with adversaries on the basis of all of these factors. Insofar as there is a common reference to these factors, it is possible for parties to take account of the existing *rapport de force* and to accommodate differences without needing to resort to overt violence.

Every phase preceding the initiation of overt violence is critical to either avoiding the violence or determining the outcomes of the violent phase. Hence each phase is viewed as indispensable, whether the actor's objective is aggressive or conservative, that is, whether the actor is concerned with extending control over theretofore uncontrolled actors or resources or simply maintaining the arrangements that currently exist.

The application of the term *covert* to any of these phases often shifts, depending upon who is using the term and to which phase it applies. In some cases, neither the target nor third parties may be aware of the activity. For example, penetration of the weapons development or strategic planning processes of the adversary or acquisition of information about the forward location of anti-aircraft defenses is effective only if it is so covert that the adversary remains unaware of it. Such activities may determine the outcome of the phase of explicit violence, should it take place, and, hence, must be considered an element of covert action. Covert activities like these may be accomplished by recruiting ideologically or economically motivated volunteers. They may also be accomplished by imposing relatively high levels of coercion on particular individuals, perhaps by threats of violence against the person or his family or by forms of blackmail.

Coercion is not unique to the military. If it is understood as the purposive attenuation of the options of the target, it becomes a potential property of all

*Table 1*. Covert Activities: Examples by Strategy

---

*Military/Paramilitary*
Sensitive intelligence collection
   Communications intercept
   Satellite reconnaissance
   Physical search
Indirect action
   Advice
   Intelligence support
   Foreign military sales and grants
   Advice, passive (manuals)
   Advice, active (advisers and training)
   Psychological operations
   Aerial supply to private armies/insurgents
   Proxy invasion
Direct Action
   Hardware salvage and collection
   Physical reconnaissance
   Psychological operations/Disinformation
   Exfiltration
   Sanctuary
   Forcible extradition (fugitive seizure)
   Taking of hostages
   Interdiction, mining
   Terror bombing
   Assassination
   Raid
   Sabotage
   Invasion
*Economic*
Sensitive intelligence collection
   Communications intercept
   Satellite reconnaissance
   Theft
   Industrial espionage; of private parties and government entities, by "friendly" and
   "unfriendly" actors
False flag export circumvention
Covert ownership of assets
Disinformation
Information system penetration and destruction
Currency destabilization
Backchannel sanctions
*Ideological*
Open broadcast (white propaganda)
Unattributed (grey) propaganda
False flag (black) propaganda

---

*continued*

*Table 1.* Continued

---

Technical assistance (equipment and expertise)
Electronic countermeasures (jamming)
Disinformation
Subsidization of individual journalists and papers
Mind control
Interest group infiltration/penetration
Direct ownership and operation of foreign press
*Diplomatic/Political*
Overt intelligence collection
Sensitive intelligence collection
   Communications intercept
   Technical collection
   Break-ins
Indirect action
   Election projects
      Political advice and technical campaign assistance
      Financial subsidy to: press, reporters, parties, candidates, informants, labor
      unions, students
   Coups support
   Policy influence
      Blackmail and entrapment
      Economic and political threat
   Assassination
Direct action
   Advice
   Fund raising on foreign soil
   Secret diplomacy
   Interest group infiltration
   Backchannel policy direction
   Assassination

---

*Note:* This table presents some of the variety of covert activities engaged in by state and private actors. The perspective taken is that of the scholar and does not necessarily reflect the spectrum of U.S. covert activities past or present. Nor is inclusion in this table intended to suggest that a particular activity is necessarily a "covert" or "special" activity for the purpose of U.S. law. For example, although we have included intelligence collection, it is not per se considered a covert activity under U.S. law. In fact, the line between intelligence collection and covert action can get fuzzy in practice. As a former intelligence officer has pointed out, "If a case officer has recruited a minister in a foreign government, and the minister brings him information but also wants to talk about his ministerial duties, inviting the advice of the case officer, is it 'covert action' to give advice even if the purpose is only to string along the minister and make him a happy spy?"

instruments of policy: the economic, the ideological (mass communication to rank-and-file as a way of undermining elite control), the diplomatic (inter-elite), as well as the military. Coercive action through each of these modalities may be accomplished covertly (see Table 1).

### WHEN ARE ACTIVITIES COVERT?

The term *covert* is used, as we have seen, in many different ways and appears to resist a fixed meaning. It has become "normatively ambiguous" in the sense that it refers simultaneously to facts and, for those for whom the term is generally or totally negative, legal conclusions about facts. The factual property conveyed by the word *covert* is that the action is accomplished in ways unknown to some parties (not necessarily the targets). The normative conclusion conveyed by the word *covert* is that the action per se and the way it has been accomplished make it unlawful.

Normative ambiguities are pathological precisely because they short-circuit appraisal. Indeed, some covert usages appear normatively benign, even in structured democratic systems in which openness is a critical component of power sharing. For example, decisions by the Federal Reserve have enormous consequences on the political economy of the United States and other countries. The decisions are accomplished in great secrecy and some can be inferred only from post hoc effects. Comparable decisions may be made on the international level by all or some of the G-7 (United States, Canada, United Kingdom, France, Germany, Italy, and Japan). Decisions in democratic governments to devalue currency are also made in complete secrecy. These essentially "domestic" activities may have significant consequences for foreign governments. At least until the present, the fact that they are accomplished secretly has not appeared to violate international law.

From a scientific standpoint, it would be more precise to use a different term to designate various factual activities and perhaps to reserve the term *covert activity* for activities deemed to be unlawful. But there are also good reasons for retaining common meanings, if they are used with care. We propose to retain the terms *covert action* and *covert activities* but to use them only to designate events and not to determine their lawfulness.

### WHO'S FOOLING WHOM?

Some international activities are accomplished covertly, but they are known to both actor and target. In some cases, secrecy is used to conceal from a constituency plans that, once under way, will be irrevocable. In some instances, one or both of the governments are concerned to conceal these earlier activities. Hence they become covert by agreement. The provision of intelligence or of political or military advice may be suppressed, because the donor or the recipient (or both) feel that knowledge of its source could undermine its own base of power. The relation between the U.S. and the Saudi governments during the past several decades comes to mind. But the nature of the collaboration need not be defensive. Assume, purely hypothetically, that during the war between Iran and Iraq, the United States determined that its interests would be served by increasing the efficiency of the Iraqi air force. If it were to have sent advisers to Baghdad, where they would have provided target analysis and advice to Iraqi forces, it might well have served the purposes of both governments to make that operation as secret as possible.

### THE UTILITY OF SECRECY

It is clear that the property of secrecy is often necessary for the success of an operation or, at least, is a factor that can reduce substantially the costs of an operation, when projected costs become a major factor in a "go" or "no-go" decision. But critics of secrecy frequently note that nothing is really secret and that in most cases the target can get wind of what is being planned. In a sense, this is true, but it overlooks the fact that the major problem decision makers face is often not the unavailability of information but a surfeit of information of varying levels of accuracy, whose truth must be evaluated. There will be reports of many "covert" operations under planning. The problem is usually to identify which are real and, moreover, which are likely to result in action.[8] Secrecy and deniability increase the target's sense of uncertainty and make its ability to prepare for contingencies more difficult and costly. It thus theoretically improves the likelihood of a successful operation. In some circumstances, it also may increase the probability of the adversary's preemptive moves, if not preemptive strikes. The general expectation of covert action may have the potential of raising the probability of conflict.

### THE COSTS OF SECRECY

If secrecy may be viewed as a useful property in many circumstances, it also has disutilities. Wholly aside from the consequence of restricting rather than sharing power in these decisions, shielding certain plans from critical scrutiny may permit inherently defective operations to be set in motion. Sunlight, as Brandeis said, is "the best of disinfectants."[9] Publicity might have identified defects and either corrected them or led to aborting the project at an early term. In this respect secrecy, whether in democratic or authoritarian systems, has a potential for increasing operational dysfunctions.

In democratic societies, the operational utility of secrecy collides with the demands for power sharing. Even when secrecy is pursued for socially and legally valid reasons, a necessary consequence is to restrict the participatory options of all those who are denied knowledge of the activity. Despite this aspect of secrecy, democratic societies have adapted themselves to the need for secrecy, but have tried to establish certain normative limits that balance interests in efficiency with interests in power-sharing. United States efforts to find the right mix are considered in chapter 6.

In international politics and law, in which formal institutions still play a reduced role and most decisions are perforce taken unilaterally, the value of power-sharing does not appear to be given as much deference. Nevertheless secrecy may be viewed as unacceptable in circumstances in which, at the very least, law and policy require that advance notice be given to a potential target so that it still can, if it is so disposed, mend its behavior and avoid whatever deprivations have been planned. Considering that the real victims in most punitive actions are civilians who had no role in the offending behavior that precipitated the action, prior notification is particularly humane. With regard to enforceable countermeasures, which we will consider in more detail in chapter 5, it is widely assumed that such measures, if they are to be lawful, must be preceded by an appropriate warning to the putative target. The requirement would plainly undermine the case for an unqualified covert countermeasure.

## NONGOVERNMENTAL ACTORS

Changes in the structure of the international arena have greatly enhanced the ability of nongovernmental and nonterritorially based actors to use the military and, in some cases, other instruments of strategy transnationally in order to secure their objectives. Many of these activities are, by their nature, covert: assassination, sabotage, for example. Governmental responses, whether proactive or reactive, to these activities must often be covert. Operations against narcotics producers and traffickers and organized transnational criminal groups, for example, may be largely conducted covertly. Similarly, operations against independent terrorist groups must sometimes be covert. In circumstances where the nongovernmental target is operating within the territory of the state whose own government is ineffective, the success of an operation may preclude cooperation with the host government, if the latter has been infiltrated.

## CHANGES IN THE GLOBAL ARENA

Until the present time, the customary version of international law with regard to the use of force, including covert activities, has served the common interests of the major players in the international system. There can be little question that the essential structure of that system, established after the Second World War, is changing. Major international actors whose power had been severely reduced after the Second World War are in the process of reclaiming positions they enjoyed prior to that conflict. The last major empire to have survived the process of decolonization is now under severe stress and may be crumbling. Increasing attention and disposable foreign aid funds are being shifted, in the Western World, from the so-called Third World to Eastern Europe. At the same time, many latent conflicts within and between Eastern and Central European and Central Asian states that had been suppressed by the Soviet Union's imperial control appear to be reviving. The diversion of Western resources from the Third World to this arena may occasion more adventures in the Third World.

One future construct of the international system in the next several decades would foresee a very high expectation of conventional violence within and between small and mid-sized actors. Insofar as these conflicts threaten to change the power balance between the larger actors, either directly or by shifting control of resources and access to markets, one would expect a variety of political efforts, overt and covert, to influence outcomes in ways that would not discriminate against national interests. In short, the possibility of an emerging consensus between the superpowers about certain types of global arrangements need not preclude an understanding that will tolerate a significant amount of covert activity.

**Chapter 2**

# The Constitutive Process
# of International Law:
# Prescription and Application

By *law* we mean the expectations that politically relevant actors in a system share concerning what is the correct way of apportioning and using power, of producing and distributing particular desired values, and of shaping certain events, in particular circumstances. These expectations are "authoritative" in the sense of being deemed right by the actors and "controlling" because the actors who entertain them are themselves politically effective.

The term *law* as we use it, does not imply approval of the policies law expresses. The observer, from the critical perspective of the scholar, will often find that particular authoritative arrangements are inconsistent with his own views or those of one or more systems of morality. Indeed, the identification of certain policies as operative law may stimulate programs to change these policies. Some writers assign a high and unvarying positive valence to anything that is characterized as "legal," but we think it more accurate from a scholarly and jurisprudential perspective and more effective from a policy perspective to resist natural and transempirical notions of law and to conceive of law in terms of authoritative and controlling policies, without regard to whether we approve of those policies.

Law, so understood, does not spring full-blown from some part of the anatomy of some fictitious entity. Law is made and changed by human beings through complex political processes in which power and authority are used by many official and unofficial actors. In national systems marked by stability and institutional differentiation, a key part of the law of the community emerges from a legislature. Statute books become reliable indicators of what the law is. In contrast, the international political and legal system is marked by much lower stability and relatively little effective institutional differentiation. Identifying the law is a much more difficult problem.

Traditionally international law was said to be made by explicit agreement or by the customary practice of effective actors. This formula had the advantage of preventing those who would codify international law at any moment from straying too far from the expectations of effective elites. Its disadvantages included, first, the automatic assumption that whatever was in treaty form continued to be an expression of law or, at least, an expression of law with the same full intensity as at the time of its conclusion and, second, a certain imprecision in inferring customary expectations from complex and often contradictory flows of practice.

Traditional inquiry assumed that formal international actors would only use the forms and language of agreement when they intended to express policies they deemed to be authoritative and controlling. In the twentieth century, that assumption has continued, though the factual basis for it has ceased. For complex reasons, which we will consider later in this chapter, a large number of states, acting in international parliamentary settings, have routinely expressed aspirational norms or short-term political judgments, in the formal language of agreements. Indeed, a certain debased "legislativistic style"[1] has come to characterize much of international political communication. Nevertheless, many scholars have continued to deploy the traditional methodology to this vast and ever-growing body of communication. Hence they find more and more of what they characterize as "international law," even though significant parts of this international law do not correspond to the expectations of the politically relevant actors in the system. Simultaneously, the always imprecise methods of inferring custom from a flow of practice have become more difficult to apply, when the behavior of more than 160 actors, each composite and incorporating many other actors, and much of the behavior, either unrecorded or inaccessible, must be accounted for.

These complex developments have challenged international legal scholarship. Some scholars have refused to face it and have continued to invoke Article 38 of the Statute of the International Court of Justice as the template for international law.[2] But Article 38 is only a choice of law clause in an arbitration agreement, and its operational authority depends on the agreement of two states to submit a particular dispute to the court. Even if one took Article 38 as a general statement of the "sources" of international law, the question of whether, at the critical moment of decision, items listed in Article 38 are *still* expressive of the expectations of relevant actors remains.

Various alternative methods have been developed to assess and up-date current expectations of politically relevant actors in the international system, whether from particular incidents[3] or by inferring expectations through the application of a communications model.[4] Whatever method is used, we would submit that the international law with which we are concerned, as unclear as it may be in certain parts, can be understood, as can the reasons for its obfuscation, only by reference to the political and legal processes that have made it and the context in which it was shaped.

And, as we said earlier, whatever method is used, it is always important to distinguish between what has occurred in the past, the conditions that accounted for it, possible changes of conditions, and the range of possible decisions in the future. One should not assume, especially in periods of rapid change in the overall environment in which decisions are being made, that past decisions will be duplicated in the future.

### EFFORTS AT CONSTITUTIVE REVISIONS
### IN INTERNATIONAL LAWMAKING

In any group, at any level of social organization, one may discern a process of decision making that is concerned less with day-to-day choices and more with establishing and maintaining over time the fundamental institutions for making decisions. Sometimes, this process is expressed in a formal constitution and that document continues to approximate the way these decisions are and are expected to be taken. More often, however, there is no document or, if there is one, the process is more fluid than the text that purports to describe it and it can best be conceived of as an ongoing constitutive process.[5] In the international constitutive process, like processes of decision at all other levels, actors use the authority and the effective control at their disposal to shape institutions to meet their common interests. The constitutive process is neither an abnegation to power nor the transcendence by law over power, but an adaptation of the two.

The installation of the United Nations was accomplished by this constitutive process. Its formal structures confirmed and reinforced the existing power distribution. The Charter was designed to assign critical powers to the Security Council and to require the agreement of all of its permanent members if those critical powers were to be used. But it is no secret that the structural arrangements which the then elite nations had agreed upon and which the Charter sought to install in world politics were frustrated early in the history of the United Nations.

The elite agreement between the Soviet Union and the other permanent members ended shortly after the ink on the document was dry, if it ever really existed at all. Indeed, only in 1990, in response to the invasion of Kuwait was the Council used as the drafters seem to have intended. Slowly, initially at the initiative of the United States, and then, with the admission of many new states as members, at theirs, the General Assembly tried to assume a different and bolder role than the drafters of the Charter had planned for it. Increasingly, the Assembly got into the lawmaking business and, increasingly, many members of the Assembly began to take for granted that when a majority of the states of the world convened in a conference forum, what they said was, if not international law, then at least evidence of international law. After 1975, the International Court, for related political and constitutional reasons, tended to support that idea.[6]

The disintegration during the last forty years of all but the last of the European empires has been accompanied by the establishment of more than one hundred new states, most of which shared the common experience of colonialism and underdevelopment. A large number of the new states in the General Assembly who were relatively weaker than those in the then Soviet and Western blocs, but whose numerical majority, in certain organized structures, permitted them to put their own aspirations into law, sought to use international politics as a way of accelerating their own development and advancing their distinctive political goals.

Nor should it be surprising that this period was marked by greater heterogeneity in perception of the past and aspiration for the future and that this heterogeneity was reflected in almost all lawmaking activities. Different identifications, different demands for future production and distribution of all the things that people value and different expectations of past and future mean radically different and frequently contradictory appraisals of the lawfulness of contemporary events, particularly those involving conflicts. This has been nowhere more dramatically evident than in appraisals of the Arab-Israeli conflict, but it extends to virtually every one of the major international conflicts of the past decades.

All of these developments accelerated attempts to change, through ambitious international parliamentary programs, almost all the law regarding the techniques by which states influence each other, including ideological methods, the so-called new international information order;[7] economic methods, the so-called new international economic order;[8] military methods, most comprehensively in the 1977 Protocols Additional to the 1949 Geneva Conventions[9] and in a number of other multilateral conventions.[10]

Many Western states and, most prominently and vigorously, the United States opposed many of these efforts on substantive policy grounds and on the essentially international constitutive ground that international law could not be made in this fashion. As an empirical matter, that was not always the case. Lawmaking, as we have remarked, is a process of communication in which the mobilization of authority and control creates and sustains expectations about what types of behavior in what contingencies shall be deemed lawful or unlawful and what sanctions will be effectively applied. Some policies that Western states opposed did become law through this process.

But this was a period of constitutive transition in which the outcomes were far from certain. Because attitudes about fundamental constitutive decisions on lawmaking were divided, there was continuing controversy and confusion, adverted to in the previous chapter, concerning what key parts of contemporary international law were. For some important matters, two versions of the law existed, and international decisions resembled a camera taking double-exposures.[11] Insofar as this situation continues, it makes the performance of legal tasks task harder, but we submit that the disengaged scholar should be able to identify, though with varying degrees of certainty and sometimes at a rather high level of generality, what, if any, norms are required by effective actors for particular matters.

## CONSTITUTIVE CHANGES CONCERNING THE USE OF FORCE

Because the bloc of new states has been composed essentially of have-nots who are seeking to use law to bring about changes, it is not surprising that they have been more open to some uses of force to accelerate the achievement of what they have expressed as legal objectives. Thus, the general restraints on the use of force which have been expressed in constitutive documents since 1945 have often been effectively suspended when matters such as self-determination or decolonization were concerned. Indeed, as we will see in chapter 3, the language in a number of resolutions and conventions opens even broader exceptions.

These various changes have combined with an essentially unresolved innovative feature of the Charter. The Charter is simultaneously statist-oriented and oriented to policies that transcend state claims, such as human rights and, preeminently, self-determination. One consequence is that substantive international law, which was marked in the past largely by static and conserving norms, is now marked by an increasing demand for change. Indeed, it is replete with norms, prescribed within the institutional framework of and drawing authority from the United Nations, retroactively characterizing existing and formally legal situations as unlawful and pathological. Many of these norms are accompanied by general obligations to behave in ways likely to aid in their realization or they require continuing judgments about situations in terms of an international standard with an accompanying obligation to act to correct the situations if they depart from that standard.

The transformation of the Charter regime, the changing international military environment, the pressure arising from aspirational and appraisal norms, the tension between them and the static statist norms and, of course, the heterogeneity of views of political actors have all contributed to an anomalous situation. The international lawmaking process has responded and adapted to it. Although formal international law, dating from 1945, has established a norm prohibiting "the threat or use of force against the territorial integrity or political independence of any state," new corollaries have established a regime in which certain uses of force by certain groups for certain purposes have been characterized by some organs as legitimate, even though they involve uses of coercion against the territorial integrity or political independence of the targeted state.

Conversely, the coercive responses by those targeted states that might formerly have been considered lawful means of self-defense, may now be characterized by this particular lawmaking process as themselves unlawful uses of force. First, the aspirational or change norms that have been produced largely in United Nations organs and agencies are used to characterize some situations as unlawful. Second, United Nations organs other than the Security Council, using the Charter paradigm of "aggression–self-defense" as the criterion for lawful uses of force under the Charter, now decide to which contingencies this paradigm will apply. The matter is rendered even more difficult for scholars and practitioners by the fact that key states, which dispose of substantial power in the international system, continue to resist these changes and to insist upon an earlier version of international law that often yields diametrically opposed conclusions concerning the lawfulness of a given case.

The end of the Cold War may signal a revival of more traditional views and the termination of these various exceptions to the unilateral use of force. But, for the moment, the situation remains confused. For the legal scholar operating in this type of complex situation, it is important to distinguish the intellectual tasks being performed.[12] One of them is goal clarification: legal scholars are obliged to clarify what policies they believe will best serve the common interests of the international community. This intellectual task requires the examination of a variety of institutional alternatives in terms of their aggregate consequences for the maintenance of minimum order and the fulfillment of the other goals of the international community.

Scholars must also examine past decisions that conformed or deviated from those goals. Although the performance of the first task necessarily requires a subjective element, the task of trend description cannot be corrupted by the observer's prejudices. The scholar must also indicate which conditions accounted for past decisions and the likely course of future decisions. Here, again, it is important to suspend one's personal preferences, lest they distort the scholarly enterprise. The scholar is entitled to express appraisals in terms of his own preferences, but they must be clearly labeled as such, and when the scholar suggests alternatives for achieving a better approximation of certain preferences, he should indicate whether those preferences are his own or those of the larger community.

## MYTH SYSTEM AND OPERATIONAL CODE IN INTERNATIONAL LAW

Before commencing our examination of decision-making trends regarding the use of force in covert fashion, it is necessary to make two other methodological points. Non-lawyers generally assume that the solution to a legal "problem" is to find a formal provision, for example, Article 2(4) of the United Nations Charter[13] or Article 18 of the Charter of the Organization of American States[14] and simply apply it. That is a grossly over-simplified way of dealing with international law, for it is based on a misapprehension of the character of law and a misunderstanding of the function of the application of norms to concrete cases.

The first misapprehension concerns what constitutes law. In all legal systems, much of what is expressed in legal formulae and is attended by signals of authority is not intended to govern, regulate, or provide effective guidelines for official or private behavior. This part of the "legal system" conveys aspirations and images, not of the way things are, but of the way group members like to believe they are. This is particularly striking in the area of public law:

> The picture produced by control institutions does not correspond, point for point, with the actual flow of behavior of those institutions in the performance of their public function: indeed, there may be very great discrepancies between it and the actual way of doing things. The persistent discrepancies do not necessarily mean that there is no "law," that in those sectors "anything goes," for some of those discrepancies may conform to a different code. They may indicate an additional set of expectations and demands that are effectively, though often informally, sanctioned and that guide actors when they deal with "the real world." Hence we encounter two "relevant" normative systems: one that is supposed to apply, which continues to enjoy lip service among elites, and one that is actually applied. Neither should be confused with actual behavior, which may be discrepant from both.

A disengaged observer might call the norm system of the official picture the myth system of the group. Parts of it provide the appropriate code of conduct for most group members; for some, most of it is their normative guide. But there are enough discrepancies between this myth system and the way things are actually done by key official or effective actors to force the observer to apply another name for the unofficial but nonetheless effective guidelines for behavior in those discrepant sectors: the operational code. Bear in mind that the terms *myth system* and *operational code* are functional creations of the observer for describing the actual flow of official behavior or the official picture.[15]

The myth system is readily retrievable through conventional research in the formal repositories of law. The operational code, in contrast, must be sought in elite behavior.

Even if there is little divergence between myth system and operational code, the differing rates of decay of text and context may limit the usefulness of formal sources of law. The proverbial decrees of the Medes and the Persians still exist; the context in which they were created and in which they had legal relevance is gone. Whether a particular exercise of lawmaking seeks to stabilize or change a situation, if it is concerned not with ornamenting myth but with doing what it says it is doing, there must be a minimum congruence between the sociopolitical context prevailing at the time and the sociopolitical presumptions of the legislation. Once legislation is expressed in relatively enduring textual form, however, its rate of decay is minimal; the rate of decay of the encompassing sociopolitical situation will always be greater and may, indeed, be extremely rapid.

With regard to the international law of the use of force, discrepancies between myth and operational code are quite apparent. As in all law, the discrepancy derives from two incompatible drives: an unwillingness on the part of a community to yield key aspirations, however impracticable, that collides with the need to establish guidelines for the actual behavior that is anticipated.

A second misunderstanding concerns how law is applied. Many non-lawyers assume that application simply involves identifying a single norm or rule and applying it to a set of facts. This misapprehends legal methodology. Complex events usually engage many community policies and norms. The responsible decision maker necessarily takes account of all of them within certain limits. The need for the maintenance of minimum order operates as an unstated rider in every decision. The decision maker does not choose an option that is likely to shatter minimum order, a fortiori when the consequence may be nuclear war. Within those parameters, the decision maker seeks to fashion an authoritative response that achieves the best possible approximation of *all* the norms engaged.

## INTERNATIONAL LEGAL APPRAISAL METHODS

Notwithstanding changes in the constitutive process of the United Nations, most instruments of strategy in international law are not, as we will see in chapter 3, deemed to be per se lawful or unlawful. If they were, judgment tasks would be enormously simplified. Because they are not, determining criteria for the appraisal of lawfulness becomes much more complex. To be sure, some General Assembly resolutions, as we will see, do purport to make per se condemnations of particular uses of force. But such resolutions are not always or even often determinative of international law, although they may reflect the aspirations of certain elites and, sometimes, their expectations. International texts, and most importantly, the operational code as evidenced by practice and international incidents must also be consulted. All three may be in conflict.

At the moment of an event and usually on the basis of limited information, intrepid jurists frequently produce a legal "answer" or *responsum,* a type of unsolicited judgment, based on logical derivation from principles, sometimes a single principle, which the jurist determines to be guiding. Consideration of the purpose of the action being appraised and its consequences is deemed inadmissible. The principles on which such opinions are based usually derive from the textual world, whose incompleteness as a guide to the expectations of effective actors we have already commented upon. It is these opinions that often appear in the media as "authoritative" characterizations of the lawfulness or unlawfulness of the event. Would that law were that simple. Would that life were.

We believe that a more appropriate approach is based on what one might call a type of modern natural law in which the purposes, including the aggregate social consequences of the relevant policies expressed in law, are taken fully into account in fashioning a decision. Moreover, the currency of that legal formulation or institutional arrangement for achieving the common interests of the world community are also considered. In our view, this has been the essential character of the international legal process in the past. Accordingly, we submit that lawfulness is, and should continue to be, determined by contextual analysis: who is using a particular strategy, in what context, for what purpose, and in conformity with what international norm, with what authority, decided by what procedures, where and how, with what commensurance to the precipitating event, with what degree of discrimination in targeting, and with what effects as a sanction and what peripheral effects on general political, legal, and economic processes.[16]

**Chapter 3**


**International Legal Regulation
of Proactive Covert Operations**


**INTRODUCTION**

Overt and covert operations can be accomplished, as we observed earlier, using any of four basic strategic modes: military, economic, diplomatic, and ideological. Whether the mode in question is used coercively or persuasively, its objective is always to attenuate the range of choice of its target by raising the cost of resisting a certain designated behavior and thus increasing the likelihood that that behavior will be forthcoming. Any strategic mode may be used for expansive or conservative purposes, that is, either to expand one's range of power or control over other valued things or to preserve them against efforts by others to secure them.

Traditionally, international decisions seem to have taken account of these two purposes but international scholarship since 1945 has not focused on this consequential (and, in our view, more important) aspect of the strategic modes. Rather, scholarship has, with a few notable exceptions, concentrated on the contingencies for the initiation of the use of force, that is, without regard for the actual objectives sought and the likely consequences. In this approach, the critical question with regard to the lawfulness of a use of force is deemed to be whether the user is reacting to another actor's internationally wrongful use of force. In order to engage the issue, we will explore that question in this chapter, but we must, in light of the method we proposed in the preceding chapter, also appraise lawfulness in terms of the aggregate consequences of the actions that have been undertaken.

In terms of the full range of strategies, it will be apparent that some modalities of proactive covert as well as overt coercion operate with a high degree of "active" toleration or, often, without effective regulation. Leaving aside questions of implementability, international norms governing the ideological instrument, for example, are still largely incipient, and regulation of economic coercion remains, whether for affirmative policy reasons or the lack of feasible alternatives, largely permissive. Although regulated by international texts and normative practice, diplomacy that engages covertly in activities deemed incompatible with the diplomatic mode still benefits from severe limitations on authorized international response.

In sharp contrast, the military modality (the direct or surrogate use of military coercion) is more complex. Here, as we will see, the distinction between the usually textual myth system and the operational code has become more pronounced and, accordingly, procedures and criteria for assessing lawfulness and unlawfulness more controversial. Since 1945, the Charter's collective security regime has remained largely stillborn. In its place, operational norms have perforce emerged that, not surprisingly, diverge in many details from the myth system. This trend is marked by the emergence of an interesting but potentially mischievous doctrine of neo-just war and intervention, which has been driven by expansion of membership and efforts at securing constitutive changes in the United Nations itself. This operational code, however, is not oblivious to formal law. It reflects, in some of its parts, basic substantive policies of the Charter, if not all of its black letter textual aspirations. It departs most dramatically from it with regard to procedures.

The operational code, which can be inferred from a flow of decisions, suggests that uses of military force in certain contingencies, most dramatically those relating to efforts that are internationally characterized as legitimate self-determination, may be tolerated and in some cases internationally endorsed and supported. There may be other categories of events for which permissive uses of force are, in certain circumstances, tolerated. The net effect is that what is arguably textually prohibited by the Charter may well be tolerated and even supported in practice in certain circumstances.

After examining the contingencies under which overt uses of coercion may be deemed internationally lawful, this chapter will consider under what circumstances, if any, states may be permitted to use coercion proactively *and covertly*. In that regard, it will be necessary to consider whether the property of secrecy, by itself, has a negative international legal valence, in the sense that otherwise lawful activities are rendered unlawful if they are accomplished covertly, or whether the property of secrecy has no independent legal valence and is subordinated to the lawfulness or unlawfulness of the act it characterizes. There may not be a single answer to these questions. Trends in the first three modalities are, as we will see, little distinguished from those relating to overt use, a conclusion that prompts us to suggest that, in the future, they should be. Trends with regard to covert military coercion are more difficult to set into a coherent pattern and to codify in normative terms. Formal legal texts provide scant guidance, but a review of selected incidents suggests some contours of contemporary attitudes regarding proactive military and paramilitary covert operations.

## MODALITIES OF COERCION

### The Economic Instrument

Empirical studies of practice with regard to the economic instrument are available, but scholarly efforts at identifying fundamental policies in this area are, with few exceptions, quite unsatisfactory.[1] Trends in international decisions governing the use of economic coercion suggest that the regime is by and large permissive. Some United Nations declarations speak of limiting economic coercion, but the law-making effect of these resolutions, in the formal terms of the United Nations Charter and as tested by a more empirically sensitive analysis of practice, would appear to be low. Moreover, the language of some of the resolutions prohibits only grave forms of coercion without indicating where and how minor economic coercion becomes grave. As for the lesser forms, one scholar has observed, "Such influences could only be fully excluded, if states of disparate economic strength would avoid all economic contacts."[2]

Charter Article 2(4)'s prohibition on the use of force does not include economic coercion. The legislative history indicates that this was not an oversight.[3] There is no analogue Charter article admonishing members to refrain from the threat or use of economic deprivation or the use of bribery. Certain resolutions, discussed below, do condemn economic coercion in general terms, but few specific instances of coercion are condemned and then only when a particular act of economic coercion is perceived as an issue between developed and less developed nations.[4]

At least one form of economic coercion, sanctions, is explicitly endorsed in Article 41 but only, of course, when called for by the Security Council. Even when employed unilaterally or regionally, some sanctions are tolerated, or endorsed, by the United Nations.[5] The Charter of the Organization of American

States, in contrast, explicitly prohibits economic coercion.[6] But that provision would appear to have fallen into desuetude.

The operational code of the political use of economic indulgence and deprivation appears no less permissive. In contemporary world politics, rewards such as most-favored-nation status, loans, credits, and foreign aid are regularly withheld or employed to coerce state elites to modulate their behavior in designated ways. Covert techniques of economic coercion, like bribery, also appear to be widely used. Some intelligence services appear to have considered payments to agents a rather mundane routine of intelligence collection and not per se covert operations, but from our perspective this is surely a common type of covert operation.[7] Many intelligence officers apparently believe that it is "cost-effective," asserting that an agent on payroll is more reliable (and more subject to control) than an ideologically motivated agent. There is no international prohibition of such forms of bribery, although nation-states may formally prohibit their officials from taking bribes and sanction internally the acceptance of bribes.

*Quod licet Jovi non licet bovi:* The gods can do things prohibited ordinary mortals. International prescriptions and operational norms are increasingly less tolerant of *private* or nongovernmental bribery. The General Assembly position on corporate bribery is set down in Resolution 3514 (XXX) (1975), which, among other things, condemns "all corrupt practices, including bribery, by transnational and other corporations" and calls upon member states to take measures against such practices. In 1977, the United States Congress passed the Foreign Corrupt Practices Act.[8] The issue in these various initiatives seems to be on the order of "who can bribe whom" rather than the lawfulness of bribery per se. There is no indication that governments and their intelligence agencies have refrained from or reduced the technique of covertly providing private payments to foreign officials for defections from public duties. When individuals who have engaged in this practice are apprehended, they may be punished at the national level, but there is no evidence that the practice itself is viewed as a violation of international law.[9]

Deprivatory techniques classically called retorsions[10] and including such measures as selective tariffs, asset freezing, embargoes, boycotts, restrictions on arms sales, expropriation, and dumping are also commonplace. Nor, as the 1973 embargo by the Organization of Petroleum Exporting Countries (OPEC) illustrates,[11] are these methods of economic coercion an exclusive modality of Western or powerful socialist states.

A number of international efforts, largely stillborn, have been mounted to restrict the unilateral use of the economic instrument.[12] A number of scholars have also targeted this practice as incompatible with minimum if not preferred world order.[13] But the opinions of scholars who have seriously studied this subject are not uniform. Some of the more thoughtful works either despair of the possibility of restriction, given the inherently competitive nature of the international market, or doubt that legal restrictions are even desirable. In Professor Seidl-Hohenveldern's opinion, for example, any further attempt to restrict economic force could even be counterproductive. "The relative freedom in the recourse to the use of economic force" diminishes the incentive of more powerful states to resolve issues with military force and "thus acts as a safety valve."[14]

There is at best only an inchoate consensus that the most extreme cases of state economic coercion are illicit. This is far from satisfactory for world public order, for, given the asymmetrical distribution of economic power, strong states may coerce smaller states and undermine their political economies without suffering even the most minimal legal condemnation.

Speaking speculatively, as we must in this area, we would surmise that where the particular unilateral economic strategy raises costs as a means of securing desired behavior, it would be viewed as lawful. Where it would seriously undermine a political economy or, if practiced widely, disrupt the international economic system, it would, like other undiscriminating strategies that injure unrelated parties, probably be viewed as unlawful. Put in different terms, the permissiveness with regard to the economic strategy may not mean that every potential use of the instrument is lawful nor that what may be accomplished overtly may, at the discretion of the actor contemplating the strategy, also be done covertly. As an example of the first proposition, we would suppose that the counterfeiting of another state's currency and the infiltration of bogus bills into the international market would be characterized by most effective actors as unlawful. We would propose, with less certainty, that the dissemination of disinformation about the quality or safety of important products of a target state or the conditions for tourists there as a way of undermining its economy, would also be viewed as unlawful. Both of these examples would presumably be accomplished in covert fashion to increase their effectiveness.

On the other hand, the proactive external movement of funds or the infiltration of funds into a country to improve its market situation as a way of influencing elections, which would again be accomplished covertly, would not appear to be considered unlawful, even though it represents a clear intervention into national electoral processes and has, on occasion, been protested. Such electoral processes have come to be one of the fundamental techniques for assessing international political legitimacy. Thus in terms of preferred policy, the relatively permissive operational code of this strategy may be seriously inconsistent with fundamental policies necessary for an acceptable world order.[15]

Nor is it certain that the property of secrecy in these types of strategic uses has no independent negative normative valence and that whatever economic strategy may be accomplished overtly may also be accomplished covertly. An overt use of the economic strategy is communicative rather than simply destructive. It sends a message to the target government that it has the option of changing certain behaviors in order to have the deprivation terminated. A covert use of the same strategy sends no message, as the target cannot know who the agent of the deprivation is or why or what action might be taken to secure its termination. Indeed, if the deprivation is sufficiently covert, the target may not even know why parts of its economy are failing. In addition, an overt use of the economic strategy is, by its very openness, available for international appraisal and, if appropriate, condemnation. A covert use of the same strategy is not.

These observations are preliminary and perforce speculative. Their only purpose is to suggest that the apparent permissiveness of the use of the economic instrument may be subject to more authoritative expectations than has been appreciated and that the assumption that what is permitted overtly may also be done covertly should be carefully scrutinized. Plainly, this is an area in which custom and operational code are not always congruent with the needs of world order. Practicable alternatives are not easy to come by, yet the need for alternatives is clear. As the international economic system becomes more interdependent, the possibilities of larger states using techniques of economic coercion covertly against smaller states abound and could make a mockery of many other formal norms. In Central Europe, for example, it is quite likely that, in the future, the Bundesbank could notify its Polish counterpart that unless Poland complies with certain German political policies, loans might not be rolled over. Since one such refusal to roll over could trigger many others, a weaker and dependent economy might find itself effectively obliged in an increasing number of cases to comply with the wishes of a stronger economy. Because activities such as these could be conducted covertly and both parties might find common though differently motivated reasons for maintaining secrecy, there could be no appraisal by the international community. In general, the question of coercive use of economic measures, whether overt or covert, requires urgent reconsideration.

### The Ideological Instrument

Conventional international law governing ideological measures—communication to an audience broader than specific elite groups—is in an incipient stage.[16] Although a number of international agreements, for example, restrict or prohibit the use of ideological means for "hostile" purposes, these provisions are frequently ignored by state elites as well as private actors.

The 1936 Convention concerning the Use of Broadcasting in the Cause of Peace prohibits the use of broadcasting to "incite the population of any territory to acts incompatible with the internal order or the security of a . . . contracting party . . . and the use of broadcasting as an incitement to war."[17] It is difficult to find in this agreement and in subsequent custom and practice an indication of more general principles of international law. In contrast, the Genocide Convention's prohibition against "Direct and public incitement to commit genocide" is an accepted principle of international law and, reservations and understandings notwithstanding, few would question the universality of the crime of genocide.[18] Moreover, the Nuremberg trials, and in particular the conviction of Julius Streicher, stand for the proposition that "incitement to murder and extermination" is a crime against humanity.[19] But the background of Nuremberg was the condemnation of aggressive war; the Military Tribunal found eleven defendants guilty of Crimes against peace, namely "planning, preparation, initiation or waging of a war of aggression, or a war in violation of international treaties, agreements or assurances, or participation in a common plan or conspiracy for the accomplishment of any of the foregoing." Disseminating Nazi ideology and propaganda alone was not used to convict on Counts I or II in the absence of evidence that the propaganda was linked to a plan of aggression or that a particular defendant had knowledge and influence over subsequent acts of aggression.[20]

The United Nations Charter makes no express mention of ideological strategy and propaganda.[21] However, the U.N. community has, on a number of occasions, expressed a norm on this subject. General Assembly Resolution 110(II) (1947) "condemns all forms of propaganda . . . which is either designed or likely to provoke or encourage any threat to the peace, breach of the peace, or act of aggression."[22] The Resolution's prescription, however, is nebulous, reflecting the tension at the time between the Communist states' desire to regulate communications with political implications and the liberal democratic Western states' preference for freedom of information.[23] Additional General Assembly resolutions have sought to define and characterize "warmongering" and "hostile propaganda" as unlawful,[24] but the prescriptive effects of these efforts are uncertain. The International Covenant on Civil and Political Rights[25] and the Draft Convention on Freedom of Information[26] state that all persons should be free to receive and impart information across state boundaries, but both documents permit the imposition of restrictions "for the protection of national security or of public order, or of public health or morals."[27]

Efforts by the United Nations Economic, Scientific and Cultural Organization (UNESCO) to draft a world information order collided with two political issues: first, fundamental differences in political outlook between centralized totalitarian governments and a Western view of freedom of expression, with that expression to be processed by a largely unregulated private media industry; and, second, divisions between developed and developing countries. The fundamental difference between free and totalitarian societies is the democratic conviction that truth is a public and evolving process, in which all should have full opportunity to participate. Totalitarian systems share the notion that information is a resource exclusively available to elites to shape public attitudes and that control may be accomplished by the generous use of Plato's "noble lie." The concern of developing countries for equitable access to the information order is expressed in Article 9 of UNESCO Resolution 3/3.1/2 (1978),[28] which calls on the international community to create "a free flow and wider and more balanced dissemination of information." Article 6 calls for a correction in "the inequalities in the flow of information to and from developing countries," while Article 2 recognizes that "the mass media throughout the world, . . . contribute to promoting human rights, in particular by giving expression to oppressed peoples . . . unable to make their voices heard within their own territories."

Many of the existing documents regarding the ideological instrument deal with methods of communication and elite control rather than content. General Assembly Resolution 37/92 addresses the "Principles governing the Use by States of Artificial Earth Satellites for International Direct Television Broadcasting."[29] Paragraph 13, for example, provides that "A State which intends to establish or authorize the establishment of an international direct television broadcasting satellite service shall without delay notify the . . . receiving State . . . and shall promptly enter into consultation with any of those States which so requests."Like preceding efforts to regulate the ideological instrument, the Resolution attempts to balance freedom of information, regulation of propaganda and forum access. Thus, activities in the field are to be carried out in a manner compatible with "the principle of non-intervention, as well as . . . the right of everyone to seek, receive and impart information and ideas as enshrined in the United Nations instruments," and "access to the technology . . . should be available to all states without discrimination on terms mutually agreed by all concerned." The Resolution also calls for the peaceful resolution of disputes. Regardless of the Resolution's prescriptive authority, which is doubtful, states still appear likely as a practical matter, to continue to resort to the readily available unilateral remedies of direct jamming and reciprocity in response to broadcast interference.[30]

The International Telecommunication Convention is the basic instrument of the International Telecommunication Union (ITU).[31] The purpose of the union is "to maintain and extend international cooperation between all Members of the Union for the improvement and rational use of telecommunication," promote technical assistance to developing countries, and "harmonize the actions of nations in attainment of those ends." Towards this end, the Convention's principal concern is allocating the radio frequency spectrum through the ITU regime. The Convention, however, also seeks to regulate use of radio waves for hostile purposes by private parties or harmful interference with the radio services of other members. Thus, "Members . . . reserve the right to cut off any other private telecommunications which may appear dangerous to the security of the State . . . " (Art. 19), and "all stations, whatever their purpose, must be established and operated in such a manner as not to cause harmful interference to the radio services or communications of other Members . . . " (Art. 35). But "Members retain their entire freedom with regard to military radio installations . . . " which "must, so far as possible, . . . observe statutory provisions relative to . . . the measures to be taken to prevent harmful interference," and the Administrative Regulations regarding the types of emission. Moreover, the majority of signatories reserved the right to take what they deem to be necessary measures in the event of noncompliance by another member.

The European Agreement for the Prevention of Broadcasts Transmitted from Stations Outside National Territories[32] seeks to address, on a regional basis, some of the loopholes in the ITU's first convention. Thus Article 2 of the agreement requires members to make punishable acts of collaboration involving the provision of transport, maintenance, and supplies to parties who illegally broadcast from floating or airborne stations outside the national territories of members or which cause harmful interference with radiocommunication service operating under the authority of a contracting party.

Similarly the 1982 United Nations Convention on the Law of the Sea[33] goes beyond the 1958 Law of the Sea Conventions in addressing broadcasting from the high seas. Article 109 would provide that all states cooperate in the suppression of "unauthorized broadcasting" and authorizes the prosecution of any person engaged in such broadcasting by, among others, "any State where the transmissions can be received." Article 109 defines "unauthorized broadcasting" as "the transmission of sound radio or television broadcasts from a ship or installation on the high seas intended for reception by the general public contrary to international regulations, but excluding the transmission of distress calls." Presumably, this definition includes private or state broadcasting on frequencies allocated by the ITU to other nations, but the Convention does not clarify what other broadcasts are contrary to "international regulations." The Charter of the Organization of American States indicates an awareness of the intervention potential of hostile propaganda, but it does not generalize this concern. Its prescriptions may have fallen into desuetude in the region.

In general, these agreements touch only tangentially some of the primary uses of the ideological instrument in the later twentieth century. Nor do they appear to have diminished enthusiasm for use of the ideological instrument as a form of covert or overt coercion or simply a conduit of information, the travails of the *Goddess of Democracy* notwithstanding.[34] A recent listing of clandestine African radio stations only begins to suggest the proliferation of broadcast capability among private actors.[35]

A major international use of the ideological instrument in covert fashion is disinformation, which has been defined as "the dissemination of false and provocative information."[36] The classic techniques of disinformation are forgery and the duping or purchase of foreign media assets, but disinformation may also involve physical acts committed for their psychological effect. Terrorism, whether by governmental or nongovernmental actors, essentially employs this technique. Military efforts at disinformation, which are included in United States doctrine under psychological operations (psyops) and by the Soviets as *maskirovka*,[37] aim to mislead foreign services concerning actual strengths and equipment capabilities in peacetime, and to mask strategic or tactical intent during war. During armed conflict, "misinformation," as it is known in Protocol I, is expressly permitted as a "ruse of war."[38] A separate legal regime, however, governs peacetime use of disinformation.

The KGB has a department dedicated to *Dezinformatsiya* whose activities have provoked substantial study.[39] But this is not a Soviet monopoly. Disinformation is employed by many state and intrastate actors.[40] Gross examples of disinformation abound and, when exposed, are widely condemned,[41] but it is not always easy, in many "grayer" cases, to differentiate disinformation from promotion, "spin control," or the suppression of some information, whose unavailability gives an entirely different face to what is accessible. The United States statutory definition of "political propaganda" would seem to reach virtually all forms of political communication.[42] The Convention on the International Right of Correction, although expressing a desire for the free flow of information and opinion, provides signatories a theoretical right to submit corrections in cases where

> . . . a Contracting State contends that a news dispatch capable of injuring its relations with other States or its national prestige or dignity transmitted from one country to another . . . and published or disseminated abroad is false or distorted.[43]

No major powers or media consumers, however, are signatories and "[i]n actual practice," the MacBride Commission concluded, "the system does not operate."[44]

We would surmise that most actors and political observers would view the grosser forms of covert ideological action as unlawful. Indeed, one incidental reason for their covert use is to protect the communicator from condemnation. As in many of the other strategies, however, the only sanctions for abuse appear to be found in those controls provided by the implications of reciprocity and threats of retaliation that are at the basis of all law.

Many of the trends with regard to this instrument of strategy have been profoundly affected by the Cold War. With its cessation, the larger pattern of tolerance may be reduced. Article 109 of the Convention on the Law of the Sea would appear an initial step in this direction. It is not clear that cessation of the Cold War will increase and intensify condemnation of the use of covert propaganda in bilateral conflicts. Plainly, however, this area urgently requires better law.

### The Diplomatic Instrument

Diplomacy is concerned with the communications between the elites of nation-states, international organizations, and peoples. The number of participants in this process is increasing. Heads of state and ministers no longer exclusively influence the outcome of elite diplomacy. Private, corporate, and international nongovernmental actors play a large and increasingly visible role.

International documents express a preference for inclusive and open diplomacy. Thus, Article 102(1) of the U.N. Charter states: "Every treaty and every international agreement entered into by any Member of the United Nations . . . shall as soon as possible be registered with the Secretariat and published by it." Parties not in compliance with 102(1) may not invoke the treaty or agreement before any organ of the United Nations. The effect of this provision, however, was substantially tempered by the International Court,[45] which has allowed agreements that were not registered to be relied upon.

In practice, the operational code of interelite communication involves a significant degree of covert action. Elites seek to "communicate" with each other in modes not addressed or anticipated in the essentially treaty conception of the Charter provision or, for example, the Vienna Convention on Diplomatic Relations.[46] Envoys are sent secretly to negotiate between nation-states. There is reason to believe that some treaties and agreements are secret or contain secret addenda. Agreements whose records are then made confidential or classified accomplish the same end.

Another form of covert coercion at the interelite level involves covert extradition. In this practice, one government effectively extradites a person to another either in the absence of an extradition agreement, or against its own law. Covert extradition involves the use of coercion against an individual by two governments, with a commensurate deprivation in the rights of the individual in both states. When conducted as a unilateral state policy, covert extradition is, in effect, covert abduction.

Elites of nation-states maintain contacts with both governing elites and opposition parties, groups, or individuals and may without themselves resorting to direct methods of coercion, encourage these actors to pursue extraconstitutional political change, sometimes by promises of rapid recognition followed by subsequent support. Such practices may violate textual norms of nonintervention in the internal affairs of other nations,[47] but as discussed later, such interventions in support of coups or other extraconstitutional changes may sometimes promote the broader policy objectives of the Charter. "Diplomatic" interventions have been both internationally condemned and endorsed, depending apparently on purposes and other contextual factors. More often, they receive neither international sanction nor condemnation.

The use of coercion against diplomats is prohibited both by customary practice and treaties codifying diplomatic and consular immunity. Diplomatic immunity applies in varying degree to persons, papers, personal property, facilities, communications, and movements. Historically, the doctrine of diplomatic immunity was grounded on a combination of three theories: personal representation, extraterritoriality, and functional necessity.[48] Today general diplomatic immunity is based on treaty as well as customary practice, and not on the fiction of extraterritoriality.

The principal textual source for the practice of diplomatic immunity is the Vienna Convention on Diplomatic Relations. Article 29 provides that "The person of the diplomatic agent shall be inviolable. He shall not be liable to any form of arrest or detention. The receiving State shall treat him with due respect and shall take all appropriate steps to prevent any attack on his person, freedom or dignity."[49]

The Vienna Convention on Consular Relations[50] applies comparable principles to consular posts. The Convention on the Prevention and Punishment of Crimes against Internationally Protected Persons, Including Diplomatic Agents[51] also explicitly prohibits acts of coercion against diplomats *and* heads of state, foreign ministers, and any representative of a state or international organization of an intergovernmental character entitled under international law to special protection, whenever such a person is in a foreign state.[52] In addition, states have signed bilateral agreements extending the customary and Vienna Convention–based rights of diplomatic immunity.[53] Immunities of members of international organizations are theoretically different from diplomatic immunity. In practice, however, many of the immunities are similar.[54]

International practice has not always lived up to the textual promises of the Vienna Convention or of the customary law of diplomatic immunity from coercion. There are numerous notorious examples of violation.[55] But given the uniformity and often universality of condemnation, the violations have, apparently, not eroded the rule. As recent events in Panama and Kuwait illustrate, even during armed conflict the norm is recognized to a degree.[56] As a result, embassies continue to be used for the purposes of political sanctuary, most recently in China, Eastern Europe, and Latin America where the tradition of political asylum has been particularly strong. Moreover, states have taken strong measures in response to violations of the norms prohibiting the use of coercion against diplomats, relying primarily on the implications of reciprocity and retaliation. International institutions, most notably the International Court, have also upheld the principle of diplomatic immunity.[57] The United Nations General Assembly includes the question of diplomatic security on its annual list of agenda items.

Violations of security of host states *by* diplomats have also been a form of covert diplomatic action. Diplomacy is frequently used to "cover," with the immunities available to it, activities that are not quite diplomatic, that is, concerned with exchanges between the authorized official elites of the sending and receiving states. The fact that many of these activities are ordinarily monitored, but not terminated, suggests the existence of a usage permitting them reciprocally. On the other hand, uses of the facilities of diplomacy to smuggle arms or drugs, to cite some obvious examples, appear to provoke stronger reactions.[58] The response available to the host state is prescribed and restricted by international convention.[59]

Unquestionably, the major pattern of coercive use of the diplomatic instrument is set at the superpower level. With the current changes in world politics, a new perception of common interest may lead to a break from these past trends and reduce the tolerance for coercive uses of diplomacy.

### The Military Instrument—Use of Force

Nowhere has the divide between textual myth system and aspirational norms, on the one hand, and operational code, on the other, been more apparent and significant for world order than in the continuing international effort to regulate the unilateral use of the military instrument. Within five years of the creation of the United Nations, a pattern was established according to which certain unilateral violations of U.N. Charter Article 2(4) might be condemned but to all intents and purposes validated, with the violator enjoying the benefits of its delict. A legal gray area extended between the black letter of the Charter and the bloody reality of world politics. Although the general Charter prohibition against unilateral action continued, and organs of the United Nations frequently condemned such action, often nothing could be or was done beyond such verbal condemnation. In a number of significant cases, the party subject to the condemnation was permitted to continue to benefit from the fruits of its illegal action. Moreover, as membership increased and the balance of states in the General Assembly shifted, new contingencies for the use of force and intervention emerged. These contingencies did not just tolerate certain unilateral uses of force but raised them to the level of a lawful duty.

Until this century, the unilateral use of force in international politics was lawful. As late as 1945, Charles Cheney Hyde, of Columbia University, could write "it always lies within the power of a State . . . to gain political or other advantage over another, not merely by the employment of force, but also by direct recourse to war."[60] States could use force, from reprisals to covert operations through to full war, as of right. After the rise of democratic polities and the development of mass industrial war, it might have become politically useful, particularly for purposes of internal mobilization, to develop doctrines legitimating particular uses of force but such justifications were unnecessary as an international legal matter.

Many recognized this as a morally unsatisfactory regime. From the middle of the nineteenth century, one tracks many efforts, official and nonofficial, to temper and restrict the theretofore unlimited contingencies for the lawful unilateral initiation of force. But even the more far-reaching of these efforts did not amount to an absolute bar on the use of force.[61]

These efforts were dramatically unsuccessful and not for want of diligence and intelligence. Law is perforce a system of authorized coercion, and it can neither be conceived of nor operate without a supportive political system coordinated with a power process. Without a central authority and an effective monopoly over the use of force to maintain community order and values, individual actors must look to their own resources. Moralizers might seek to prohibit a *jus ad bellum* but those responsible for security and their constituents could be expected to resist the prohibition until they were assured that someone else was able and willing to shoulder their task.

This structural problem was addressed directly in the League of Nations and, more boldly and explicitly, in the Charter of the United Nations. The United Nations Charter provided a centralized system in which unauthorized uses of force by any state were dealt with by the Security Council which was to have, under the Charter conception, access to the military assets necessary to restore peace. The language of the Charter was quite conservative: the contingencies to which the Security Council was to react, "threat to the peace, breach of the peace, or act of aggression," were all coercive efforts to change the status quo and all were presumptively unlawful.

With a centralized system, like that conceived in the Charter, there was no longer any need for unilateral resort to force by self-help. Hence the prescription of Article 2(4) of the Charter was not only morally elevated but politically feasible and responsible: "All members shall refrain in their international relations from the threat or use of force against the territorial integrity or political independence of any state, or in any other manner inconsistent with the purposes of the United Nations." Some might be inclined to assume that in terms of outcomes, there should have been no difference between Charter law and customary law, for rights which states would formerly have had to protect on their own by force under customary law would now be protected by the Security Council under the Charter. If the Charter worked, customary rights to resort to coercion would not only have been rendered unlawful; they would have been rendered superfluous.

The Charter regime may be compared with customary international law at the time. Even after the prohibition of aggression, customary law allowed the use of force, for self-defense, of course, as well as for "self-help," the protection and realization of other international rights. Charter law, in contrast, prohibited the unilateral use of force for any reason other than for self-defense and that right depended, not on a prior unlawful act or even a concrete territorial incursion, but on a prior "armed attack." Armed attack, in this system, became a technical concept that the U.N. apparatus would have to illuminate.

Article 2(4) may have prohibited states from unilaterally deciding when to use force; but it did not prohibit the United Nations from prescribing how force could be used, whether for self-defense or for any other purpose. The point of emphasis is that a uniquely structured organization, composed of a Security Council and a General Assembly, with an intricate and changing relationship between the two, now claimed the authentic and final competence to interpret the words in the Charter.

In short, the Charter and the creation of the United Nations established a new set of words about when and how military force could be used and endowed a new set of institutions with the competence to interpret and apply those words. And there were ample opportunities to do just that, for Article 2(4) of the Charter notwithstanding, the question of the use of force continued to present itself.

The General Assembly's Resolution 2625 on Friendly Relations in 1970 provided that

> [e]very State has a duty to refrain from organizing or encouraging the organization of irregular force or armed bands, including mercenaries, for incursion into the territory of another State. . . . Every State has the duty to refrain from organizing, instigating, assisting or participating in acts of civil strife or terrorist acts in another State or

acquiescing in organized activities within its territory directed towards the commission of such acts, when the acts referred to in the present paragraph involve a threat or use of force.

But, interestingly, only four years later, the Assembly in its Declaration on Strengthening International Security[62] made clear that the blanket prohibition on coercion might cease to operate when it infringed on the rights of peoples "to determine their own destinies." Indeed, Resolution 2625 authorized and mandated support for coercion directed at "self-determination and freedom and independence." In 1981, the Declaration on the Inadmissibility of Intervention and Interference in the Internal Affairs of States again exempted self-determination cases.[63]

Both the Charter, its reformulations by the Assembly and customary conceptions of international law with regard to the use of the military instrument rested on a set of inherited assumptions about how military conflict is conducted: conflict is territorial, between organized communities, conducted by certain types of specialists in violence or "regular forces," who are clearly identified. They concentrate their efforts against each other in a war zone, defined by something called the forward edge of the battle area and a rear area. The conflict itself is preceded by formal notification, suspended by some formal arrangement, and terminated in an explicit and often ceremonialized fashion.

Changes in military technology and political dynamics made many of the key assumptions underlying the basic rules about when and how to use force obsolete. On the one hand, the nuclear balance reduced the profitability and, to some extent, the likelihood of conventional warfare between the two major antagonists, but it did not reduce the conflict itself. Instead, a variety of nonconventional methods were developed or refined, some conducted by proxies, with careful concealment of the identity and activities of the principal. Many of these methods were associated with the independence or changed governments of the new states and underwent a mythicization. Developments in communications and transportation enhanced the possibilities of infiltration and subversion, of protracted low-level conflict by well-supplied proxies, of pre-programmed "popular" uprisings, followed by "invitations" from local inhabitants and so on. International politics includes many nonstate categories of actors, many of whom increasingly seek to use nonconventional methods of coercion as a way of achieving their political objectives. The ease of communications, the relative miniaturization of weapons of increasing destructiveness and refinements in methods of pursuing general objectives of mass terror have permitted many groups, some with aspirations to become states, others with anarchist or nihilist objectives, to become involved in military activity.

## SOME AUTHORITATIVE AND CONTROVERSIAL EXCEPTIONS

As these changes in the military and technological environment occurred, the smaller states, through the United Nations and other international parliamentary arenas, sought to change the international law of force to make it better reflect their values and objectives. Some of the resulting new "rules" were never more than aspirations. Others were successful legislative exercises and more closely approximated an operational code. In particular cases, the outcome of the application of all of them turned, as one would expect, on contextual factors. A few examples will suffice to demonstrate the point.

### Self-Determination

Consider first the General Assembly's Declaration on the Principles of International Law concerning Friendly Relations (1970), a document that the United States supported and that has frequently been presented by states and, on occasion, by the International Court of Justice as a codification of contemporary international law. The Declaration provides in pertinent part:

> By virtue of the principle of equal rights and self-determination of peoples enshrined in the Charter of the United Nations, all peoples have the right freely to determine, without external interference, their political status and to pursue their economic, social and cultural development, and every State has the duty to respect this right in accordance with the provisions of the Charter.

The operational implications of this right are spelled out three paragraphs later.

> Every state has the duty to refrain from any forcible action which deprives peoples . . . of their right to self-determination and freedom and independence. *In their actions against and resistance to such forcible action in pursuit of the exercise of self-determination, such peoples are entitled to seek and to receive support in accordance with the purposes and principles of the Charter* (italics supplied).

Note here the beginning of an attempt at inverting customary law. "Peoples" have the right to "self-determination" and "freedom and independence." The state against which these groups are struggling must refrain from any action that impedes the struggle, that is, it must refrain from actions that could otherwise be characterized as self-defense. Third states are obliged to help the struggling groups, but cannot be held legally responsible by the targeted state.

This "inversion" is not limited to a few historical atavisms. Although decolonization may have had a historically specific reference for some drafters and been limited to Portuguese territories and the apartheid government in South Africa, terms such as "self-determination" and, even more, "freedom and independence" are open ended and can be applied to any group to which a majority of the General Assembly wishes to apply it. In a classic definition of law in the legal realist perspective, Justice Holmes said that law is nothing more pretentious than the prediction of what a court will in fact do.[64] If you wished to know which groups would be deemed in the future to be struggling for their "freedom and independence" and, hence, to be the beneficiaries of the new regime, the current General Assembly became a better indicator than legislative history.

The Convention against the Taking of Hostages of 1979[65] even more explicitly sets out the implications of the inversion. Article 1(1) defines the offense prohibited by the Convention as follows:

> Any person who seizes or detains and threatens to kill, to injure or to continue to detain another person (hereinafter referred to as the "hostage") in order to compel a third party, namely a State, an international intergovernmental organization, a natural or juridical person or a group of persons, to do or abstain from doing any act as an explicit or implicit condition for the release of the hostage commits the offense of taking of hostages ("hostage taking") within the meaning of this Convention.

But Article 12 of the same Convention provides in pertinent part:

> . . . the present Convention shall not apply to an act of hostage-taking committed in the course of armed conflict as defined in the Geneva Conventions of 1949 and the Protocols thereto, including armed conflicts mentioned in Article 1, paragraph 4, of Additional Protocol I of 1977, in which peoples are fighting against colonial domination and alien occupation and against racist regimes in the exercise of their right of self-determination, as enshrined in the Charter of the United Nations and the Declaration of Principles of International Law concerning Friendly Relations and Cooperation among States in accordance with the Charter of the United Nations.

We cite these instruments to make clear that a conception of international law as it relates to the use of the military instrument was emerging from the institutions of formal international law making over a period of time. That conception was straying quite far from customary international law. Indeed, a type of *just war* was being created.

A parallel development can be found with regard to the way the new just wars were to be fought: the law of armed conflict or *jus in bello*. Two Protocols additional to the Geneva Conventions, in particular Protocol I,[66] besides introducing new norms of humanitarian conduct for medical assistance and the identification of the missing in action, challenged conventional views regarding the norms to govern the conduct of insurgent conflict. Protocol I seeks to internationalize "armed conflicts in which peoples are fighting . . . in the exercise of their right of self-determination" (Article 1(4)) thus facilitating fulfillment of the obligation of states to provide assistance to such peoples embodied in G.A. Res. 2526 (Friendly Relations). Contemporaneous statements by delegates confirm this intention. In addition, Articles 43 and 44 relax the customary and Geneva-based requirements that combatants wear a fixed distinctive sign and carry their arms openly in order to obtain combatant status, developments that favor the irregular soldier, often identified with wars of national liberation.[67] The distinction between camouflage and the feigning of noncombatant status, however, remains ambiguous under this emerging law of armed conflict. This tension is captured in Article 37 of the Protocol which permits "ruses of war" but prohibits "perfidy," leaving it unclear which acts qualify as one or the other.[68] At this point one can only surmise which of the initiatives of Protocol I will be endorsed by customary practice as law.

### Brezhnev and Reagan Doctrines

Outside the United Nations structure, some states began to justify unilateral intervention on the grounds of unilaterally characterized claims of self-determination, even if those claims had not received international organizational endorsement, that is, by the Committee of Twenty-Four.[69] The Brezhnev and Reagan doctrines contain both defensive prescriptions relating to self-described critical defense zones *and* self-styled self-determination, national liberation or freedom fighter corollaries. "Genuine revolutionaries," the Brezhnev Doctrine went, "as internationalists, cannot fail to support progressive forces in all countries in their just struggle for national and social liberation."[70] Mutatis mutandis, the United States perspective, expressed by President Reagan's Freedom Fighter Corollary has a parallel structure. In a speech on March 1, 1985, Reagan said, "Freedom movements arise and assert themselves. They're doing so on almost every continent populated by man—in the hills of Afghanistan, in Angola, in Kampuchea, in Central America. . . . They are our brothers, these freedom fighters, and we owe them our help."[71] The Reagan administration, however, was not the first to hear the call and provide different forms of covert support to selected insurgencies against existing governments. The Truman, Eisenhower, Kennedy, Johnson, Nixon, Ford, Carter, and Bush administrations have, at times, been similarly engaged.[72]

Mikhail Gorbachev has denounced the Brezhnev Doctrine. The United States, to date, has not renounced the Reagan Doctrine. It would, however, appear that with the end of the Cold War neither of the erstwhile superpowers will continue to engage in this particular type of action under an open and flaunted "doctrine." Nevertheless, one notes patterns of intervention continuing under explicit or implicit regional equivalents of Brezhnev doctrines: for example, China in Cambodia and Israel in Lebanon. International tolerance for these particular assertions is uncertain.

### Humanitarian Intervention

With the paralysis of the United Nations security system, other *proactive* contingencies outside the scope of self-determination legitimizing the use of unilateral coercion emerged and reemerged. Thus humanitarian intervention, replacement of an elite in another state, uses of the military within spheres of influence and critical defense zones, and treaty obligations have all been cited, since 1945, as authorizing proactive military interventions.

At least since Grotius, in theory, and the Greek insurrection of 1827, in practice, international decision making has uneasily recognized a right of one state to intervene in another state in response to violations of human rights that "shock the conscience of mankind." Although the technique is necessarily the same as the forceful implementation of the doctrine of diplomatic protection of nationals, under the doctrine of humanitarian intervention the intervenor need not have a direct link to the persons who are the object of the protective action.

The validity of the doctrine, however, has been questioned by some legal scholars in light of Article 2(4)'s prohibition on the unilateral use of force and postwar practice.[73] But a significant group of scholars continues to support its validity.[74]

Some support for the doctrine may be found in the U.N. Charter itself, which creates an incipient form of action for human rights deprivations. Article 55 of the Charter reaffirms that the United Nations shall promote "Universal respect for, and observance of, human rights and fundamental freedoms for all." Article 56 transforms that commitment into an active obligation for joint and separate action in defense of human rights. "All Members pledge themselves to take joint and separate action in cooperation with the Organization for the achievement of the purposes set forth in Article 55."

Moreover, the Preamble of the Charter includes a commitment "to ensure, by the acceptance of principles and the institution of methods, that armed force shall not be used, save in common interest."

Finally, insofar as human rights deprivations giving cause to humanitarian intervention constitute a "threat to the peace" or "breach of the peace" or "act of aggression," the Security Council, under Chapter VII of the Charter, is seized with jurisdiction. Should the Council be unable to function, the secondary competence of the General Assembly, under the Uniting for Peace Resolution,[75] arguably becomes operative. Under its terms, the Assembly may execute duties and arrogate powers comparable to those of the Council, insofar as its action is consistent with the major purposes and principles of the United Nations.[76]

As with other norms expressed by competing Charter language, to ascertain the doctrine's validity, one must look to practice, community expectations, and the overall policies behind the Charter and not confine oneself exclusively to strict textual analysis. The continuing validity of the basic policies underlying humanitarian intervention is reiterated in the operational articles of the Charter and the Genocide Convention. The cumulative effect of the Charter on customary humanitarian intervention is to create a coordinate responsibility for the active protection of human rights: members may act jointly with the Organization in what might be termed a newly organized, explicitly conventional, humanitarian intervention or singly or collectively in the customary international law of humanitarian intervention.

Humanitarian intervention is a malleable doctrine and plainly susceptible to abuse. Mere invocation of the name of the doctrine does not automatically sanctify a use of force. Each case must still pass international and legal scrutiny by demonstrating that the circumstances were so exigent as to displace the countervailing norms of nonintervention and state sovereignty. In our view, the doctrine continues to reflect community expectations, provided it is invoked in exigent circumstances and for humanitarian purposes and is not used as a veil for occupation, as proved to be the case in Vietnam's invasion of Cambodia.[77] International relief efforts to aid the Kurds in northern Iraq confirm this trend.

### Critical Defense Zones

The Soviet Union, throughout the Cold War, and the United States, for more than a century, have claimed exclusive prerogatives to "protect" designated geographic perimeters, or critical defense zones.[78] Although often identified as the Brezhnev and Reagan doctrines, these defensive claims are historical in nature and have been exercised under other rubrics. In the future, short of a major change in the structure of international politics, they will likely be exercised under still other rubrics, though the geographic scope may change.

The doctrines purport to be rooted in the right of self-defense, but the two nations also claim a right to take proactive measures in support of these claims and have done so. Soviet military and diplomatic interventions in Hungary, Czechoslovakia, East Germany, and Poland, for example, even when not explicitly founded on a defensive zone rational, appear to have been based on such thinking. A comparable United States claim is witnessed in the frequent intervention by military force in the 1920s in Latin America and during the Cold War, in Guatemala (1954), Cuba (1961), the Dominican Republic (1965), Nicaragua (1980s), Grenada (1983), and later in Panama (1989–90).

Both doctrines are based in part on security and allegedly defensive strategic considerations. Each expresses the view that the approach by an adversary into its own buffer areas would pose an unacceptable security risk, a risk so great that it would require the threatened state to resort to an anticipatory action that would be unlawful in other circumstances, and in particular, had it been taken by other actors. Both are premised on military and strategic theories that may be obsolete.

There are significant differences between the U.S. and Soviet formulas. All of the unilateral American doctrines considered up to now are territorially specific: they relate to the Western hemisphere, as they have done since the Monroe Doctrine. Exercises beyond that hemisphere, for example, Korea and Vietnam, had treaty bases, unequivocal invitations from governments, and a measure of multilateral if not international support. (Note, however, that the Carter Doctrine shifted to the Persian Gulf as did the so-called Reagan Corollary.)[79] The Brezhnev doctrine, in contrast, managed to convey a certain regional redolence, but in fact it was drafted in terms of a potential worldwide jurisdiction: any state that became a member of the so-called socialist commonwealth came permanently under the Brezhnev doctrine.

These claimed zones can be deemed lawful only in so far as they can be related directly and plausibly to superpower defense and the avoidance of nuclear war. Thus, the exclusion of an adversary's influence may be justified in terms of the maintenance of world order, but the aggressive realignments of unaffiliated states and interventions in the internal public order of states within critical defense zones could not be thus justified.

The operational code suggests a remarkable degree of tolerance for certain applications of the Brezhnev and Reagan doctrines even when their practice violates this norm. The United States and the majority of members of the United Nations essentially accommodated themselves to all cases of Soviet "defensive" intervention, except Afghanistan, although there was considerable protest regarding Soviet covert complicity in the declaration of martial law in Poland. The analysis, however, is more difficult when the critical defense zone claim is linked to other norms.

Note, for example, the merging of two doctrines of intervention in Secretary Baker's signal to the Soviet Union in the wake of the overthrow of the Ceausescu regime in Romania. Asked whether the United States would approve if the Soviet Union sent troops to support prodemocracy forces in Rumania, Baker responded: "They are attempting to put off the yoke of a very, very oppressive and repressive dictatorship. So I think that we would be inclined probably to follow the example of France, who today has said that if the Warsaw Pact felt it necessary to intervene on behalf of the opposition, that it would support that action. . . ."[80]

Israel has made a corollary tactical claim to a defensive zone in Lebanon and with regard to the proximity of Jordanian antiaircraft batteries to the Israeli border. Absent the overarching rationale of preventing nuclear war, these Israeli claims are less justifiable under the operational international norm, especially when they entail the occupation of alien territory, and they have been widely condemned. Jordan and the larger international community, however, have seemed tolerant of the Israeli position in southern Lebanon, in contrast to their response to the 1982 invasion of Lebanon, where tolerance quickly tapered off after Israel advanced beyond a border zone deep into Lebanon.[81]

Whether the tolerance for critical defense zones will continue as the threat of nuclear war decreases is open to question. Clearly this attenuation of the competence of smaller communities has been tolerated because avoiding nuclear war at all costs was viewed as a matter of the most urgent common interest. With the reduction of that threat, there may be a parallel reduction in the tolerance for this particular form of extension of national power abroad.

## APPLICATIONS TO COVERT ACTIONS

International law, as we have seen, tolerates degrees of coercion short of military force in the diplomatic, economic, and ideological modalities. Nor has there been, in operational terms, an absolute prohibition on the use of force or intervention. That is not to say that "everything is permitted," that is, all proactive uses of force are lawful or effectively unregulated. It is to say that the operational code in these matters is discrepant in key ways from textual law and the myth system and that determinations of lawfulness in particular cases must, in our view, use a more comprehensive, consequentialist, and policy-sensitive approach consistent with the method proposed in chapter 2.

Do these same distinctions also apply directly or mutatis mutandis to covert operations? That is, if a state is lawfully permitted to engage in force overtly, let us say to remove tyrannical rulers such as Idi Amin, Jean Claude Bokassa, the Khmer Rouge, Ferdinand Marcos, or Manuel Noriega, may it, with the same objective, go about the matter covertly?

Analysis of specific incidents of "exposed" covert operations is, of course, an indispensable part of any cogent test of international expectations. The research problems here are formidable. Available information may be disinformation and possibilities for cross-checking are limited. The unavailability of information is, itself, subject to more than one interpretation.[82] Public condemnations may conceal private approval and, in some circumstances, covert support. Within the confines of our subject, it is impossible to undertake a comprehensive trend study. Below are factual reports on eight incidents on which information was available; five are illustrations of political intervention, tracing, in chronological order, international reaction regarding coups; the sixth, an abortive "rescue" mission, did not excite international condemnation, suggesting that factors such as objective, alternative, and consequence are weighed into international appraisals of the lawfulness of covert actions. The two other incidents, one involving an act of sabotage against a nonstate actor, the other the international kidnapping of a war criminal, suggest interesting normative limits to permissible covert operations. Five of the incidents involved covert actions by the United States; two of these actions were widely condemned.

We need hardly add that none of these incidents are put forward as summaries of statements of current law. The international reactions represent the views of effective elites at the time of their occurrence and provide some ongoing trend data of normative expectations. Changes in conditioning factors can be expected to elicit comparable changes in such expectations.

### Iran, 1953

During the Second World War, Iran was divided into British and Soviet spheres of influence. Soviet occupation troops, however, did not leave the country until 1946 and then only after a Soviet puppet regime in Azerbaijan collapsed. For its part, the United Kingdom continued to influence Iranian politics through its control of the oil industry.[83]

After the Second World War, Iran was nominally ruled by Shah Mohammed Reza Pahlavi. The instruments of government, however, were parliamentary. De facto power was in the hands of a prime minister, appointed by the shah, and in the lower house of Parliament, the Majlis. In 1951, the Majlis nationalized the oil industry then dominated by the Anglo-Iranian Oil Company, which in turn was controlled by the British government. When the prime minister was assassinated in 1951, the shah was persuaded to appoint the popular nationalist, Mohammed Mossadegh, as prime minister. The Majlis soon gave him dictatorial powers.

At first, American policy and public opinion warmed to Mossadegh. In 1952, *Time* named him "Man of the Year." Then Washington cooled. Iran's oil dependent economy faltered after British technicians withdrew and the British government leveraged the purchase of oil. There was nationalist rioting often directed at British and American interests. As Mossadegh lost control, Washington grew concerned that the prime minister was under the influence of the *Tudeh*, the Iranian Communist Party. American aid was curtailed and oil purchases suspended. In 1952, Mossadegh dissolved the parliament. One year later he won what was generally recognized as a rigged election. The Eisenhower administration decided to intervene. Contact was made with the Shah. On August 13, 1953, the Shah dismissed Mossadegh and appointed

General Zahedi in his place. When Mossadegh refused to step down, however, the Shah withdrew to the sanctuary of the summer palace. There followed five days of civil unrest and uncertainty until United States-instigated demonstrations eventually turned the tide. Mossadegh was arrested and the Shah returned to Teheran.

Details of the United States role in the events of August were secret. On the other hand, news accounts of the time do indicate that the United States, and to a lesser degree Britain, were deeply involved in Iranian affairs, employing methods of economic and political persuasion. Nevertheless, there was no contemporary suggestion of international condemnation or concern in the press. The United Nations, still dominated by the United States, did not include Iran among its seventy-two provisional agenda items issued on September 16 for the 8th General Assembly. Resolutions on Tunisian and Moroccan independence were considered during the fall of 1953, but nothing regarding Iran.

By 1980, when the ICJ was considering the hostage case, the actual events of August 1953 were well known.[84] Although Iran was not represented at oral proceedings and did not submit formal pleadings, Iran's position was defined in two letters to the court from its minister of Foreign Affairs. In the first letter, dated December 9, 1980, the Iranian government argued that

> the Court cannot examine the American Application divorced from its proper context, namely the whole political dossier of the relations between Iran and the United States over the last 25 years. This dossier includes, *inter alia,* all the crimes perpetrated in Iran by the American Government, in particular the coup d'etat of 1953 stirred up and carried out by the CIA.[85]

Although the court noted that Iran could have appeared before the court to explain "on what legal basis it considered these allegations to constitute a relevant answer to United States claims," the court nevertheless rejected Iran's contextual defense.

> . . . even if the alleged criminal activities of the United States in Iran could be considered as having been established, the question would remain whether they could be regarded by the Court as justification of Iran's conduct and thus a defense to the United States' claims in the present case. The Court, however, is unable to accept that they can be so regarded. This is because diplomatic law itself provides the necessary means of defense against, and sanction for, illicit activities by members of the diplomatic or consular missions.[86]

### Eichmann, 1960

On May 23, 1960, Israeli Prime Minister David Ben-Gurion announced to the Knesset that ". . . one of the greatest of the Nazi war criminals,

Adolf Eichmann . . . was found by the Israeli Security Services . . . and is under arrest in Israel. . . ."[87] Ben-Gurion did not indicate where or how Eichmann was found. A government spokesman, however, acknowledged that Eichmann had been taken "without the assistance of foreign governments." Within days, the Associated Press and *Time* reported that Eichmann had been abducted on a Buenos Aires street by a team of Israeli commandos.

The Argentine government protested to Israel and recalled its ambassador from Tel Aviv. There followed an exchange of notes between the two governments. Israel expressed regret for any violations of Argentine law or sovereignty but argued that "consideration be given to the fact that the volunteers, themselves survivors of this massacre, put this task before everything else." The Argentine government should "show understanding in the face of these historic and moral reasons." In addition, an Israeli note stated, the volunteers took Eichmann out of Argentina with his "full conformity."

The Argentine government in response stated that it "perfectly understands the sentiments the Jewish people may harbour towards a man charged with extermination in the concentration camps," but "the fact that a State sends its agents into the territory of another State to carry out without authorization actions of any nature, and particularly those which are coercive, cannot be legitimately included in the framework of international juridical relations." Argentina asked that Israel make reparation by returning Eichmann. Israel could then request Eichmann's extradition.[88] But if Eichmann were extradited on a charge of genocide, he must be tried in Germany or by an international court in accordance with the terms of the Genocide Convention of which both Israel and Argentina were signatories.

A spokesman for the Foreign Ministry in Bonn had earlier indicated that West Germany would supply evidence to Israel for Eichmann's trial. In addition, a German extradition request was unlikely, as no extradition treaty existed between West Germany and Israel. Latin American suggestions that Eichmann be placed in the custody of the Argentine embassy in Tel Aviv pending a ruling on jurisdiction by the International Court were rejected by Israel.

When Israel did not respond to its note of June 8, the Argentine government requested an urgent meeting of the Security Council to consider the matter. On June 22, the Argentine representative to the United Nations submitted a draft resolution for the Council's consideration. The resolution declared that "acts such as that under consideration . . . may, if repeated, endanger international peace and security." In addition, Israel was requested to "make appropriate reparation in accordance with the U.N. Charter and the rules of international law." At the suggestion of the United States delegate, this draft resolution was amended to include preambular language noting that the council was "mindful of the universal condemnation of the persecution of the Jews under the Nazis, and of the concern of people in all countries that Eichmann should be brought to appropriate justice." Language was also added expressing the hope "that the traditional friendly relations between Argentina and Israel will be advanced."

During the ensuing debate, the Soviet delegate criticized Argentina for not arresting Eichmann itself, while the French and Polish delegates criticized Argentina for requesting Eichmann's return. In contrast, the delegates from Italy, Ceylon, Ecuador, Nationalist China, and Tunisia supported Argentina on the issue of state sovereignty. The United Kingdom supported the Resolution as amended. The resolution was adopted by a vote of 8–0 with the Soviet Union and Poland abstaining.[89] Argentina did not vote.

Argentina and Israel, however, continued to disagree on the form of reparation, with Israel arguing that the resolution was itself satisfaction. In July, the Israeli ambassador to Buenos Aires was declared persona non grata. A joint statement issued on August 3 declared the incident closed and included an Israeli admission that Israeli nationals had "infringed the fundamental rights . . . of Argentina."[90] Full diplomatic relations were restored in October.

Eichmann was tried and convicted of war crimes, genocide and membership in Nazi organizations under Israel's 1950 Nazis and Nazi Collaborators (Punishment) Law.[91] He was executed on May 31, 1962.

### Bay of Pigs, 1961

On the morning of April 17, 1961, a brigade of 1,400 Cuban exiles landed at Bahia de Cochinos, Cuba. Their objective was the overthrow of Fidel Castro either by direct force of arms or by instigating a popular uprising. As a third option, the exiles would withdraw to the Escambray Mountains and carry on a protracted guerrilla campaign much as Castro himself had done from the Sierra Maestra. In preparation for the landing, Cubans piloting unmarked B-26 aircraft attacked Cuban airfields on April 15. To cover the origin of the attack, one pilot continued on to Florida to announce his defection and request asylum.[92]

The brigade was recruited, trained, and equipped by the Central Intelligence Agency (CIA). The concept of operations, conceived during the Eisenhower administration, was inherited by the Kennedy administration. To keep the operation secret, the exiles' ground combat element was trained in Guatemala; the Brigade's air element flew out of Nicaragua. The air element consisted of eight surplus Korean vintage B-26 bombers conspicuous for their availability throughout Latin America and therefore, in theory, not readily traceable to the United States. As one more concession to the desire for secrecy, the landing site was changed from the city of Trinidad at the base of the Escambray Mountains to the Bay of Pigs eighty miles to the west. Trinidad was thought "too spectacular" a location by the president who wanted to reduce the political risk of the operation, including the potential for anti-American reactions in Latin America and at the United Nations.[93]

But even with all of these adjustments, the invasion was still "too large to be clandestine and too small to be successful."[94] As early as October 1960 newspapers in Guatemala were carrying stories about preparations for the invasion. In December, the United States media joined in. Nor did the preparations escape Cuban attention. In a letter to the president of the General Assembly dated March 13, Cuban Minister for External Affairs Raul Roa complained about

> the preparations for the invasion of Cuba, the imminence of which is proclaimed by the United States press, radio and television and by the leaders of the counter-revolutionaries and mercenaries hired by the Central Intelligence Agency. . . . It is well known that this invasion force has been trained by United States technicians at its bases in Florida and Guatemala.[95]

On April 12, Kennedy declared at a press conference, "There will not be, under any conditions, an intervention in Cuba by the United States Armed Forces. . . . The basic issue in Cuba is not one between the United States and Cuba. It is between the Cubans themselves."[96]

When the Brigade landed at the Bahia de Cochinos, the Cuban response was immediate and effective. Within hours, 20,000 potential opponents of the regime were detained. There was no popular uprising. On the landing beaches, the exiles met stiff resistance, if they made it to the beach at all. The Cuban forces soon contained the beachhead with an estimated 20,000 men supported by armor. Cuban T-33 jet trainers controlled the air. Although the fighting was at times fierce, the brigade ceased to exist as a fighting unit within two days. Nor were its survivors able to escape to the Escambray Mountains some eighty miles to the east and across a swamp. Of the exiles, 114 were killed and 1,189 captured. Cuban casualties, acknowledged as 87 killed and over 200 wounded, were probably higher.[97]

Reaction to the invasion was strongest in Latin America. United States relations "soured" throughout the region.[98] Anti-American or pro-Castro demonstrations occurred in Buenos Aires, Bogota, Mexico City, Caracas, Montevideo, and Santiago.[99] The Venezuelan Chamber of Deputies passed a resolution condemning "any foreign armed intervention" in Cuba.[100]

The invasion was met with "widespread disenchantment" in Western Europe. The *Frankfurter Neue Presse* wrote "Kennedy is to be regarded as politically and morally defeated." Presaging later reaction to the Rainbow Warrior incident, however, the European response was in part directed at the failure of the operation, not necessarily its existence. As Schlesinger summarizes, "The New Frontier looked like a collection not only of imperialists but of ineffectual imperialists—and, what was worst of all, of stupid, ineffectual imperialists."[101]

Premier Khrushchev sent a warning to President Kennedy on April 22:

> If you consider yourself to be in the right to implement such measures against Cuba which have been lately taken by the United States of America, you must admit that other countries, also, do not have lesser reason to act in a similar manner in relation to states on whose territories preparations are actually being made which represent a threat against the security of the Soviet Union. If you do not wish to sin against elementary logic, you evidently must admit such a right to other states.

At the United Nations, the General Assembly expedited consideration of an existing agenda item (Number 90) originating from an October 18, 1960, Cuban complaint regarding acts of United States intervention, including an alleged air drop of weapons into the Escambray Mountains and the landing of mercenaries from Florida.[102] The First Committee of the General Assembly held twelve meetings between April 17 and April 21 to consider the invasion.

The General Assembly chose not to condemn the invasion in adopting a draft resolution submitted by Argentina, Chile, Colombia, Honduras, Panama, Uruguay, and Venezuela which read in part

> The General Assembly . . . [d]eeply concerned over the situation disclosed therein, which is disturbing world public opinion and the continuation of which could endanger world peace . . . [e]xhorts all Member States to take such peaceful action as is open to them to remove existing tension.

The seven-power resolution was amended at the request of the Sudan to include the phrase "which is disturbing world public opinion" in lieu of "which is disturbing the American continent." The United States joined the majority of sixty-one voting in favor of the resolution. Cuba and twenty-seven other nations voted against the resolution. There were ten abstentions.[103]

A Mexican draft resolution had been stronger. It read in part

> The General Assembly . . . [f]irmly believing that the principle of non-intervention in the internal affairs of any State imposes an obligation on Members of the United Nations to refrain from encouraging or promoting civil strife in other States . . . [m]akes an urgent appeal to all States to ensure that their territories and resources are not used to promote a civil war in Cuba.[104]

But the Mexican draft failed to achieve the necessary two-thirds vote in the General Assembly (42–31–25). Romania and the Soviet Union also submitted draft resolutions to the First Committee condemning the armed attack on Cuba and demanding the cessation of assistance but chose not to press for votes on their resolutions.

What was, perhaps, most remarkable about reaction to the Bay of Pigs was the paucity of United States domestic criticism. If little consideration was given to the principle of nonintervention prior to the invasion, just as little was said about it afterwards. Some in Congress were soon calling for a blockade of Cuba or an invasion. A May 3 Gallup poll gave the administration an unprecedented 82 percent approval rating.[105]

The Bay of Pigs is the rare covert operation for which there is ample source material, albeit, until now, almost exclusively from a United States perspective. Immediate postmortems focused on the lack of ammunition on the beach, itself the product of poor embarkation procedures, the decision to move the landing site from Trinidad to the Bay of Pigs, the use of obsolete and ineffective equipment, and the president's decision not to order United States air strikes. More generally, the planners failed to find a successful balance between secrecy and effectiveness, in the end achieving neither.

Less was said of Castro's role. Cuban forces responded quickly, were well led, fought hard, and did not, as U.S. planners had hoped, defect. The Bay of Pigs was as much a Cuban victory as a United States defeat.

Subsequent memoirs and studies offer valuable insight into weaknesses in the covert decision-making process. Irving Janis found in the Bay of Pigs a classic example of what he calls "groupthink," a process by which "members of any small cohesive group tend to maintain esprit de corps by unconsciously developing a number of shared illusions and related norms that interfere with critical thinking and reality testing." This led to a sense of invulnerability, an illusion of unanimity, the suppression of personal doubts, and docility in the face of suave leadership. Within the cycle of covert decision making, the risk of "groupthink" is heightened.[106] Treverton's review of the Bay of Pigs focuses on the detrimental bureaucratic factors. He describes the growth in momentum behind the operation until it was seemingly irresistible, as well as the professional incentives within the clandestine services to see the project through.[107]

Less concern has been paid to the legal implications of the invasion, perhaps because there was little to debate about.[108] The Bay of Pigs was among the most patently "Cold War" of United States covert operations. Unlike the Cuban quarantine which would follow eighteen months later, the operation had little basis in international law, and no effort was made to marshal regional support or approval for the undertaking. Indeed, the Kennedy administration made few pretenses about the invasion being consistent with either international or domestic law.[109]

If there was any basis in international law for the operation it rested on the principle of self-determination. Kennedy in response to Khrushchev's note, wrote

> I believe, Mr. Chairman, that you should recognize that free peoples in all parts of the world do not accept the claim of historical inevitability for communist revolution. What your Government believes is its own business; what it does in the world is the world's business. The great revolution in the history of man, past, present and future, is the revolution of those determined to be free.[110]

In this instance, however, the self-determination argument was a questionable one. As events demonstrated, the exiles had little popular support in Cuba *at the time* of the invasion, what existed may have been reduced by Castro's extensive police action. Some of Kennedy's aides were suspicious of the insurrection argument and told the president so. Schlesinger reports, "In his judgment, the critical point—the weak part of the case for going ahead—lay in the theory that the landings would touch off a mass insurrection against the regime. How unpopular was Castro anyway? I mentioned a series written by Joseph Newman, who had just visited Cuba for the *New York Herald Tribune*, citing a piece which reported the strength of sentiment behind Castro."[111]

On the subject of United States law, Attorney General Robert Kennedy was asked if the Cuban operation was a violation of United States neutrality laws.[112] His reply was a triumph of hair splitting.

> . . . the neutrality laws were never designed to prevent individuals from leaving the United States to fight for a cause in which they believed. There is nothing in the neutrality laws which prevents refugees from Cuba from returning to that country to engage in the fight for freedom. Nor is an individual prohibited from departing from the United States, with others of like belief, to join still others in a second country for an expedition against a third country.
>
> There is nothing criminal in an individual leaving the United States with the intent of joining an insurgent group. There is nothing criminal in his urging others to do so. There is nothing criminal in several persons departing at the same time.
>
> What the law does prohibit is a group organized as a military expedition from departing from the United States to take action as a military force against a nation with whom the United States is at peace.[113]

If the administration played fast and loose with international law and the neutrality laws, it was more attentive to the existing mechanism of congressional oversight. This mechanism, later dubbed "the buddy system" by Senator Mondale, consisted of little more than informal and selective notification of key committee chairmen. What is striking about the Bay of Pigs, however, is that Senate Foreign Relations Committee Chairman J. William Fulbright was brought into the executive decision-making loop prior to the president's own decision. When Fulbright expressed concern about invasion reports in the press in late March 1961, Kennedy personally briefed the chairman on the proposed operation. Fulbright, in turn, offered the president a memorandum stating his opposition to the concept. Fulbright also attended what Schlesinger describes as "the climatic meeting" on April 14 where he spoke emphatically against the operation. Fulbright's participation in the Bay of Pigs decision offers an interesting contrast to oversight during the Iran desert operation and the Libyan raid, when congressional leaders first learned of the operation after some of the aircraft were airborne.

### Trujillo Assassination, 1961

Rafael Leonidas Trujillo had controlled political power in the Dominican Republic since 1930. Relatives held and profited from positions throughout the government. Trujillo himself was reported to have $800 million in overseas accounts and holdings. His regime was brutal by any standard; Trujillo was alleged to have authorized the deaths of at least 1,000 political opponents in 1930 alone. In 1937, 15,000 Haitian sugar workers were killed in the Dominican Republic when they refused to return to Haiti. A diplomat with the Dominican Republic's United Nations Mission in New York seeking political asylum in February 1961 charged that "human rights are continuing to be violated. . . . Jails continue full of political prisoners who are submitted to horrifying tortures."[114]

Trujillo also tried to carry his reign of terror abroad. In June 1960 agents of the Dominican Republic were implicated in an attempt to assassinate Venezuelan President Romulo Betancourt. As a result, in August 1960, the foreign ministers of the Organization of American States (OAS) voted to impose an arms embargo against the Dominican Republic and sever relations with the Trujillo regime. In January 1961, by a vote of 14–1–6, the OAS recommended that members suspend shipments of oil, oil products, and trucks to the Dominican Republic.[115]

"For most of his tenure, the United States Government supported [Trujillo] and he was regarded throughout much of the Caribbean and Latin America as a protegé of the United States."[116] In 1960, however, the Eisenhower administration, concerned with the prospects of another Cuba, began to consider political action to remove Trujillo.[117] Contact was made with Dominican dissidents through the embassy in Ciudad Trujillo. The dissidents requested sniper rifles with scopes as well as other weapons. In July 1960, the senior United States diplomat in the Dominican Republic advised Washington that the dissidents ". . . were in no way ready to carry on any type of revolutionary activity in the foreseeable future except the assassination of their principal enemy."[118]In a later cable the Consul General concluded:

> From a purely practical standpoint, it will be best for us, for the OAS, and for the Dominican Republic if the Dominicans put an end to Trujillo before he leaves this island. If he has his millions and is a free agent, he will devote his life from exile to preventing stable government in the D.R., to overturning democratic governments and establishing dictatorships in the Caribbean, and to assassinating his enemies.[119]

Support for the dissidents continued into the Kennedy administration. The Church Committee summarized:

> Prior to the failure of the Bay of Pigs invasion on April 17, 1961, a number of significant events occurred. These events included meetings with Dominican dissidents in which specific assassination plans were discussed, requests by dissidents for explosive devices, the passage by the United States officials of pistols and carbines to dissidents inside the Dominican Republic and the pouching . . . of machine guns which had been requested by the dissidents for use in connection with an assassination attempt.[120]

Permission to pass the machine guns to the dissidents was never granted. Indeed, late in April, the consul general received instructions to "turn off the assassination attempt."[121] A May 13 State Department document titled "Program for Covert Action for the Dominican Republic" refers to the pistols and carbines passed to the dissidents as "personal defense weapons attendant to their projected efforts to *neutralize* Trujillo."[122] On May 29, the day before the assassination, a cable from Washington reportedly with President Kennedy's own imprimatur advised:

> . . . we must not run the risk of U.S. association with political assassination, since U.S. as a matter of general policy cannot condone assassination. This last principal is overriding and must prevail in doubtful situation. . . .
>     . . . [C]ontinue to advise dissident elements of U.S. support for their position.[123]

Whether these decisions represented a change in policy, a change in tone, or an effort to distance the United States and the presidency from an event the consul general had anticipated for some time[124] was not clear to the players in Ciudad Trujillo. The Church Committee report indicates that these late modulations were prompted by concerns that the dissidents were not ready to fill the vacuum should Trujillo perish and, perhaps, a new caution about undertaking foreign adventures in the wake of the Bay of Pigs. State Department documents, however, demonstrate that at least some policy officials were animated by concern that the United States should not "lend itself to direct political assassination," risk further moral tarnishing in the eyes of the world, and could ill "afford a precedent which may convince the world that our diplomatic pouches are used to deliver assassination weapon[s]."[125]

Trujillo was ambushed and assassinated by dissidents during the night of May 30, 1961. On May 31, President Kennedy's press secretary made the first public announcement of Trujillo's assassination. The announcement preceded release of the news in the Dominican Republic by several hours. There was, however, no international concern expressed regarding United States complicity in the assassination.[126] In contrast to the international reaction to the alleged plot to kill President Betancourt the previous year, no action was taken by the OAS with regard to the assassination. To the contrary, on June 5, the OAS approved a request made on June 2 by the United States that a fact-finding mission be sent to the Dominican Republic to investigate police terror.[127]

### Chile, 1964–1973

Between 1964 and 1973, the CIA spent $13.4 million on covert operations in Chile.[128] These operations can be divided into three general phases. During the period, 1964–1970, United States operations focused on "election projects" designed to keep Eduardo Frei and the Christian Democrats in office and Salvador Allende and the Marxist party out of office. Money was channeled to Frei and his allies,[129] and some campaign expertise was provided in areas like polling.

In September 1970, Allende received a plurality of the votes cast in Chile's presidential election. Under the Chilean constitution, when a candidate failed to receive a majority of popular votes a joint session of Congress would choose between the first and second place finishers. The Congress had never failed to select the candidate with the most votes in the initial popular ballot.[130] During the period between the September election and the scheduled October 24 congressional vote, United States covert operations turned towards "spoiling operations" to prevent Allende from assuming power. This campaign proceeded on two levels, the so-called Track I and Track II. In fact, the Select Committee would conclude that these tracks had much the same objective: encouraging the military to move against Allende. What was different was the organizational structure within the United States government and the degree of CIA participation in Chile. Track I consisted of efforts to bribe members of the Chilean Congress, an increase in funding channeled to the media for propaganda, and efforts to encourage a military coup, provided Eduardo Frei concurred. Track II involved direct contacts between the CIA and coup plotters.

In October 1970, operatives provided three submachine guns and six tear gas grenades to a group of military officers involved in a coup plot. The officers had twice before tried to abduct the army chief-of-staff, General Rene Schneider, who was a constitutionalist and opposed coups.[131] The weapons were, it was subsequently said, meant largely as symbolic support. As it turned out, on the same day as the exchange of weapons, Schneider was killed during an attempted abduction by another group of officers.

Allende assumed office and, among other things, nationalized the copper industry. United States covert activities turned towards the "political and economic destabilization" of Chile. Towards this end $8 million was provided to opposition political parties and to media for propaganda. The United States also imposed overt economic sanctions on Chile, including a substantial reduction in foreign assistance.[132] In time, the Chilean economy began to suffer, a product of Allende's own policies as well as United States' actions. A strike by Chilean truck drivers from July to September 1973 precipitated a final crisis. On September 11, 1973, military forces under General Pinochet seized control of the government in a violent coup. President Allende was either murdered, killed in combat in the palace, or committed suicide. Extensive human rights abuses, including torture and summary execution ensued.

Almost immediately, there were allegations of United States complicity in the coup.[133] In a short time, the entire previous period of covert intervention came under congressional scrutiny. Although United States domestic attention did address international law,[134] the domestic focus was on separation of powers issues and the absence or failure of internal control and oversight of covert operations.

In Rome and Paris, thousands of demonstrators marched in the streets denouncing the CIA for overthrowing Allende. Charges of illegal intervention came from the communist bloc countries. The Cuban representative to the United Nations denounced the coup before the General Assembly referring to the "many plots hatched by the United States Embassy . . . which tried to stop him [Allende] from acceding to the presidency," followed by "a large-scale operation designed to ruin the economy and provoke a coup d'etat."[135] Chile's new United Nations representative countered that Cuba had been training Chilean insurgents. The United States representative denied "categorically that the United States was involved in any way in the events which have occurred in Chile."[136]

In July 1973, two months before the coup, the United Nations Economic and Social Council had approved a year-long study of the conduct of multinational companies in the developing world. Chile had requested the study as a result of interference in Chilean politics by International Telephone and Telegraph (ITT) and Kennecott Copper.[137] No comparable U.N. study of state intervention, however, was initiated in the wake of the September coup and the allegations of

U.S. covert complicity that followed. The General Assembly and Security Council took no action.

The international response to the coup focused instead on allegations of widespread human rights abuses in post-coup Chile. France, Italy, Yugoslavia, Cuba, and the Soviet Union refused to recognize the new government. Mexico recalled its ambassador, and Sweden and Finland suspended their foreign assistance. Brazil and Uruguay, however, recognized the new government on September 13, and Panama, Haiti, Venezuela, South Korea, and the United States did the same on September 24. In 1974, the United Nations passed a General Assembly Resolution calling for the release of political prisoners in Chile and restoration of human rights, and the OAS sent a team of investigators to report on human rights conditions in Chile.

### Iran, 1980

After two years of student and religious unrest, the Shah turned power over to a regency council under Prime Minister Bakhtiar and fled Iran on January 16, 1979. Two weeks later, the Ayatollah Khomeini returned from exile in Paris having already named a provisional government. Forces loyal to the Shah, however, continued to fight at least until February 11, the nominal anniversary of the Iranian Revolution. Unrest continued and on February 14 an armed group seized the United States embassy in Teheran and its seventy occupants. Within hours, however, a contingent of Revolutionary Guards returned control of the embassy to the United States. One month later an Islamic Republic was founded and endorsed by a plebiscite.

After leaving Iran, the Shah proceeded to Egypt, Morocco, and Mexico before being admitted to the United States for medical treatment on October 22. On October 30 the government of Iran requested that the Shah be returned to Teheran. Demonstrations in front of the United States embassy began shortly thereafter. On November 4, 1979, a group of demonstrators, characterized as student militants, overran the United States embassy and took its occupants hostage. Other American diplomatic personnel, including the chargé d'affaires were detained in the Iranian Foreign Ministry. One day later, the American consulates in Tabriz and Shiraz were also seized. In all, sixty-nine United States citizens were held captive.[138] As the International Court of Justice would determine later, the Iranian government took no protective action to either forestall the seizure or end it.[139]

In the immediate aftermath of the seizure, the Security Council unanimously passed a resolution calling on Iran to release the United States personnel, calling on both governments to resolve their dispute through peaceful means and requesting that the secretary-general use his good offices to help secure the purposes of the resolution.[140] A second resolution, passed on December 31, reiterated the provisions of Resolution 457 and called for a vote on economic sanctions against Iran if the hostages were not released by January 7.[141] The secretary-general's trip to Iran, however, proved fruitless. On January 13, the Soviet Union vetoed a United States–sponsored resolution calling for economic sanctions against Iran.

Meanwhile, the United States instituted proceedings against Iran at the ICJ and requested and received an order of "provisional measures," directing Iran to restore the premises to the United States and to release the hostages. However, "the Court's Order of 15 December 1979, for the immediate restoration of the Embassy to the United States and the release of the hostages, was publicly rejected by the [Iranian] Minister of Foreign Affairs and . . . ignored by all Iranian authorities."[142]

The United States also took certain unilateral political and economic measures against Iran pursuant to the president's authority under the International Emergency Economic Powers Act[143] and the "Hostage Act of 1868."[144] United States' efforts to organize multilateral sanctions outside the structure of the United Nations, however, met with little immediate support. Iran threatened to cut off oil shipments to any nation that joined the U.S. sanctions.

As the hostage crisis continued into 1980, an election year, President Carter imposed further political and economic sanctions against Iran. On April 17 in a televised news conference, he indicated that the measures "are a continuation of our efforts to resolve this crisis by peaceful means." But, the president added, "If a constructive Iranian response is not forthcoming soon, the United States should and will proceed with other measures." In response to a question, the president reiterated that if these sanctions were not "successful then the only next step available . . . would be some sort of military action."[145] On April 22, 1980, the foreign ministers of the European Economic Community voted to impose phased political and economic sanctions against Iran, and on April 23 and 24, Canada and Japan imposed their own sanctions on Iran. Statements by members of the administration suggested that these allied sanctions might prompt reconsideration or postponement of military options.[146]

In the early morning hours of April 25, 1980, the White House announced that a covert military operation to rescue the hostages in Iran had been aborted. The statement indicated that the mission was "ordered for humanitarian reasons, to protect the national interests of this country and to alleviate international tensions." A force of some 180 men flying in eight helicopters and six C-130 transport aircraft had penetrated Iranian territory as far as the Dasht-i-Kavir, a salt desert near Tabas, two hundred miles southeast of Teheran. The

C-130s had taken off from Egypt. Other members of the rescue team and Iranian agents were already in place in Teheran, having entered the country under cover in the preceding weeks or months. As a result of equipment failure, however, the main body of the force had to withdraw from Iran. In the process of withdrawal, a C-130 collided with a helicopter at the checkpoint known as Desert One, and eight members of the force were killed.

Immediate reaction to the rescue mission ranged from support to condemnation. Official statements from the governments of Israel and West Germany were sympathetic. Britain chose not to condemn the raid, whereas French reaction was limited to the fact that it had not received prior notification of the operation. In contrast, Italy was opposed to the use of force "in any circumstance for the liberation of the hostages." On May 18, however, the European Community voted to impose limited economic sanctions against Iran as "a gesture of support for the U.S. effort to free the American hostages."[147] These sanctions fell short of the plan voted on April 22.[148]

In contrast, Warsaw Pact reaction was uniformly negative. Soviet commentary in Tass referred to "an aggressive, hegemonic foreign policy," and "a broader plan for staging an antipopular coup in Iran." Romania condemned the operation as a violation of Iranian territorial sovereignty not justified by the hostage situation. Czechoslovakia argued that the United States may have "created an exceptionally serious situation."

Islamic and Near Eastern reaction was generally critical of the operation. Those governments voicing criticism included: India ("military adventurism"), Pakistan ("shock and dismay" and support for Iran's struggle to defend its sovereignty), Libya, and South Yemen. Yasir Arafat apparently sent a message to Ayatollah Khomeini referring to the "brutal onslaught of Iran." Egyptian President Sadat, alone, spoke of "hard luck" which "should not dishearten more action to free and rescue the hostages." He offered the United States continued use of Egyptian facilities. In May, the foreign ministers representing over thirty members of the Conference of Islamic States unanimously adopted a resolution condemning the "recent military aggression" of the United States against Iran. A separate resolution expressed opposition to any action that threatened Iran's territorial integrity.[149]

At the United Nations, the United States reported on April 25 to the Security Council regarding the operation "pursuant to Article 51 of the Charter." The United States argued that the mission was conducted "in exercise of its inherent right of self-defense with the aim of extricating American nationals who have been and remain the victims of the Iranian armed attack on our Embassy."[150] The Security Council took no further action. No resolutions were considered or passed by the General Assembly. As discussed in chapter 5, the International

Court in its May 24, 1980, opinion on the merits of the hostage case expressed concern about the United States incursion into Iran, especially because it had occurred while the court was preparing its judgment. The court noted that under such circumstances the operation "is of a kind to undermine respect for the judicial process in international law."[151] The court, however, declined to rule on the legality of the operation. Nor, in the opinion of the court, did the operation have any bearing on the conduct of the Iranian government on November 4, 1979.[152]

### Poland, 1981

At midnight on December 13, 1981, the Polish government declared a state of emergency and imposed martial law. A curfew was imposed, basic civil liberties suspended, gatherings banned, and the umbrella resistance organization Solidarity suspended. Thousands of persons were arrested, including labor leaders, activists, and members of the government. There were also reports of casualties. After the coup, government authority was centralized in the hands of a military council under the direction of General Wojciech Jaruzelski.

Initial press reports speculated that the crisis was precipitated by Solidarity's December 12 proposal for a national referendum on the Communist Party, General Jaruzelski, the Soviet alliance, and free elections. There were, however, indications that the imposition of martial law had been in the offing for months, planned covertly in the Soviet Union,[153] notwithstanding official Soviet descriptions of events in Poland as "an internal affair." On December 20, Poland's ambassador to the United States defected and charged "'This carefully orchestrated crackdown is not an internal Polish issue,' but a 'flagrant' violation of the Final Act of the Helsinki Accords" (which requires signatories to refrain from intervention in the internal affairs of other countries).[154] Three days later Poland's ambassador to Japan also defected. He accused the military, under Soviet pressure, of planning for martial law since March 1981. On December 28, a Polish general who defected in August, reported that Polish army uniforms had been sent to the Soviet Union, and that Soviet soldiers in Polish uniforms were guarding key installations.

United States response to the covert Soviet role was immediate and distinct from its equally swift criticism of martial law.[155] On December 17, President Reagan charged that "It would be naive to think that this could happen without the full knowledge of the Soviet Union."[156] On December 23, in a nationally televised address, President Reagan announced the imposition of sanctions against Poland and warned that if martial law continued, the United States would consider sanctions against Moscow. On December 29, President Reagan imposed sanctions against the USSR, stating that "the Soviet Union does not understand the seriousness of our concern and its final obligations under both the Helsinki Final Act and the United Nations Charter."[157]

Initial European response to Soviet involvement in the coup, as distinct from condemnation of conditions in Poland, was muted. On December 18, for example, Chancellor Bruno Kreisky of Austria indicated concern that the Soviet Union would intervene, whereas Chancellor Helmut Schmidt of West Germany advocated a policy of strict noninterference in Poland. In contrast, there was "sharp" debate over the Soviet role at the Madrid conference on European Security and Cooperation, but no allied support for United States sanctions against Poland. As one government spokesman put it, "West Germany did 'not share the view that the Soviet Union is to be considered the prime author of the imposition of martial law.' Canada was still arguing that what was going on in Poland was an internal matter."[158]

European response to the Soviet covert operation changed within a month. On January 4, 1982, the European Community's ten foreign ministers issued a communique calling on Polish authorities to end martial law and noting "with concern and disapproval the serious external pressures and the campaign directed by the U.S.S.R. and other Eastern European countries against the efforts for renewal in Poland." On January 5, President Reagan and Chancellor Schmidt issued a joint communique expressing agreement on "the responsibility of the Soviet Union for developments in Poland." A NATO foreign ministers' communique of January 11, asked the Soviets to permit Poland "to solve its own problems free from foreign interference." "Economic relations with Poland and the Soviet Union," the communique continued, "were bound to be affected." Each member, however, was to determine what sanctions to impose, if any, according to its own "situation and legislation."[159]

In the General Assembly, consideration of the "Poland situation" was limited to statements in plenary session. In contrast, in November and December 1981, the General Assembly adopted a general prohibition on intervention, condemned Israel and South Africa for specific instances of alleged coercion, and called for the withdrawal of foreign troops from Afghanistan.[160] Nor was the "Poland situation" included on the Security Council's agenda in 1981 or 1982, or "brought to the attention" of the Security Council during 1981 or 1982.[161] In his first annual report in September 1982, Secretary-General Perez de Cuellar cited the United Nations' failure to resolve international crises throughout the world but did not cite Poland. Nor did the United Nations Human Rights Committee include Poland among the twenty-two named countries in its 1982 annual report on human rights abuse.[162]

## Rainbow Warrior, 1985

The Greenpeace[163] vessel *Rainbow Warrior* was part of a flotilla that planned to protest and perhaps disrupt impending French nuclear tests on the South Pacific atoll of Mururoa. Because of its size and its desalinization plant, the *Rainbow Warrior* was to serve as a mother ship for the protest. On July 10, 1985, French military officers sank the *Rainbow Warrior* while it lay at anchor in Auckland harbor, New Zealand. A Dutch photographer on board the *Rainbow Warrior* drowned.

Two French military officers were arrested in New Zealand while traveling under false names on false passports and charged with murder under New Zealand law. In Australia, a search of a French-registered yacht revealed evidence of plastic explosives. The vessel and its crew of three disappeared, however, before Australian officials decided to detain them.

New Zealand protests to the French were immediate. The officers were arrested and prosecuted. After pleading guilty to charges of manslaughter and willful damage to a ship by means of an explosive, the officers were sentenced to ten years incarceration. Having originally denied complicity in the operation, the French government eventually accepted responsibility for the officers' actions and requested their release to French authorities on the grounds that the officers were following military orders. When negotiations faltered, the French threatened to terminate New Zealand's butter quota and other trade concessions scheduled to expire within weeks.

After a period of negotiations, the dispute was submitted to the secretary-general for, in effect, implementation of a prior agreement between the two countries. The two officers were transferred to the French on the condition they be assigned to a French military facility on the South Pacific island of Hao for "a period of not less than three years" ("pour une période minimale de 3 ans."). In addition, France paid an indemnity to New Zealand of $7 million and publicly acknowledged that ". . . the attack carried out against the 'Rainbow Warrior' took place in violation of the territorial sovereignty of New Zealand and that it was therefore committed in violation of international law." The French government, however, also asserted that "[t]he attack against the 'Rainbow Warrior' originates in the illegal actions of the 'Greenpeace' organization. It could not moreover be understood without recalling the intervention of certain New Zealand authorities in French internal affairs, especially with respect to the nuclear tests conducted on Mururoa."[164] The French government also paid the survivors of the Dutch photographer $400,000. An arbitral tribunal awarded Greenpeace damages of $8.1 million.

International public and press appraisal of the French operation was lively, ranging from outrage at France's unlawful behavior to scorn for the incompetent manner in which the mission was executed. The press, however, was ahead of government elites in criticizing the French. With the exception of New Zealand and Australia, which protested vigorously and brought their outrage to the attention of the General Assembly, state response to the incident was mild. Soviet spokesmen were silent. The United Kingdom did not go beyond calling on France to compensate the victims of the explosion. The State Department and the White House chose not to comment at all.

The *Rainbow Warrior* incident is cited by some authors as authority for the sanctity of territorial sovereignty, a limitation on permissible acts of defense in the name of national security and even evidence of a "trend to punish those responsible for terrorist acts."[165] France did pay reparations and offer satisfaction in the form of a verbal *mea culpa* to New Zealand. The incident, however, might also stand for the proposition that the international community is in some instances willing tacitly to tolerate covert actions in support of "national security," or in any event treat such incidents differently from other violent crimes. Perhaps out of consideration for their own nuclear concerns, the United States and Soviet Union, both sometime targets of Greenpeace operations, remained silent throughout the incident.

Although the French officers pleaded guilty to manslaughter and damage to a ship by means of an explosive, ultimately they were not treated as common criminals or terrorists. Major Mafart was promoted. By 1988, both French officers had been unilaterally repatriated back to France.[166]

## FACTORS CONDITIONING ELITE RESPONSE

Analysis of these and other incidents within the context in which they occurred suggests that the elite expectations regarding the operational code of covert operations and the reactions of politically relevant strata to particular operations have depended on a number of variables, which may be considered briefly and, perforce, tentatively.

1. The context of many of these actions was either Cold War or some other form of less comprehensive overt but suspended conflict. In other words, a set of shared expectations in which the likelihood of violence was deemed high and was, accordingly, prepared for. The Cold War, through its various transformations, was marked by a clear delineation of the adversaries, a constant state of preparedness for overt conflict, a common interest in avoiding it, an assignment of some geo-strategic value to every part of the globe, and an implicit "rules of the game" code that included toleration for covert actions below a certain threshold that did not introduce a major change in the power balance. Covert

actions in this context were frequently appraised differently from comparable actions in other contexts.

In cases of long-term *bilateral* but suspended conflict, which we distinguish from the "serial conflicts" of military historians, a comparable tolerance and expectation appears to have operated between adversaries. The rest of the international community which, as it were, sat in continuous judgment in both public and private settings, also seems to have viewed these actions differently. Thus, covert actions in the Israel-Arab conflict were appraised differently than, let us say, the French covert action in New Zealand. The United States action in Iran in 1980 would appear to have been appraised in terms of the same sort of context.

If we have identified a key conditioning factor here, it may provide some predictive as well as past explanatory value. If the Cold War does end, the threshold of tolerance for covert actions between continuing competitors such as the United States and the Soviet Union may become much lower. Espionage may continue and even increase, but, according to this hypothesis, covert operations between the two states will decrease.

2. Just as covert operations have been driven by the Cold War, the Cold War has also determined through which end of the binoculars an operation is viewed by the international community. When President Reagan declared in 1983: "I do believe in the right of a country, when it believes that its interests are best served, to practice covert activity," the president's press secretary quickly qualified that the "President had meant the statement to apply only to the U.S."[167] A comparable understanding and tolerance if not outright sympathy for the covert actions of friends against *their* adversaries seems to operate.

United States government activities in Iran and Chile, for example, received a different level of international scrutiny at the time than did Soviet activities related to the imposition of martial law in Poland. Yet, the motives behind both operations were arguably equally exclusive: military dictatorship was the expected result in both cases, and human rights abuse followed. This is not to discount that other factors such as Poland's geographic location and considerations of economic stakes also influenced European analysis and the mildness of the response. The evolution and escalation in international reaction to coups from Iran to Chile to Poland may also reflect a decline in tolerance for the coup as a form of great power covert operation, even in a sphere in which a power claims special privileges. Recall, however, that the Soviet role in Poland was only condemned in earnest at United States urging.[168]

3. In all contexts, however, some modalities of covert operations are little regulated and generally tolerated. This is especially true of the diplomatic, ideological, and economic modalities. Secret diplomacy, for example, only

evokes general international outcry when the content or consequence of the diplomacy is offensive.

4. Political assassination by state agents is generally condemned as a violation of international law and, where it is widely practiced, as a cascading threat to world public order. Evidence of commitment to this norm is found in the Convention on the Prevention and Punishment of Crimes against Internationally Protected Persons, Including Diplomatic Agents (1973),[169] the Convention to Punish Acts of Terrorism Taking the Form of Crimes against Persons and Related Extortion That Are of International Significance (OAS),[170] and Article 23(b) of the Annex to Hague Convention IV.[171] Confirmation of that commitment is provided by practice. The Israeli assassination of Khalil al-Wazir in Tunisia, for example, was condemned by the Islamic world but also by Western states, including the United States, and the Soviet Union. In addition, the Security Council by a vote of 14 to 0 "condemn[ed] vigorously the aggression."[172] But when Professor Kazem Rajavi was assassinated on April 24, 1989, in Geneva, Switzerland, probably by Iranian operatives, there was no condemnation. And the flurry of murders of Libyan nationals opposed to the Qaddafi government in Libya prompted little international comment. Part of this may be structural. Unless an international actor with access to formal arenas is willing to take up the case, it never gets brought to the court of public opinion. When one's own ox is gored, cries of indignation are immediate and loud.

Yet on closer view, one finds some striking qualifications even in governments that do protest. Senator Church, for example, made clear that the Select Committee to Study Governmental Operations was condemning some assassinations but not proposing an absolute ban. Senator Church said that he was "not talking about Adolf Hitler or anything of that character, nor are we condemning actions taken in a grave national emergency when the life of the republic is endangered."[173] These scenarios rest on uncertain definitions and pose difficult legal and moral problems. The Trujillo incident is a case in point.

Western moral tradition has long debated and, in some cases, recognized a right of subjects to remove a wicked ruler.[174] The question arises whether this right embraces assassination initiated or assisted by outside governments. If there is a case for assassination, it is most compelling where in fact the existing government is internationally condemned as tyrannical and there is ". . . no way ready to carry on any type of revolutionary activity . . . except the assassination of their principal enemy," as the United States consul general reported from Ciudad Trujillo. But who is to decide these many questions?

One is tempted to infer from practice operational distinctions between lawful and unlawful assassinations. Compare, for example, the international response to the attempt on the life of Romulo Betancourt to the assassination of Rafael

Trujillo. This distinction is intriguing, but not conclusive, for other factors may have influenced judgment. The year was 1961. President Kennedy had just launched the Alliance for Progress and the United States enjoyed a position of leadership and control within the OAS. Cold War considerations also clearly informed the actions and reactions of the United States as well as other OAS nations to some Cuban style insurgencies. The Church Committee, for example, concluded "the plots occurred in a Cold War atmosphere perceived to be of crisis proportions."[175] Finally, the full precedential import of state-supported assassination, however morally defensible some might sometimes have found it, would not be realized for another ten years, until Munich. "International terrorism" is often assassination conducted by adversaries.

A second issue regarding assassination is definitional. What is it? And do the norms change in time of armed conflict? The Church Committee publicly considered five incidents of alleged political assassination but did not consider the so-called Phoenix program in Vietnam, which seemed to tolerate "assassination," even if it did not expressly authorize it, in the context of the guerrilla war in the South. The committee's draft statute criminalizing under United States law the assassination of foreign officials included within its definition of "foreign official" persons belonging to an insurgent force, an unrecognized government, or a political party. But the statute did not apply to officials of a government or movement engaged in a war or hostilities with the United States. Finally, if "assassination" is an international crime, does such a prohibition translate across cultures and religions? The experience of Salman Rushdie suggests, for example, that although the words *justice* and *murder* may occur in every culture, the content of the notions may not be universal.

We do not suggest that the material we have reviewed supports the proposition that assassination is a preferred or lawful activity to be condoned by state actors. On the other hand, we were surprised to find that elite expectations are perhaps less defined than expected. The area is murky, and one must extrapolate with care. Assassination, in our opinion, is viewed as unlawful, but it is not clear that every act of discrete, politically motivated killing will be characterized as assassination. However, that subset of "assassinations" that might be deemed lawful would appear to be limited if it exists at all. Tyrannicide in the case of the wicked dictator presents the most compelling moral setting, yet its legal appraisal is no easier. Applications are difficult. One person's tyrant is another's hero. It is humbling to note that Muammar Qaddafi emerged in a poll in 1990 as widely admired by young people in Third World countries and that Saddam Hussein enjoyed substantial popularity in parts of the Arab world.

In our view, assassination should be viewed as an unlawful covert action and should not be given any color of law. Nevertheless, it is clear that there is a certain conditional tolerance for this at the elite level, a trend that prevents us from saying that it is prohibited as a matter of law.[176] Because of difficulties of definition, legal analysis of the lawfulness of such issues is best resolved with a contextual reading of each case that relies on both political context and reference to the traditional doctrines governing the use of force: proportionality, necessity, and discrimination concerning the target.

5. Security Council Resolution 138, Question Relating to the Case of Adolf Eichmann, has been found by at least one United States Circuit Court to stand for the proposition that international kidnapping in the name of law enforcement is a violation of international law.[177] Indeed, when set against the enormity of Eichmann's offense against humanity, the resolution is all the more compelling as a precedent for the principle of absolute state sovereignty.

Symbolic reparations between states, however, can be an ineffective enforcement or restraint mechanism and, for the individual seized, an irrelevant one. Moreover, contemporary state practice may suggest that "forcible extradition," while often protested vociferously on the bilateral level, is tolerated on the international level, provided a minimal or proportionate use of force is involved in the seizure and the norm that the seized person violated is deemed to be one of general concern.

We conclude that there is a norm against forcible extradition, but the intensity with which it will be demanded in particular cases depends on many variables. Conclusions of lawfulness seem to be affected by the particular answers to the questions "who" seizes "whom", "why," and "how". In our view, the *Toscanino* court should be seen as abundantly optimistic when it writes, "The Resolution [U.N. Doc. S/4349] merely recognizes a long standing principle of international law that abductions of persons located within the territory of another violate the territorial sovereignty of the second state and are redressable usually by the return of the person kidnapped." If anything, covert extradition appears to be on the rise.[178]

6. The Rainbow Warrior incident may be much more instructive about the future, for it did not involve a state target, but rather a private target within the jurisdiction of another state, whose neutralization required the preparation and implementation of a raid that had to be concealed from both the target and the host state. The indignation of the host state, New Zealand, at the violation of its jurisdiction was all the more understandable, because, for some two decades, it had opposed the French nuclear tests, which it continued to view as violating its international rights. New Zealand viewed Greenpeace as a nongovernmental knight in shining armor. The reactions of other state actors, some of whom may themselves have been past or prospective targets of Greenpeace or have contemplated such actions against terrorists or drug traders, appeared to have been

much more subdued than the media and popular reactions. One finds here certain structural similarities between this incident and Arab-Israeli covert operations *inter se* in Western Europe and other parts of the Mediterranean. The mysterious sinking of the ill-fated PLO ferry *Al Awda* (formerly *Sol Phryne*) in Cyprus and the virtual absence of international reaction may be considered in this regard.[179]

7. Covert operations appear to be more often condemned when they involve independent and disproportionate violations of other norms governing violence, such as murder or assassination. Compare, for example, the relative treatment of Eugene Hasenfus, who was shot down while dropping supplies to the Contras to that of French officers Mafart and Prieur implicated in the explosion and (apparently unintended) death aboard *Rainbow Warrior*. In like manner, one suspects that covert surveillance of one's own citizens on foreign soil has sometimes been grudgingly tolerated. As the Letelier case indicates, assassination is not.[180] Reactions in all three of these cases must be gauged by reference to contemporary political responses whether protest, silence, or diplomacy.

8. Though governments continue to use coercion against each other, they seem to share a common interest in keeping the tools and prerogatives of coercion in governmental hands. State covert operations are more likely to be tolerated than private covert operations with the same objectives and employing the same means. Chile is a case in point. The United Nations investigated ITT and Kennecott efforts to destabilize Allende, which, in turn, contributed to passage of General Assembly Resolution 3514, Measures against Corrupt Practices of Transnational and Other Corporations, Their Intermediaries and Others Involved. There was, however, no comparable investigation of foreign state interference in Chile.

9. As one moves along the continuum from covert and localized to overt and generalized conflict, attitudes about the lawfulness of covert actions change. Covert operations in support of overt military operations are often analyzed as single, integrated operations, their validity tested against that of the overall mission. This, despite the fact that the law of armed conflict frequently segregates unlawful parts of otherwise lawfully conducted missions. Discrete covert operations in support of the aborted United States hostage rescue mission were neither challenged nor condemned as they became known.[181] So too, Israeli operations prior to the Entebbe raid were not discussed independently of the merits of the overall mission.

Some recognition of this attitude is reflected in the Protocols Additional to the Geneva Conventions. Protocol I, for example, is textually tolerant of covert deployment of forces preceding an attack. Article 44.3 provides in pertinent part:

> . . . there are situations in armed conflicts where, owing to the nature of the hostilities an armed combatant cannot so distinguish himself, he shall retain his status as a combatant, provided that, in such situations, he carries his arms openly:
> (a) during each military engagement, and
> (b) during such time as he is visible to the adversary while he is engaged in military deployment preceding the launching of an attack . . .

In the context of Entebbe and Iran, Article 44.3 can be viewed as incident neutral and not necessarily "pro-terrorist." However, the gray area between war and peace that has been a basic feature of international politics since 1945 makes the implementation of this sort of provision difficult.

## INTERNATIONAL LEGAL APPRAISAL

### Proactive Overt Uses of Force

As one would imagine, the views of jurists on the issue of coercive proactive covert operations diverge greatly and passionately. For those who reject *any* unilateral use of force that is not self-defensive in the sense of the *Caroline*[182] incident, the question of the possible lawfulness of proactive covert actions simply does not arise. If one adopts a strict textual interpretation of international law, one need look no further than the United Nations Charter for the answer to these questions. Article 2(4) proscribes the use of force except in self-defense and "armed attack" is the threshold for self-defense. In this particular reading, Article 2(4) would effectively rule out any lawful unilateral proactive use of force, whether covert or not.

That approach rests on a rigid and noncontextual reading of Article 2(4), a method of interpretation we would not endorse in any circumstances. As a general matter, one should not seek point-for-point conformity to a rule without constant regard for the policy or principle that animated its prescription. Article 2(4) does not even address the majority of covert operations that may be politically and ideologically coercive in effect but do not employ military force. Yet many of those covert operations should, in our view, be deemed unlawful. Would world order be served by their blanket authorization? The consequence of the textualistic legal approach does not serve the interests and fundamental objectives of the United Nations and contribute to the fulfillment of an inclusive or common interest in the maintenance of minimum world order.

The challenge to scholars and students of this area of the law is to clarify, with as much specificity as possible, the policies and the contingent events that will render proactive strategy applications lawful. It is beyond peradventure that the fundamental postulate of political legitimacy of our century is the right of peoples to shape their own political community and freely to choose governments that are responsive to their wishes and consistent with overarching international human rights norms. Those who require textual authority for this proposition may find it in the United Nations Charter, the Universal Declaration of Human Rights, the Covenants, the Declaration on Friendly Relations, the Helsinki Accords, and many others. International events in the past three years confirm that those documents express the deepest yearnings of most people in this century.

It is equally clear that most people about the planet survive in circumstances and under governments that fall far from this international standard. Anyone who is animated by the fundamentally liberal impulse to help others by mobilizing government support when autonomous social and market forces themselves are not likely to remedy serious social pathologies can hardly look across political boundaries at the travail of fellow human beings without demanding some effective remedy. Given the inability of international organizations until now to fulfill the promises and achieve the standards of that system, either individual states (or nonstate entities) must act or the promises must be abandoned. Indeed, there may be no escape from this. Eisuke Suzuki has argued that "in a global state of interdependence and simultaneity, a traditional proscription of 'foreign intervention' in internal events has become obsolete."[183] "External actors are decision-makers that influence the course of events by modulating their behavior and symbolic communications toward contending groups in the contestation for power."[184] Consistent with such reasoning, to not intervene is in effect a decision to throw one's own national support behind the currently predominant contestant, however illegitimate its claim to authority.

In a decentralized constitutive system with the black letter of the Charter, the resolutions of the General Assembly, the claims of superpowers, and the emergent operational code so often incongruent, the critical question is not whether coercion has been or should be applied, but whether it has been or will be applied in support of or against community order and basic policies, and whether the application will be accomplished in ways whose net consequences include increased congruence with community goals and minimum order. Genuine self-determination is one of these community goals, in our view, the basic postulate of political legitimacy in this century.

We do not minimize the dangers of even a qualified authorization to use force unilaterally, a fortiori covertly in an international political system that lacks the institutions to control potential abuses. It is the same institutional weakness that presses one to act unilaterally in these circumstances. Fortunately, the international social process is increasingly integrated with a system of communications that transmits events rapidly to all parts of the planet and retransmits reactions to those initial communications. This system acts as a type of international decision-making process and may have the potential for providing rapid and effective judgments about unilateral uses of force. If there is general agreement on the criteria to be applied in such appraisals, the prospect of condemnation may act as some restraint. This is, we acknowledge, far from a satisfactory arrangement, particularly when confronted with totalitarian societies such as Iraq's under Saddam Hussein. But the alternatives seem even less desirable. A blanket prohibition on the unilateral use of coercion in the "right" circumstances and for the "right" reasons simply immunizes evil from remedy. We would distinguish, however, responsible state action from freelance private acts by anarchists or issue zealots. Permitting episodic covert actions without appraisal appears, to us, to incorporate the worst of all the alternatives.

Though all interventions are lamentable, the fact is that some may serve, in terms of aggregate consequences, to increase the probability of the free choice of peoples about their government and political structure. In some instances, it may be the only possibility. Other interventions have the manifest objective and consequence of doing exactly the opposite. There is, thus, neither need nor justification for treating in a mechanically equal fashion, United States covert operations in postwar Greece or Italy, which sought to enable the exercise of self-determination, on the one hand, and Soviet covert intervention in Poland or Cuban operations in Central America, which undermine popular movements and impose undesired regimes on coerced populations, on the other. A mechanically equal assessment of U.S. actions in Grenada and Panama and Soviet actions in Hungary, Czechoslovakia, and Afghanistan ignores objective and consequence which is what politics, morals, and law are all about. It is like equating a mugger's knifing of a citizen on the street with a surgeon's removal of a tumor from that ailing citizen, because both actions involve one human being's putting a knife into another. The strikingly different appraisals of these various cases by the international legal system should occasion no surprise.

### Proactive Covert Uses of Force

The fact that some interventions may be lawful does not necessarily mean that a covert intervention in the same circumstances would also be lawful. Secrecy has tactical advantages but may also involve costs to many other policies. Strict utility theory may argue in favor of covert operations to achieve outcomes otherwise obtainable by a sanctioned use of force. If, for example, the elite of one nation has a dispute with the elite of another nation and diplomatic means have failed, resort to covert action is less costly in terms of deprivation of values and lives than military intervention. Moreover, because covert operations may employ instrumentalities short of military force, they do not authorize the unilateral or community response that would be triggered by direct armed attack.

But there are serious costs as well. An overt operation must be preceded by a community decision condemning the target to whatever deprivations are to be applied, thereby reinforcing both the norm in question as well as community procedures for decision making. A covert operation does not accomplish any of these important objectives. The architects of overt actions can be identified and subjected to appraisal and, if appropriate, legal action. Not so with covert operations. Domestically, covert operations divert decision from broad community participation to a much narrower group, with the concomitant risks of "groupthink," which may have occurred during United States planning for the Bay of Pigs.

A crude comparison may be drawn between a police vigilante action that "takes out" a presumed "bad guy" and legal, overt apprehension of the same person and his trial. The fact that the latter course may consume an enormous amount of the criminal justice budget and even the lives of some policemen is generally deemed to be an acceptable social cost. Playing by the rules in domestic settings may be both policy and utility responsive.

But is it always policy responsive in an international setting? If, to make the discussion simpler, we address only the problem of the wicked homicidal dictator, we discover that overt means carry their own heavy costs. Economic deprivatory strategies, like all economics, presuppose a universe of rational actors who seek to optimize wealth and the conditions for securing it. The use of overt and covert economic strategies against a thug will have no effect, for, as reported about Noriega or Idi Amin in Uganda, he may not care that his country is being impoverished. As sanctioning states tighten the economic screws, the victims are innocent. In the meanwhile, the wicked dictator may continue to wreak havoc on his people. In other circumstances, the suffering community may simply lack the means of removing the wicked dictator.

The same sorts of considerations arise with regard to tyrants. As we saw in our review of the Trujillo incident, the option of simply banishing the dictator was deemed by local opposition leaders as well as observers in the United States embassy as ineffective. Trujillo had cached large reserves abroad and from a base in, let us say Spain, could be expected to harry the succeeding government mercilessly and obsessively. What should one do in such circumstances?

In these circumstances, none of the choices available to decision makers is particularly attractive. Each option has serious short- and longer-term social costs. Massive invasion has its own direct and peripheral costs. Covert operations may sometimes minimize destruction of total values in disputes between elites regarding elite objectives. They may sometimes be the only feasible means to accomplish a mission. They may also minimize the risk of arena escalation. But, as we have seen, they have their own costs. And they are far from negligible.

In our view, the legality of any proactive covert operation should be tested by whether it promotes the basic policy objectives of the Charter, for example, self-determination; whether it adds to or detracts from minimum world order; whether it is consistent with contingencies authorizing the *overt* use of force; and whether covert coercion was implemented only after plausibly less coercive measures were tried. Covert measures must meet the requirements of the law of armed conflict such as proportionality and discrimination. Insofar as the measure concerned requires notification and the opportunity for the putative target to change its offending behavior, a covert measure should be preceded by a warning, as for example, was President Carter's rescue mission.

# Chapter 4

## International Legal Regulation of Reactions to Covert Activity

Low-intensity conflict, like many other legal and military terms of art, is used in a comparative and relative sense to distinguish conflicts in which the types of armament and intensity of destruction are relatively confined.[1] Low-intensity conflict is an ambiguous term, encompassing a range of political, economic, and military modalities; one man's low-intensity conflict may be another man's high-intensity or total conflict. The term has not proven particularly satisfactory or clear in the context of United Nations practice.

Our concern in this chapter is with the emerging international law regarding lawful *reactions* to the covert military operations of others, and how the United Nations has chosen to define that problem. Because covert operations are generally low intensity in character, one must examine the problem in that context. Lawful reactions to covert operations employing the diplomatic, economic, or ideological instruments are largely governed by the Vienna Convention on Diplomatic Relations, by norms of reciprocity, and by counter-measures, the subject of the next chapter.

In international law, the terms of art that have been devised to control lawful responses to low-intensity conflict are "armed attack" (the necessary precipitating event) and "self-defense" (the lawful response). The term *armed attack* was fashioned to give decision makers a range of appreciation and discretion when encountering uses of the military instrument. The term is not precise.

The General Assembly has addressed the issue of low-intensity conflict in terms of general prohibitions against indirect aggression and in some instances covert coercion. These broad prohibitions are defined with reference to state support for armed bands. As will be recalled, General Assembly Resolution 2625 (Friendly Relations)[2] proclaims inter alia

[e]very State has a duty to refrain from organizing or encouraging the organization of irregular forces or armed bands, including mercenaries, for incursion into the territory of another State.

Every State has the duty to refrain from organizing, instigating, assisting or participating in acts of civil strife or terrorist acts in another State or acquiescing in organized activities within its territory directed towards the commission of such acts, when the acts referred to in the present paragraph involve a threat or use of force.

The right of self-help is also textually constrained. Thus, "States have a duty to refrain from acts of reprisal involving the use of force" and "a threat or use of force . . . shall never be employed as a means of settling international disputes." But the section of the resolution denoted "General Part" states that: "Nothing in this Declaration shall be construed as prejudicing in any manner the provisions of the Charter . . . " including the right of self-defense.

The Declaration on the Strengthening of International Security[3] reaffirms that

[s]tates must fully respect . . . the right of peoples to determine their own destinies, free of external intervention, coercion or constraint, especially involving the threat or use of force, overt or covert . . . [and] . . . that every State has the duty to refrain from organizing, instigating, assisting or participating in acts of civil strife or terrorist acts in another State.

This resolution urges states to seek peaceful settlement of disputes and reaffirms that force will not be used in contravention of the Charter.

With the "Definition of Aggression" Resolution,[4] the General Assembly tried to move toward a more precise threshold to determine when the use of force in self-defense would be consistent with Article 51 of the Charter.[5] Although nowhere explicitly stated, the Report of the Special Committee on the Question of Defining Aggression and its commentary imply that armed attack is "aggression," and it triggers the right, under Article 51, to self-defense. A key part of the regime of Article 51 is unilateral action, which presupposes unilateral determination that certain acts constitute aggression. But Resolution 3314 decrees that not all uses of force constitute "armed attack" and/or are aggression. One of the consequences of this innovation was to attempt to reduce substantially the competence of the state which deemed itself under attack to characterize the event as aggression and to respond in self-defense. In this respect, the right of self-defense was attenuated.

This also had implications for the question of whether covert action might be deemed to be aggressive. As long as questions such as this remained within the unilateral competence of the state which believed itself under attack, that state would resolve the matter on a case-by-case basis. But with an attenuation of the rights of Article 51, the meaning of the Charter with regard to covert action became a more urgent question.

On its face, it is not clear whether the Charter's prohibition on the use of military force incorporated "covert coercion" or indirect aggression and whether such coercion would give rise to a right of self-defense.[6] Put more concisely, it is unclear whether low-level acts of coercion were "aggression" with all that this entailed. While drafting the Resolution, the so-called six powers of the Special Committee moved to include in Article 1 the proposition that "the term aggression is applicable, without prejudice to a finding of threat to the peace or breach of the peace, to the use of force in international relations, *overt or covert, direct or indirect,* . . . (emphasis supplied)." This proposal was defeated as was an additional amendment that referred to force "however exerted." States feared the language was too broad and would too easily lead to a breach of the peace being regarded as an act of aggression.[7]

The net result of this exercise was to shift the focus of Article 51 from consequences for the targeted state to *mode* of attack by the erstwhile aggressor. Henceforth, only specific types of indirect aggression conducted at specified levels of intensity were to be included in the definition. By apparently developing an objective criterion, the drafters here may have thought that they were introducing a degree of international supervision and control to what theretofore had been a matter of unilateral appreciation that might be subject to abuse. At the same time, however, they were closing the safety valve that had made the Charter system acceptable. That would have been justified if an international enforcement system could move into the vacuum created and itself effectively respond to the sorts of contingencies for which the right of self-defense was designed. Yet the overall paralysis of the international security machinery continued. As a result, the progress made here was only apparent. However, the question of covert coercion per se was not addressed. Article 6 retained qualifying language to the effect that nothing in the definition enlarges or diminishes the scope of the Charter. Though this stated the obvious, it must have provided some consolation to the losers.

Not surprisingly, Article 3(g) has presented interpretative problems in the context of low-intensity conflict. Article 3 states inter alia that

Any of the following acts . . . qualify as an act of aggression . . . .

(g) The sending by or on behalf of a State of armed bands, groups, irregulars or mercenaries, which carry out acts of armed force against another State of such gravity as to amount to the acts listed above, or its substantial involvement therein.

Competence to proscribe other uses of force is left to the Security Council. As Benjamin Ferencz reports, the phrase "substantial involvement therein" was a compromise *between* the threshold phrase "invasion or attack" and a more restrictive formulation built around the phrase "or its open and active participation therein." A group composed of African and Arab states who wished to maintain flexibility and an impunity that would allow them to support national liberation movements favored the former phrase whereas the Western states sought inclusion of the latter.[8] As we will see, the version favoring the more limited authorization for self-defense was eventually adopted by the ICJ in the *Nicaragua* case.

The Declaration on the Inadmissibility of Intervention and Interference in the Internal Affairs of States (1981) includes a more comprehensive prohibition against the use of covert coercion adopting terms similar to those favored by the six powers for the Definition of Aggression. The resolution, however, returns to the earlier formula of making the declaration contingent on already existing Charter rights and exempting "the right and duty of States fully to support the right to self-determination . . . as well as . . . peoples to wage political and armed struggle to that end, in accordance with the purposes and principles of the Charter" from its application.[9]

Following adoption of these earlier resolutions, the General Assembly has sought to limit the right of coercive self-defense to "armed attack." As a result, legal attention has focused more on mode and less on where, in the continuum of coercion, the threshold of the term *armed attack* lies. Moreover, merely characterizing certain actions, as for example, "armed bands" or "irregulars" seems to create an assumption that they *do not* constitute an "armed attack." Yet even that has changed. As a consequence, from the Definition of Aggression to the Merits Phase of *Nicaragua,* the threshold for lawful armed response to covert action, as articulated in the language of the United Nations and its organs, has become higher.

One of the consequences of these resolutions was to encourage states to report incidents of covert coercion and actions by limited overt armed force; this was, after all, the remedy that replaced self-defense for these contingencies.[10] Ironically, these same reports, gathered pursuant to agenda items on implementation of the Declaration on the Strengthening of International Security and Good Neighborliness, also make clear that the norms in these resolutions have been ineffective. Whether the complaint entailed initial or reactive force, there has been little condemnation of, or response to, incidents that did not appear to engage Cold War interests or, more recently, self-determination or apartheid. In a curious example of legal iatrogenics, the result has been to force the target of covert armed aggression itself to respond with covert and low-intensity options, a regime that not only does not appear to deter low-intensity adventurism, but actually increases the volume of unregulated coercion. The armed attack threshold appears to increase the use of covert coercion in response to covert coercion in lieu of overt armed force or that hybrid form of covert action dubbed "overt covert" action.

The new pattern of application of these particular norms in the reactive mode can be gained from an examination of recent decisions by the political organs of the United Nations and the judgments of the International Court. We start with an incident from southern Africa, the international response to the South African incursions into neighboring African states on May 19, 1986. The dispute here derives from claims based on extant statehood (South Africa's) and claims based on violations of transnational values (racism and egregious human rights violations) and self-determination. We are interested here, not in the absolute or relative justice of particular claims, but in the legal paradigms that emerge from them and their implications for the future.[11]

South African troops had attacked the African National Congress (ANC) installations in downtown Harare, Zimbabwe, mounted helicopter and ground attacks near Gabarone and Mogditshane, Botswana, and mounted air attacks on housing settlements and refugee centers in Makeni, near Lusaka, Zambia. There was ample evidence that the ANC operated from those places and that the ANC was mounting incursions of forces, whether regular or irregular, and directing irregular activities within metropolitan South Africa.

The South African representative at the Security Council, Mr. Von Schirnding, defended his government's action as follows.

> . . . South Africa will not tolerate activities endangering our security . . . we will not hesitate to take whatever action may be appropriate for defense and security of our own people and for the elimination of terrorist elements who are intent on sowing death and destruction in our country and in our region. We will not allow ourselves to be attacked with impunity. We shall take whatever steps are appropriate to defend ourselves.

The converse claim, the basic African formula for the lawfulness of what groups like the ANC are doing, may be taken from an Organization of African Unity (OAU) resolution about the South West African People's Organization (SWAPO) in 1979; The OAU

> calls upon all progressive and peace-loving countries to render increased and sustained support in material, financial and military and other assistance to SWAPO . . . to facilitate the intensification of its legitimate armed struggle for the liberation of the people of Namibia.

The international reaction in this case is very instructive. The United States condemned the attacks, distinguishing them from the Libyan raid which the

United States had just mounted and which South Africa invoked as a justifying precedent. The United States characterized the ANC indirectly not as terrorists but as "some dissident groups." The United States expelled the South African military attaché in Washington and recalled its military attaché in Pretoria. The United Kingdom and the European Economic Community also condemned the raid. Canada temporarily recalled its ambassador from Pretoria. Argentina broke diplomatic relations. But a draft resolution prepared in the Security Council was vetoed by the United States and the United Kingdom.

This incident is instructive because it confirms the inversion of the traditional formula of international law for matters such as these. The irregular forces with sanctuary in a neighboring state who episodically invade the target state are now engaged in a lawful activity. The target state's responses, involving "going to the source," are unlawful.

Cases and incidents like these involve two innovations. First, it is quite clear that an aspirational norm is being used to recharacterize, retroactively, a hitherto lawful situation as unlawful. The state defending itself from change is per se the lawbreaker. The effect of this change is to shift the law in favor of the party that the United Nations chooses to view as struggling for "freedom and independence." Second, but only by implication, the content of the Charter conception of aggression and self-defense is being changed to preclude incursive responses by the victim into the territory in which the attacker has found haven. The effect of this innovation is to allow the low-level and protracted belligerent to operate with impunity outside the target state, whereas the target state is permitted to apprehend its adversary only *within* its own territory.

If the reaction to South Africa had been characterized as an internationally authorized departure from existing law, a type of *lex specialis* permitting the use of coercion to terminate apartheid, which everyone condemned, the generative legal consequences would have been much smaller. But the claims in that case were phrased in the most general terms, implying, if they were to be accepted, that new general principles were operating and that they would henceforth apply in all appropriate cases. This is what occurred. The revision of the formal theory of self-defense, which underlies cases such as the South African incursions of May 1986 developed over a period of time.

It is not clear from its text whether the Charter merely acknowledges the continuing legal effect of the customary right of self-defense or suppresses it and establishes an entirely new Charter-based "right." The issue is not theoretical or abstract, for suppression of the customary doctrine would limit the competence of a state contemplating self-defense to the new threshold fashioned by the term *armed attack*. As we have seen, the United Nations has claimed the competence to define the contingency for lawful self-defense, through the technical term *armed attack*.

Article 3(g) of the Definition of Aggression, considered briefly above, establishes what initially appears to be a quantitative threshold for the right of self-defense. Thus an armed attack includes

> The sending by or on behalf of a State of armed bands, groups, irregulars or mercenaries, which carry out acts of armed force against another State *of such gravity as to amount to the acts listed above [i.e., an actual armed attack conducted by regular forces, Article 3(a)] or its substantial involvement therein* (italics added).

In its affirmative part, this definition reinforces the mode rather than consequence criterion by saying that the mere fact that armed bands emanate from another state and engage in military activities in your state does not constitute "armed attack," the contingency that would justify pursuit or incursion into the other state's territory. Such responses will be deemed aggressive only when the attack by irregulars is of such gravity as to amount to an actual armed attack. More generally stated, only when this unspecified threshold is exceeded is the victim state entitled to act in self-defense. Obviously, this is a formula favorable to low-intensity conflict, which by definition does not often reach the level of "armed attack."

The implications of this innovation were made explicit and carried to their next logical phase by the International Court in its judgment on the merits in the *Nicaragua* case (June 27, 1986). There, the court takes the Charter definition and transforms it into customary law and vice versa, thereby excluding, it would seem, the old customary rights, including the general right of reprisal. Consider the court's statement at paragraph 181.

> However, so far from having constituted a marked departure from a customary international law which still exists unmodified, the Charter gave expression in this field to principles already present in customary international law, and that law has in the subsequent four decades developed under the influence of the Charter, to such an extent that a number of rules contained in the Charter have acquired a status independent of it. The essential consideration is that both the Charter and the customary international law flow from a common fundamental principle outlawing the use of force in international relations.

This merger, as it were, purports to exclude any unilateral rights to the use of force that derived from customary law and to superordinate the Charter regime and the Charter apparatus for its illumination. What then, in the court's view, is the Charter conception of the contingency for the right of self-defense?

The court narrows even more the General Assembly's conception. It excludes from "armed attack" and hence from the right of self-defense, many of the methods of low-intensity conflict. First, the court insists that acts of armed bands must "occur on a significant scale." Second, the court excludes by definition from the category of armed attack "assistance to rebels in the form of the provision of weapons or logistical support."

The language of the court here is instructive. "Such assistance may be regarded as a threat or use of force, or amount to intervention in the internal or external affairs of other states." Now these are all matters that bring into operation a contingent competence of the United Nations. If the target state thinks it can secure assistance from the United Nations, it can repair there, assuming that the United Nation's security machinery is effective (it rarely has been) and that the United Nations has not decided that the group attacking or assisting the military action in the target state is not "struggling for its freedom and independence." The point of emphasis is that what the attacking group is doing does not amount to armed attack and hence does not warrant any response that can be characterized as self-defense. Unilateral action is precluded. If a state responds to these low-level activities by force, its action itself is apparently a violation of international law.

The legal theory that has emerged is thus one that is tolerant of different forms of protracted and low-intensity conflict. While that conflict may be internationally unlawful and may give rise to a variety of protests, it does not, according to the theory developed by the court, permit the victim state to resort to levels of coercion contemplated in the right of self-defense. Moreover, the asymmetry that has been established here is one that, *pace* the court, is identical in both conventional international law (the Charter) and customary international law.

Many of these developments have presented new strategic problems for states that "have," are concerned with conserving what they have, and hence view themselves as largely in a defensive posture. On the one hand, such states are likely to see themselves as those most committed to the status quo and, hence, to limiting the unilateral use of force to bring about authoritatively approved if not authorized changes. The law they wish is the "inherent" right of self-defense that they believed was incorporated in the Charter.

But the change vector in contemporary international law has undermined the inherent conservatism of the older legal order. In many circumstances, more states committed to the changes sought by those engaged in nonconventional warfare have been willing to provide certain types of aid to those engaged in unconventional activities: base camps, military supplies and logistical support, intelligence support, and sanctuary. To be sure, activities like these had taken place before. But the formal legal sanction has encouraged more states to engage in them and made it easier for irregular forces requiring aid to agitate for its supply.

It is no surprise, then, that states which have been the targets of attack emanating from such sanctuary areas have sought to establish a norm or corollary, if you like, permitting them to go to the source of the attacks on them, even if that meant a physical intervention in the territory and jurisdiction of another state. The claim is substantially the same, whether it is made by Israel with regard to Palestine Liberation Organization (PLO) bases in Lebanon or Tunisia; by South Africa, with regard to ANC bases in Swaziland, Botswana, Zimbabwe, Mozambique, or Angola; by the Soviet Union against Afghan resistance concentrations in Pakistan; by the United States against Nicaragua for its involvement in El Salvador or by Nicaragua against contra formations in Honduras. The claim has been based on either broader conceptions of the law of the Charter, which we have considered earlier, or on the revival, or as some have contended, the survival of customary international law.

The Soviet Union was the first explicit dissenter to a comprehensive conception of Article 2(4). Its doctrine of wars of national liberation claimed to be an exception to it. But Moscow now finds that its perception of its interests have changed and that, in the future it might itself be the target for this kind of action. The Soviet Union has, it would appear, begun to reappraise and to take a more critical view of its long-held views. Conversely, the United States, during the period of its support of "Freedom Fighters" hither and yon, itself took advantage of the new international law.

Changes are underway and they are no where more apparent than in the vacillations of the U.S. Executive. In October 1985, Israeli planes flew 1,500 miles to bomb PLO Headquarters, south of Tunis. The *New York Times* reported that between thirty and sixty people were killed. Israel apparently assumed that in a belligerent situation in which an adversary had made clear its intention to attack it, the target was not obliged to wait until the attacker selected a particular moment in order for it to have a right to respond. It, *pace* Israel, could select its own moment for self-defense. This appeared to be a legal view shared by many Western governments. At the same time, however, like the South African situation, many governments and key strata in many Western states have wearied of the Israeli-Palestinian conflict and would like to see a settlement allowing the establishment of a Palestinian community.

The initial White House response to the raid was that it was "a legitimate response against terrorist attacks." The next day, Secretary of State Shultz defended the Israeli action, while the White House began to inch away. The subsequent White House statement characterized the raid as "understandable as an expression of self-defense" but added that the bombing "cannot be condoned." The Security Council condemned the Israeli action by a vote of fourteen to zero. The United States abstained, even though the language of the resolution still condemned Israel's "active armed aggression."

Within a week, the *Achille Lauro* was hijacked by members of the PLO. Two days later, the hijackers surrendered in Egypt as part of a deal that was apparently cut before the Egyptians knew that the hijackers had murdered an American national. The Security Council unanimously condemned the hijacking of the ship. A day later, United States planes diverted the Egyptian plane carrying the hijackers to Tunisia. The plane was forced to land in Italy where those PLO operatives directly involved in the hijacking were arrested and eventually prosecuted. The diversion, though not a territorial intervention, was criticized by the Egyptians and by many Arab governments but widely acclaimed in the United States and Western Europe.

One may interpret U.S. actions here as vacillation, Rough Riderism or a combination of both. We believe that they are a belated and groping response to a complex problem that will have to be addressed by whoever is in the White House, whether or not the underlying controversy concerns Israel. Events such as the Libyan raid by the United States and the diversion of the Egyptian plane carrying the hijackers of the *Achille Lauro* must be seen in two ways. On the one hand, they may be viewed as episodic and opportunistic reactions to unconventional and low-intensity methods of warfare. In a more profound if not necessarily conscious sense, however, they represent an effort on the part of the United States to restructure the process of international lawmaking about the military instrument, shifting it away from organized arenas in which numerical majorities have yielded outcomes incompatible with what the United States perceives to be its interests and moving the issue back to a customary law arena in which effective political power, rather than voting power, trumps.

On a case-by-case and incident-by-incident basis, the United States is trying to lay the basis for a different international law in this regard. Although this method circumvents the numerical majority whose policies are unacceptable, it lacks, like the spasmodic method in which anti-apartheid law was fashioned, a coherent conception of what the law should be for a wide variety of future factual situations in which the United States may be proacting as well as reacting. This effort at a constitutive shift of lawmaking is part of a trend including other similar moves taken by the United States since it rejected the First Additional Geneva Protocol and the Law of the Sea Convention.

Given the structure of international politics, this American *démarche* will not be completely successful unless the Soviet Union joins it. That seems increasingly possible as the power of Russia further declines and President Gorbachev's attention remains at home. If *détente* becomes *entente,* the United States and the Soviet Union may, with their allies, press for a revision of the efforts at amending the Charter we have reviewed and the reinstallation of severe limitations on low-intensity conflict and enhancements of unilateral rights of self-defense, closer to the customary international law conception. If this pattern of collaboration does not develop, the United States and some of its allies will be pressing their own view of law against that established by a numerical majority of states. The USSR did this for more than thirty years, with its doctrine of "wars of national liberation." That ambiguous symbol proved useful to many struggling groups and was ultimately adopted as their vision of law. The U.S. version may or may not undergo a comparable adoption. Whatever happens, this version will confuse the process by which international law is made and the specific law on this subject.

In addition to this constitutive shift, the United States is signalling its dissatisfaction with much of the content of the new law concerning the low-level use of the military instrument that has emerged, even while it continues to use this type of low-intensity force, or to support its use, on a selective basis. Although U.S. actions signal *eo ipso* that it believes that the old regime is no longer workable, they do not indicate what the new law in the new environment should be. This is dangerous, for current actions inevitably generate normative expectations; what serves interests in the short run may well disserve them in the longer run.

What the content of the new law will be with regard to reactions to low-level military use is as yet unclear. But it now seems probable that the theory developed by the General Assembly and the International Court of Justice will be unacceptable, at least to the United States. That fact alone, given the ineluctable relations between politics and law, will mean that this effort at lawmaking will probably be ineffective and will be amended. Even if the revised prescriptions are closer to those contemplated in 1945, the demand for "exceptions" that benefit groups seeking to overturn governments and enjoying the support of large parts of the international community will continue to operate, for authority conceptions will be influenced by the United Nations.

In the short term, however, the tolerance for low-intensity conflict implicit in the developments we have recorded will probably lead to a net increase in violence in international politics. Targets of low-intensity warfare will themselves have no choice but to resort to the same techniques. As a result, arena-restricted conflict, a major goal of the law of war and a more urgent one in the modern technical environment, will expand over a wider geographical area, as both protagonists and antagonists conduct wars of low-intensity conflict about the globe.

# Chapter 5

# Countermeasures and
# Covert Actions

Under the regime envisaged by the drafters of the United Nations Charter, a state's principal right to use force unilaterally was in self-defense. As illustrated in the preceding chapter, a line of decisions, culminating in *Nicaragua,* has sought to narrow the operation of this right even further by creating a new and higher legal threshold, by redefining the technical term *armed attack* and using it as the prerequisite for unilateral resort to self-defense. The events precipitating a lawful self-defensive action must, according to this innovative view, have exceeded that threshold prior to the initiation of the unilateral act of self-defense. It is unclear whether this standard will become international law or will remain stillborn, like much of the General Assembly's legislative program in the 1970s, having been rejected by indispensable actors in the international prescriptive process.

Ironically, as the General Assembly and the International Court were seeking to contract both the Charter-based and the customary right of self-defense, they and the International Law Commission were creating and expanding an alternative ground for the unilateral use of force with few of the constraints they had imposed on self-defense: the so-called countermeasures.

The development of this form of unilateral action must be seen in the context of "reprisals." In addition to self-defense, customary international law provided another contingency for the use of reactive armed force: the "nonbelligerent right of armed reprisal" in response to international wrongful acts.[1] The nonbelligerent reprisal was distinct from the reprisal competence of a belligerent during war in response to violations of the law of war.[2] Traditionally, reprisal in war has been associated with efforts to deter the first use of illegal or inhumane weapons such as gas. Reprisals must be distinguished from retorsions. Retorsions are unfriendly, but not unlawful acts, undertaken for remedial motives, for example, suspension of foreign aid or arms sales in response to human rights abuses. In contrast, a reprisal is an unlawful act that is justified as a response to the prior unlawful act of another state.

The customary distinction between nonbelligerent reprisal and self-defense was one of motive. Self-defense, in theory, was protective in nature and used to thwart an immediate attack or threat of attack; reprisal was remedial or retaliatory. A reprisal that was proportionate to the precipitating wrongful act, reasonably necessary (a concept perforce different from its application in other situations of armed conflict), and, in certain situations, preceded by a prior demand for reparation or cessation was deemed to be a lawful use of force.

Some scholars believe that the Charter, especially the second and third paragraphs of Article 2, prohibits armed reprisal per se.[3] If the collective security system and the U.N. enforcement of international rights had obviated war, they had, it was reasoned, also obviated a state's need to resort to all forms of military force to vindicate its rights. But when the Charter's collective security system proved unable to operate, the vacuum was filled with a set of discrepant practices.

States were resorting to what amounted to acts of reprisal, and whether explicitly or implicitly, claiming a right to do so. But the legal term *reprisal* was no longer being used for legal justification. In some cases, this term was eschewed for policy reasons. The United States, for example, does not engage in reprisals. All its factual reprisals are matters of self-defense. In other cases, the term itself simply did not fit the facts. In what had come to be called low-intensity conflicts, for example, undeclared guerrilla wars, and within the terrorism counterterrorism cycle, both sides were using relatively low-level and intermittent applications of coercion in ways to which notions of deterrence, retaliation, anticipatory self-defense, and aggression could be applied only with great difficulty and adjustment. Using the terms of traditional legal analysis, it is often difficult to determine in these sorts of conflicts, where the cycle of incidents began, and with which or whose wrongful act.[4] Because so much violence was unilateral, there was a great deal for jurists to do. But without a set of legal criteria for appraising lawfulness, international decision makers were discovering that they had hobbled themselves.

At least part of what used to be called the nonbelligerent reprisal or the right of state reprisal in peacetime has been subsumed under the new doctrine of countermeasures. The countermeasure is a conglomeration of older notions of self-defense, retorsion, reprisal, and reciprocity, but it incorporates new contingencies for its operation and new conceptions of lawful levels of intensity. A review of law-making efforts, international jurisprudence, commentary, and incidents indicates that more than a semantic change is involved. First, the scope and form of countermeasures is more expansive. They are not limited to wrongs that were inflicted by acts of armed force. Countermeasures are deemed to be a legitimate response to economic and political wrongs as well as military infractions. Second, while maintaining some of the superficial elements of reprisal, for example, unfulfilled demand, the new doctrine, as expressed in the International Law Commission's Draft Articles on State Responsibility, appears, in a number of ways, to be more permissive than its predecessor. A broader discretion is assigned to the injured state with regard to contingencies for and the targets of its countermeasures.

The ICJ has cited the doctrine of countermeasures, as we will see, in the *Case concerning United States Diplomatic and Consular Staff in Teheran* (United States v. Iran) and *Military and Paramilitary Activities in and against Nicaragua* (Nicaragua v. United States).[5] The doctrine, however, is an incipient one, and it is still too early to assess whether it will take hold and how it will develop. It has not supplanted claims of self-defense or the other exceptions that have been invoked by actors to justify uses of coercion. Some of the purported limitations on self-defense that we considered in the previous chapter have not yet led states to plead countermeasures as an alternative ground.

## DEVELOPMENT

The term *countermeasures* was first used explicitly in the *Air Services*[6] and *United States v. Iran*[7] cases. But because states had been using what amounted to countermeasures, then called reprisals, long before these decisions, scholarly commentary on the subject of countermeasures should begin by discussing the critical modern international decisions on nonbelligerent and belligerent reprisals: the *Naulilaa Incident*[8] and *Cysne*[9] cases, two decisions of the Portugal/Germany Arbitration Tribunal. In both decisions, the tribunal upheld the principle of the limited right of unilateral armed reprisal but found that as that right was applied in those cases, Germany had violated international law.

The *Naulilaa Incident* was precipitated by the killing of three German officials in then Portuguese Angola and the internment of two others. In response, the Germans attacked and destroyed a fort and four Portuguese outposts and caused considerable loss of life. The lawfulness of the German action was submitted to arbitration. The tribunal noted that "reprisals are an act of taking the law into its own hands by the injured State, an act carried out—after an unfulfilled demand—in response to an act contrary to the law of nations by the offending state. . . . They would be illegal" if the earlier act "had not caused the motive."[10] As applied to this case, however, the tribunal found that Germany lacked such a motive. Moreover, the reprisals were not proportionate to the offending conduct of the Portuguese authorities and violated the rule that a reprisal be preceded by an unfulfilled demand.

The *Cysne* involved the sinking of a Portuguese vessel of that name by a German U-boat in 1914. The Declaration concerning the Laws of Naval War (London Declaration) proscribed certain articles as "absolute contraband" subject to the law of war. The Germans, however, unilaterally added to this list and sank the *Cysne* which was carrying those items to the United Kingdom. Germany defended its action as a lawful reprisal in response to British violations of the London Declaration. The tribunal, however, ruled that "only reprisals taken against the provoking state are permissible."[11] Portugal could not be considered the provoker and, indeed, had yet to enter the conflict.

Countermeasures have also been equated with measures of self-help. In the *Corfu Channel Case,*[12] the International Court of Justice was asked, among other things, to determine whether the United Kingdom had violated Albanian sovereignty when it swept the Corfu channel for mines on November 12 and 13, 1946. Although the United Kingdom did not explicitly claim a right of reprisal in this case, the court did address the United Kingdom's extended claim of self-defense, that is, a right of self-protection or self-help.

Against the backdrop of the impending Greek civil war, Albanian coastal batteries fired on British naval vessels transiting the straits of Corfu in May 1946. The British navy next asserted its right of "innocent passage" through the straits in October 1946, but, this time, it proceeded with armament in fore and aft position. Two destroyers struck mines and were heavily damaged and forty-four crew members killed. Subsequently, the United Kingdom argued before the court that its mine-sweeping operation was justified on the grounds of self-protection and self-help. The court held that "the action of the British navy constituted a violation of Albanian sovereignty," but it refused to impose any further sanction upon the United Kingdom, other than the verbal rebuke of the judgment. Moreover, the court did not deem the mines that the United Kingdom had unlawfully swept inadmissible as evidence. On the contrary, it relied upon the evidence of the mines and based a number of factual conclusions upon them. The *Corfu Channel Case* has recently been cited in support of a United States right to take positive counteraction against the laying of mines in the Persian Gulf.[13]

As international tribunals were moving towards a concept of permissible countermeasures, the United Nations was trying to extend a prohibition against armed reprisal in the absence of Security Council authorization. The first steps were taken by the Security Council within the context of the Middle East conflict. Security Council Resolution 56 (1948), for example, declared that "No party is permitted to violate the truce on the ground that it is undertaking reprisals or retaliations against the other party."[14] Sixteen years later, in response to the Harib Incident, the Security Council adopted Resolution 188, which "[c]ondemns reprisals as incompatible with the purposes and principles of the United Nations."[15] In 1966 the Council "[e]mphasize[d] to Israel that actions of military reprisal cannot be tolerated."[16]

The General Assembly also explicitly prohibited the right of armed reprisal. General Assembly Resolution 2625 (Declaration concerning Friendly Relations) proclaims that "States have a duty to refrain from acts of reprisal involving the use of force." General Assembly Resolution 3314 (XXIX 1974), the Definition of Aggression, does not directly address the issue of reprisals, but it does state "No consideration of whatever nature, whether political, economic, military or otherwise, may serve as a justification for aggression." In addition, "The first use of armed force by a State in contravention of the Charter shall constitute prima facie evidence of an act of aggression." Such statements are notoriously circular. "Force in contravention of the Charter" is not all force nor is every use of force "aggression." In effect, these pronouncements only served to further delimit the classical doctrine of reprisal. They did not clarify what was permissible under an emerging doctrine not yet identified as countermeasures.

A positive doctrine of countermeasures began to emerge with greater clarity in the *Air Services Award* and the ICJ's decisions in *United States v. Iran* and *Nicaragua v. United States*. Air Services involved a dispute between France and the United States over interpretation of a 1946 Air Services Agreement as well as the validity of United States countermeasures taken in response to French actions to uphold their interpretation of the agreement.[17] The Direction générale de l'Aviation civile (DGAC) had refused to approve Pan Am's 1978 service flight plan and had then barred a Pan Am flight from disembarking its passengers at Orly Airport in Paris. The aircraft was surrounded by police and the captain instructed to return to London. Pan Am's flights to and from Paris were subsequently suspended. In response, the Civil Aeronautics Board (CAB) ordered Air France and Union de transports aériens to file all their existing flight schedules to and from the United States. A second CAB order, barring Air France from operating its three weekly flights from Paris to Los Angeles during the period for which Pan Am would be barred from operating its flights, was issued but not implemented.

Before the tribunal, France presented four arguments against what it considered United States acts of reprisal. First, France argued that the decisions of DGAC did not contradict the agreement and therefore could not justify reprisals. Second, the United States actions did not pass the test of necessity as other legal channels were available to settle the dispute.[18] Third, "the retaliation procedure should have been preceded by an unsuccessful formal request, as required by international law." Finally, the measures taken by the United States were disproportionate to the alleged wrong.[19]

In response, the United States argued that France's combined actions represented a prior breach of an international obligation; France suffered no injury as a result of United States actions; and,

> the theory of reprisals as represented by France, if correct, applies to armed reprisals only; in the present context, that theory could not be accepted until the institutions of international adjudication have evolved to the point where there are international tribunals in place with the authority to take immediate interim measures of protection, for otherwise a respondent State would lack any incentive to co-operate in the expeditious conclusion of arbitration proceedings.[20]

France countered that it was seeking reparation for moral damage and that the CAB orders did cause it material damage. Moreover, the CAB orders remained in force, presenting the possibility of future damages.[21]

In assessing "the principle of the legitimacy of the 'counter-measures'" the tribunal enunciated a general rule before applying it to the case at hand. "If a situation arises which, in one State's view, results in a violation of an international obligation by another State, the first State is entitled, within the limits set by the general rules of international law pertaining to the use of armed force, to affirm its rights through 'counter-measures.'"[22] These general rules include a requirement that countermeasures must contain some degree of equivalence or proportionality with the alleged breach, a factor determined by looking at the principle involved as well as the injuries. The "aim of counter-measures is to restore equality between the Parties and to encourage them to continue negotiations with mutual desire to reach an acceptable solution." A state, however, need not necessarily exercise a prior duty to negotiate, arbitrate, or submit a dispute for judicial settlement before undertaking countermeasures. And, by implication, a state must not always honor "the very general obligation to negotiate" set forth in Article 33 of the United Nations Charter.[23] On the basis of these remarkable general statements, "The Arbitral Tribunal does not believe it is possible, in the present state of international relations, to lay down a rule prohibiting the use of counter-measures during negotiations."[24] Nor must states necessarily refrain from countermeasures "where there is arbitral or judicial machinery which can settle the dispute," and in some cases even when proceedings are in progress. If, however, "the proceedings form part of an institutional framework ensuring some degree of enforcement of obligations, the justification for counter-measures will undoubtedly disappear." Reworded, "the position changes once the tribunal is in a position to act." But, "[a]s the object and scope of the power of the tribunal to decide on interim measures of protection may be defined quite narrowly, however, the power of the Parties to initiate or maintain counter-measures, too, may not disappear completely."[25]

*Air Services* was a commercial case before an arbitral tribunal. Moreover, the tribunal's decision itself was narrowly tailored, providing "that, *under the circumstances in question,* the United States Government had the right to undertake the action that it undertook . . . " (emphasis supplied).[26] The ICJ's ruling in *United States v. Iran* offered further validation for the doctrine, although the question of countermeasures was not itself an integral element of the case. *United States v. Iran* also begins to define judicially the permissible limits of countermeasures. We have considered part of this incident in chapter 3, and it will suffice to review it only briefly.

On November 4, 1979, the United States embassy compound in Teheran was seized by student militants. On the following day the United States consulates in Tabriz and Shiraz were also seized. On November 9, 1979, the United States permanent representative to the United Nations requested that the Security Council urgently consider the situation. A resolution calling for economic sanctions against Iran was voted on by the Security Council on January 13, 1980. The vote was ten in favor, two against, with two abstentions; the USSR, a permanent member of the Council, vetoed the resolution.

On November 29, 1979, the legal adviser of the Department of State filed an application instituting proceedings against the Islamic Republic of Iran before the ICJ asserting Iranian violations of international legal obligations to the United States as provided by five treaties and conventions including a bilateral Treaty of Amity, Economic Relations, and Consular Rights.

Prior to its application before the ICJ, however, the United States initiated certain unilateral actions against Iran, including the identification of Iranian students not in compliance with visas for the purposes of deportation, discontinuance of oil purchases, and a freeze on official Iranian assets in the United States. Following the indication of provisional measures by the court, the United States took other unilateral actions against Iran including the severance of diplomatic relations, a prohibition on exports from the United States to Iran, and cancellation of all visas for Iranian travel to the United States. In addition, the United States considered making reparations to the hostages and their families using the frozen Iranian assets. As a result of these unilateral United States actions, Iran challenged whether it was "open to the United States to rely on the 1955 Treaty." The court implicitly validated the United States measures, noting that they were measures taken in response to what the United States *believed* to be a prior wrongful act.[27]

More problematic for the court was the United States attempt to rescue the hostages on April 24–25, 1980, an action the United States justified at the time on humanitarian grounds and as self-defense. Although the court declined to rule on the legality of the operation, it noted with dismay that

> the Court was in course of preparing the present judgment adjudicating upon the claims of the United States against Iran when the operation of 24 April 1980 took place. The Court therefore feels bound to observe that an operation undertaken in those circumstances, from whatever motive, is of a kind calculated to undermine respect for the judicial process in international relations . . . [28]

The United States operation occurred within that time period which *Air Services* suggests is the least legitimate for the exercise of countermeasures. The court was "in a position to act," arguably before it was known whether the proceedings "ensured some degree of enforcement." If, however, the United States had acted after the court's decision of May 24, 1980, an application of the doctrine of *Air Services* may have produced a different outcome, assuming for the moment that military countermeasures are not prohibited per se by the Charter.

Judge Morozov (USSR), in dissent, offers a different and more restrictive reading of countermeasures than the majority in *United States v. Iran*. The United States, he argued, violated general international law and the Charter by imposing unilateral coercive measures against Iran including economic sanctions and military attack, all while the judgment of the court was pending. The freeze order, for example, was impermissible because its real purpose was domestic in nature (to underwrite a program against Iran for the hostages, the hostage families, and other U.S. claimants), and the United States decided unilaterally to undertake these actions after the Security Council failed to adopt similar sanctions.[29]

Countermeasures have been given a more systematic and codified form in the ongoing work of the International Law Commission.[30] The Draft Articles on State Responsibility[31] go beyond a codification of the case law and engage in a fair amount of "progressive development," in particular, with regard to the issue of the "impatient plaintiff," on which the United States had been rebuked. Article 10, of part two of the Draft Articles prepared by Professor Riphagen, pertaining to "the content, forms, and degrees of international responsibility," waives the requirement that the injured state exhaust the international procedures for peaceful settlement of a dispute in cases where "(b) . . . the State alleged to have committed the internationally wrongful acts fails to comply with an interim measure of protection ordered by such international court or tribunal."[32]

The commentary explains,

(7) [T]he third party may not be empowered to order *effective* interim measures of protection either on behalf of the claimant State or on behalf of the defendant State. In such a case, the claimant State has no choice but to take such measures unilaterally . . . (emphasis supplied).

(8) Finally, if the interim measures of protection ordered by the third party are not complied with, the system breaks down and the right to take measures of reprisal appears.[33]

The ICJ returned to the issue of countermeasures in 1986 in the Merits Phase of *Nicaragua v. United States*. In this case, however, the question of countermeasures was ancillary to the question of permissible self-defense. The court's brief dictum on countermeasures involving the use of force is found in paragraphs 248 and 249.

248. [H]aving rejected it [United States support for the Contras] on those terms [self-defense], the Court has nevertheless to consider whether it may be valid as action by way of counter-measures in response to intervention.

249. While an armed attack would give rise to an entitlement to collective self-defence, a use of force of a lesser degree of gravity cannot . . . produce any entitlement to take collective counter-measures involving the use of force. The acts of which Nicaragua is accused . . . could only have justified proportionate counter-measures on the part of the State which had been the victim of these acts, namely El Salvador, Honduras or Costa Rica. They could not justify counter-measures taken by a third State, the United States, and particularly could not justify intervention involving the use of force.

The court's language reiterates the principle of proportionality, required of both reprisals and countermeasures. The language also suggests that an armed attack may give rise to a right of proportional, and therefore military, action. But a military provocation less than an armed attack does not authorize a lower-level military response under the rubric of armed attack. The court restricts the right to take countermeasures to the victim state; Nicaragua's prior acts could only justify countermeasures effected by the victim state, El Salvador, but not by a third state, the United States.[34] This, Judge Schwebel argued in dissent, has dangerous implications for State B when faced with subversion short of armed attack from State A acting in conjunction with a Great Power.

[T]hird states could not use force, whether or not the preservation of political independence—or territorial integrity—of State B depended on the exertion of such measures. In short, the Court appears to offer—quite gratuitously—a prescription for overthrow of weaker governments by predatory governments while denying potential victims what in some cases may be their only hope of survival.[35]

The court's analysis regarding third state use of countermeasures is not persuasive. The presumption that the United States was not engaged in collective self-defense at the request of El Salvador, which the court rendered *juris et de jure* by not permitting El Salvador even to argue for its right to intervene, was outcome-determinative and of dubious lawfulness. Indeed, in subsequent phases of the case, judges who had voted against El Salvador on this point expressed their regret. Moreover, doctrines, variously styled self-defense, countermeasures, and something called counter-intervention, appear to be used interchangeably in the court's consideration of countermeasures,[36] thus limiting its comprehensibility and precedential value. In contrast, the International Law Commission has seemed to be quite comfortable with a right of countermeasures for states who are party to a violated treaty but not themselves directly deprived by the violation.

The ICJ proved more tolerant of United States use of the economic instrument against Nicaragua. The court, however, analyzed the United States embargo from the standpoint of nonintervention rather than countermeasures, leading to the following conclusion:

> 276. While the acts of economic pressure summarized in paragraphs 123 to 125 above are less flagrantly in contradiction with the purpose of the Treaty, the Court reaches a similar conclusion in respect of some of them. A State is not bound to continue particular trade relations longer than it sees fit to do so, in the absence of a treaty commitment or other specific legal obligation; but where there exists such a commitment, of the kind implied in a treaty of friendship and commerce, such an abrupt act of termination of commercial intercourse as the general trade embargo of 1 May 1985 will normally constitute a violation of the obligation not to defeat the object and purpose of the treaty. The 90 per cent cut in the sugar import quota of 23 September 1983 does not on the other hand seem to the Court to go so far as to constitute an act calculated to defeat the object and purpose of the Treaty. The cessation of economic aid, the giving of which is more of a unilateral and voluntary nature, could be regarded as such a violation only in exceptional circumstances.

## DOCTRINE

What are now called countermeasures are the stuff of international politics, part of the endless process of reciprocity and retaliation that lies at the base of all political organization. Unfortunately, international case law on countermeasures is sparse and not always instructive. Many cases tell us what is not permissible, but not what is or will be in a given context, or what criteria the jurist may deploy to make such assessments. International legal commentary does not measurably help to flesh out the doctrine but it does serve to confirm contemporary acceptance of countermeasures. But neither the Restatement of the Law (Third) nor the International Law Commission's Commentary on its Draft Articles on State Responsibility resolve questions regarding the use of forceful or covert countermeasures.

Countermeasures are discussed in the Restatement (Third) under "Unilateral Remedies":

(1) Subject to Subsection (2), a state victim of a violation of an international legal obligation by another state may resort to countermeasures that might otherwise be unlawful, if such measures
  (a) are necessary to terminate the violation or prevent further violation, or to remedy the violation; and
  (b) are not out of proportion to the violation and the injury suffered.
(2) The threat or use of force in response to a violation of international law is subject to prohibitions on the threat or use of force in the United Nations Charter, as well as to Subsection (1).[37]

According to this formulation, a legitimate countermeasure is a measure necessary to *remedy* a violation and proportionate to (1) a prior violation of an international obligation (2) by another state, subject to the international and Charter prohibitions regarding the threat or use of force. The Comments to the Restatement offer a more restrictive reading of necessity than either *Air Services* or Article 10 of the ILC Draft Articles discussed above. According to the American Law Institute, "counter-measures are to be avoided as long as genuine negotiation or third-party settlement is available and offers *some promise* of resolving the matter"[38] (emphasis supplied).

The International Law Commission, which continues to deliberate on this subject, offers a more permissive and contextual reading of countermeasures. Article 3, part 1, of the Draft Articles establishes an internationally wrongful act of a State as the threshold requirement for countermeasures. A wrongful act includes two elements. First, "conduct consisting of an act or omission is attributable to the state under international law," what the ILC Commentary terms the subjective element. Second, "the conduct constitutes a breach of an international obligation," the objective element.

Because countermeasures "always involve action which under different conditions . . . would represent a breach of an international obligation and an infringement of another's subjective right," Chapter 5 of the Draft Articles addresses "Circumstances Precluding Wrongfulness." That is, under certain circumstances, otherwise wrongful acts are justified. These circumstances in-

clude cases of legitimate consent, countermeasures, force majeure and for-
tuitous event, distress, state of emergency, and self-defense.[39] Article 30 (part
1) addresses countermeasures.

> Article 30. Countermeasures in respect of an internationally wrongful act
> The wrongfulness of an act of a State not in conformity with an obligation of that
> State towards another State is precluded if the act constitutes a measure legitimate
> under international law against that other State, in consequence of an internationally
> wrongful act of that other State.

According to the Commentary, countermeasures in response to internationally
wrongful acts may take one of two forms: (1) "Counter-measures having the
purpose of restoring balance in the positions of the author State and the injured
State (reciprocity);" and, (2) "countermeasures having the purpose of influencing a decision of the author State to perform its (new) obligations (reprisal)."[40]
Countermeasures in the form of reprisals must meet the special conditions of
Article 9 and Article 10 (part 2).

The ILC commentary is not precise, however, in defining what constitutes a
countermeasure that is "legitimate under international law." The right is not
unlimited but requires compliance with a qualified exhaustion of remedies and
a curious proportionality test, which allows the state applying countermeasures
to take account of both the intention and the consequences of the precipitating
act. "The injured State may not *normally* employ countermeasures . . . without
having first attempted and failed to obtain reparation" (that is, exhausted its
remedies; italics supplied).[41] The forms that countermeasures may lawfully
take vary according to the nature of the precipitating wrongful act (proportionality to intention and effect). Thus "justification for the 'weaker' countermeasure by way of reciprocity, or for the 'stronger' countermeasure by way of
reprisal, is connected with the intention and effect of the internationally wrongful act to which it is a response."[42]

There are, however, "a whole series of internationally wrongful acts which
. . . do not justify resort, or at any rate immediate resort—to punitive measures
or enforcement."[43] The Draft Articles do not specify what those acts are, and in
particular, do not indicate what precipitating acts permit "immediate resort" to a
countermeasure and what acts justify "punitive measures." Finally, the permissible scope of peripheral injury varies depending on whether the countermeasure is unilateral, or a sanction adopted by a competent international organization. In the latter case, countermeasures may infringe on the rights of a third
state, but in the former case, the rule of *Cysne* applies. "Only reprisals taken
against the provoking State are permissible."

Unresolved were questions concerning who would determine the existence of a prior wrongful act, whether an exhaustion of all alternative remedies was required prior to the use of armed force, and whether the act of reprisal had to be proportionate to the prior wrongful act or the purpose the reprisal intended to achieve.

## UNITED STATES POSITION

The United States position on reprisals during the period 1953 to 1975 is summarized in a 1979 report by the deputy assistant legal adviser for European affairs, Department of State:

Initially, the United States joined in the adoption of Security Council resolutions which isolated and condemned as illegal Israeli armed reprisals regardless of the provocations involved. [1953–1964] . . .

While the United States has modified its initial position of willingness to isolate armed reprisals and condemn them as illegal by insisting on a balanced condemnation of both the provocative acts, especially acts of terrorism, and the armed reprisal, the United States has not changed its position that reprisals involving the use of force are illegal . . .

In addition to the above possible examples of United States conduct of reprisal actions involving the use of force and threat of such uses of force, it is clear that the United States recognizes that patterns of attacks or infiltration can rise to the level of an "armed attack" thus justifying a responding use of force in the exercise of the right of self-defense . . .

In conclusion, it is clear that the United States has taken the categorical position that reprisals involving the use of force are illegal under international law; that it is generally not willing to condemn reprisals without also condemning provocative terrorist acts; and that it recognizes the difficulty of distinguishing between proportionate self-defense and reprisals but maintains the distinction. Where the United States has itself possibly engaged in reprisal action involving the use of force, characterization of the action has been confused by equating it also with self-defense. These so-called reprisal incidents took place in the context of a war justified by the United States Government as collective self-defense, and on this basis, could be distinguished from the reprisal raids conducted by Israel. It is also clear that the United States has determined that patterns of attacks can constitute a level of "armed attack" justifying the use of force in self-defense.[44]

When in 1974 Professor Eugene Rostow suggested that the United States endorse a right of reprisal under Article 51 of the Charter, Acting Secretary of State Kenneth Rush responded

As you know, it is the established policy of the United States that a state is responsible for the international use of armed force originating from its territory, whether that force be direct and overt or indirect and covert.

You would add a complementary principle, namely, that where a state cannot or will not fulfill its international legal obligations to prevent the use of its territory for the unlawful exercise of force, the wronged state is entitled to use force, by way of reprisal, to redress, by self-help, the violation of international law which it has suffered.

As you know, Resolution 2625 also contains the following categorical statement: "States have a duty to refrain from acts of reprisal involving the use of force." That injunction codifies resolutions of the Security Council which have so affirmed.

The United States has supported and supports the foregoing principle. Of course we recognize that the practice of states is not always consistent with this principle and that it may sometimes be difficult to distinguish the exercise of proportionate self-defense from an act of reprisal. Yet, essentially for reasons of the abuse to which the doctrine of reprisal particularly lends itself, we think it desirable to endeavor to maintain the distinction between acts of lawful self-defense and unlawful reprisal.[45]

As we will see in the next section, United States practice has differed markedly from its stated legal position.

## PRACTICE

This chapter cannot survey in comprehensive fashion the emerging practice of countermeasures. The limited case law and commentary reviewed is selected to illustrate changing perspectives and general rules. We focus here on five incidents that either entailed countermeasures in response to covert actions or were themselves covert military reactions to wrongful state acts and, as such, could be characterized as countermeasures. State actors, however, rarely invoke the doctrine of countermeasures to justify their actions. This has led in some cases to the invocation of the doctrine of self-defense as justification. The net result is a dilution in the clarity of international norms.

The first two incidents, the Cuban quarantine and the Libyan air raid, received world attention and considerable legal commentary. They illustrate the merger of the traditional distinctions between self-defense and reprisal. The third, fourth, and fifth incidents received little notice at the time and little commentary after the fact. They are illustrative of what one might call the tactical use of countermeasures, both economic and military.[46]

These incidents, alongside the Hostages case, suggest the contours of an emerging code that implicitly accepts the use of economic, diplomatic, and some military countermeasures. Each example presents a unilateral or multilateral response to what was believed to have been a prior unlawful act by another state short of armed attack. Moreover, the measures were arguably proportionate, and reasonably necessary. In two of the cases, the countermeasures followed a demand for restitution. Finally, contrary to the norm expressed in *Nicaragua* and the Restatement (Third), these incidents suggest a tacit acceptance of countermeasures employed by third states against defendant states, on behalf of victim states or victim populations.

### Cuban Quarantine, 1962

The Cuban quarantine was not, of course, a covert operation, although it was a reaction to one. The blockade's success and lawfulness depended on its overt nature. The incident, however, illustrates the potential and creative evolution of the law of reprisal, identified here again by a different name, quarantine.[47]

In early July 1962, the Soviet leadership decided to install medium-range missiles in Cuba. The idea was Khrushchev's own and was intended to "restrain the United States from precipitous military action against Castro's government . . ." and to "equalize what the West likes to call 'the balance of Power.'"[48] The decision was followed by a concerted effort to spread disinformation about Soviet intentions, while Soviet vessels were transporting missile components to Cuba. Thus, the Soviet ambassador to Washington "requested to see Robert Kennedy to reassure the American Government: No ground-to-ground missiles would be positioned in Cuba." An official statement by *Tass* explicitly stated "that there is no need for the Soviet Union to site defensive weapons—weapons designed to administer retaliatory blows—in any other country (Cuba, for instance)." And, Khrushchev sent a personal message of reassurance to President Kennedy and traveled extensively away from Moscow.[49]

Although the United States government was aware of a Soviet military buildup in Cuba,[50] it was not until October 14, 1962, that photographs taken from a U-2 reconnaissance aircraft offered conclusive evidence that the Soviets were installing medium- and intermediate-range missiles in Cuba as well as supplying the Cubans with Ilyushin-28 (IL-28) bombers.[51] On October 16, President Kennedy reviewed the photographs and convened the first meeting of what would become the Executive Committee of the National Security Council. The crisis became public on October 22, 1962, when President Kennedy announced on national television and radio that

> Within the past week unmistakable evidence has established the fact that a series of offensive missile sites is now in preparation on that imprisoned island (Cuba) . . .

"Acting, therefore, in the defense of our own security and of the entire Western Hemisphere," Kennedy announced the following measures:

> First: To halt this offensive buildup, a strict quarantine on all offensive military equipment under shipment to Cuba is being initiated . . .

Second: I have directed the continued and increased close surveillance of Cuba and its military buildup . . .

Third: It shall be the policy of this nation to regard any nuclear missile launched from Cuba against any nation in the Western Hemisphere as an attack by the Soviet Union on the United States, . . .

Fourth: As a necessary military precaution I have reinforced our base at Guantanamo, . . .

Fifth: We are calling tonight for an immediate meeting of the Organ of Consultation, under the Organization of American States, to consider this threat to hemispheric security and to invoke Articles 6 and 8 of the Rio Treaty in support of all necessary action. The United Nations Charter allows for regional security arrangements—and the nations of this hemisphere decided long ago against the military presence of outside powers . . .

Sixth: Under the Charter of the United Nations, we are asking tonight that an emergency meeting of the Security Council be convoked without delay to take action against this latest Soviet threat to world peace . . .

Seventh and finally: I call upon Chairman Khrushchev to halt and eliminate this clandestine, reckless, and provocative threat to world peace . . . [52]

The same evening the United States requested by letter that the United Nations Security Council meet to deal with "the dangerous threat to the peace and security of the world caused by the secret establishment in Cuba . . . of long-range ballistic missiles." Cuba also requested a meeting of the Security Council "to consider the act of war unilaterally committed by . . . [the United States] in ordering the naval blockade of Cuba." The Soviet Union made a similar request the following day. Between October 23 and October 25, the Security Council met four times. Separate resolutions were submitted by the United States, the Soviet Union, and Ghana and the United Arab Republic acting together.[53] None of the resolutions, however, was brought to a vote.

On October 23, the Council of the Organization of American States, meeting as the Provisional Organ of Consultation under Article 12 of the Rio Treaty, unanimously passed a resolution

2. To recommend that the member states, in accordance with Articles 6 and 8 of the Inter-American Treaty of Reciprocal Assistance, take all measures, individually and collectively, including the use of armed force, which they may deem necessary to ensure that the Government of Cuba cannot continue to receive from the Sino-Soviet power military material and related supplies which may threaten the peace and security of the Continent and to prevent the missiles in Cuba with offensive capability from ever becoming an active threat to the peace and security of the Continent.[54]

The following day six Latin American nations offered military assistance to the United States to help carry out the quarantine.[55] Naval forces from Argentina, the Dominican Republic, and Venezuela eventually took part in the naval operation.[56] Brazilian Premier Hermes Lima, however, supported "Cuba's right to carry out its political experiment."[57]

On October 23, President Kennedy issued a proclamation imposing a naval blockade on Cuba effective at 10:00 A.M. the next day. The proclamation stated that

> Any vessel or craft that may be proceeding toward Cuba may be intercepted and may be directed to identify itself, its cargo, equipment and stores . . . to submit to visit and search, or to proceed as directed. Any vessel or craft which fails or refuses to respond to or comply with directions shall be subjected to being taken in custody. Any vessel or craft which it is believed is en route to Cuba and may be carrying prohibited material or may itself constitute such material shall . . . be directed to proceed to another destination of its own choice and shall be taken in custody if it fails or refuses to obey. . . . Force shall not be used except in case of failure or refusal to comply with directions, . . . regulations or directives . . . after reasonable efforts have been made to communicate them to the vessel or craft, or in case of self-defense. . . . Force shall be used only to the extent necessary.[58]

On October 23, Secretary of Defense McNamara reported that as many as twenty-five Soviet vessels were en route to Cuba, while Sorensen reports that eighteen Soviet dry cargo ships, five with large hatches, were en route to Cuba. Shortly after the quarantine became effective, sixteen of the eighteen cargo vessels were reported to have stopped dead in the water or to have altered course. Within two days they had turned around and headed for the Soviet Union. The first contact between vessels occurred on October 25, when the tanker *Bucharest* crossed the quarantine line, but on presidential direction was allowed to proceed to Cuba without inspection. On October 26, the first vessel was stopped and searched. This was the Lebanese registered *Marcula* which was found to be carrying truck parts and was permitted to proceed to Cuba.[59]

An end to the crisis was largely facilitated through an exchange of notes between Chairman Khrushchev and President Kennedy on October 26, 27, and 28 which ended with a Soviet agreement to dismantle the missile sites in Cuba.[60] Negotiations, however, continued into November regarding the verification and site inspection provisions of the agreement, as well as the fate of the IL-28 bombers. On November 7, 1962, Khrushchev announced that all the Soviet missiles had been removed from Cuba. At sea, United States naval vessels stopped Soviet vessels outbound from Cuba to inspect for missiles and other contraband. Within three days, forty-two medium-range ballistic missiles had passed through the quarantine. Thirteen days later, President Kennedy ordered the blockade lifted effective November 21.[61]

The Cuban quarantine prompted considerable legal discussion.[62] Some commentators asked whether international law figured in the crisis at all.[63] Others evaluated the legality of the United States quarantine under the doctrines of pacific blockade and belligerent blockade.[64] One participant in the crisis chose to characterize the quarantine as an act of reprisal.

According to Theodore Sorensen, a member of the Executive Committee, "The quarantine was a new form of reprisal under international law, an act of national and collective self-defense against an act of aggression under the UN and OAS charters and under the Rio Treaty of 1947."[65]

The quarantine as an act of reprisal, however, received little attention. Professor Quincy Wright questioned the legality of the quarantine as a pacific blockade on the grounds that

> [u]nder general international law, states are free to engage in trade in any articles whatever in time of peace. . . . An effort to justify the quarantine by the historic doctrine of pacific blockade, therefore, fails because the United States did not make it clear what illegal act of Cuba it was trying to remedy . . . [and] non-coercive means of settlement had not been exhausted . . .

This critique would also hold true with regard to the traditional doctrine of reprisal which requires a wrongful act prior to exercising a right of reprisal. But if stationing missiles with offensive capability in Cuba was a wrongful act warranting a proportional act of reprisal, the Soviet Union could claim that its effort to place missiles in Cuba was, by reciprocal logic, itself an exercise of a correlative right of reprisal for United States missiles in Turkey. Here, the covert nature of the original Soviet gambit is significant and may otherwise elevate an unfriendly but legitimate act of military aid into a wrongful act of aggression.[66] The exhaustion requirement, for which the quarantine was also criticized by Skubiszewski,[67] is balanced by the principle of necessity. Moreover, the quarantine, as exercised, utilized a minimum of force and was arguably proportional to the installation of forty-two missiles and forty-two bombers, all nuclear-capable.[68]

Regardless, state response to the United States–led quarantine suggests that as a matter of state practice the quarantine was generally viewed as a lawful response to the Soviet buildup in Cuba. McDougal notes

> both this first provisional decision by a claimant target state and the measures it actually takes are subject to review for their necessity and proportionality by the general community of states. . . . Fortunately, today the authority structures of the United Nations, despite all their other weaknesses, do provide quickly available and convenient fora for general community review of the lawfulness of particular claims to employ the military instrument.[69]

Mallison echoes this sentiment, arguing that

> [i]t should be emphasized that the mere unilateral assertion of claims to national authority beyond territorial jurisdiction is not sufficient to establish international legality. It is rather the reasonableness of the claim and the consequent toleration of the acquiescence in it by other states which establishes its lawfulness. [70]

In this regard, United Nations inaction on the Soviet, American, and the joint resolution of Ghana and the United Arab Republic as well as the unanimous vote of the Organization of American States support a conclusion that the quarantine was consistent with existing expectations of lawfulness. Thus, the quarantine, as distinguished from the Libyan raid discussed below, underlines the traditional distinctions between self-help, self-defense, and reprisal.

> Self-help presupposes unlawful behavior directed at the identity, critical value position, or complex of key rights of the self-helper. It is justified when termination, abatement, or restitution can be reasonably effected only by the injured party's immediate recourse to its own resources.

But in contrast to reprisal, "[t]he self-help action is lawful if it conforms to what the community might have done (and *only* what it might have done) had adequate control been at its disposal."[71] In the case of the quarantine, the United States arguably had to react before the Soviet missiles became operational or potentially lose its responsive options short of direct force. In contrast, as we shall see, there was no comparable sense of impending necessity before the Libyan raid. Moreover, the Cuban quarantine may be seen as stemming from the specific delegated enforcement authority of the OAS. No comparable claim could be made for the Libyan raid.

As an indicator of future international expectation regarding use of the naval blockade as a lawful countermeasure, the quarantine must be evaluated in the context of the time.[72] First, neither the United Nations nor the OAS explicitly endorsed or condemned the quarantine. Secondly, the United States still exerted considerable control over the agenda of the United Nations and held preeminent influence over the agenda of the OAS. This should discount the precedential value of the quarantine, but not eliminate it. Contrary to some assertions, the OAS was not a rubber stamp for the United States. Recall, that no less than six states abstained from a United States measure to expel Cuba from the organization. Finally, there is no telling to what degree the state representatives at the United Nations and OAS agreed with Dean Acheson that "[t]he survival of states is not a matter of law."[73]

### Raid on Libya, 1986

At 2:00 A.M. on April 15, 1986, United States aircraft attacked Tripoli and Benghazi, Libya.[74] Over thirty attack aircraft took part in the approximately ten-minute-long raid. The aircraft were launched from carriers off the coast of Libya and from airfields in the United Kingdom. Because France had refused to allow the aircraft overflight privileges, the planes had proceeded down the Atlantic coast and through the Straits of Gibraltar.

The raid was aimed at five military targets, including El Azziziya barracks, which served as both Colonel Qaddafi's residence and military headquarters. Civilian homes and five foreign embassies were also hit during the strike. The French embassy was particularly hard hit. Civilian casualties were estimated by news sources in Tripoli at the time as approximately 130. Qaddafi's wife and two sons were reported wounded and an adopted daughter killed during the raid.

The overt act had some covert intentions. Secretary of State Shultz was quoted as saying three days after the raid, that Qaddafi had not been a "direct target" of the raid, but if "a coup takes place [as a result of the raid] that's all to the good."[75]

In a nationally televised address the same evening as the raid, President Reagan referred to the Libyan targets as "headquarters, terrorist facilities and military assets." President Reagan said that he had warned Qaddafi that he would hold Qaddafi's regime accountable for any new terrorist attacks launched against United States citizens and that evidence of Libyan complicity in the April 5 bombing of La Belle disco in Berlin was "direct, it is precise, it is irrefutable." In this bomb attack, 2 Americans and a Turkish woman were killed and 229 others wounded, including 78 Americans. "Self-defense is not only our right, it is our duty," Reagan said. "It is the purpose behind the mission undertaken tonight, a mission fully consistent with Article 51 of the United Nations Charter." Reagan added, "We always seek peaceful avenues before resorting to the use of force, and we did. We tried quiet diplomacy, public condemnation, economic sanctions and demonstrations of military force."

In the wake of the raid, reported "terrorist" incidents increased. In Beirut, one American and two British hostages were found dead with notes indicating they had been killed in revenge for the raid. The Revolutionary Organization of Socialist Moslems claimed to have executed another hostage in retaliation. Other attacks, or attempted attacks, on American and British targets occurred within days in Turkey, Costa Rica, Pakistan, North Yemen, and Mexico. There was, however, no direct evidence that Colonel Qaddafi or the Libyan government had ordered these attacks.

Reaction to the United States raid was generally negative in the West. The Italian, Spanish, and Dutch governments criticized the use of force. NATO Secretary-General, Lord Carrington, stated shortly after the raid that "the situation in the Atlantic alliance is very serious and as bad as I can remember."

France and West Germany were more ambiguous in their reaction. A French government statement referred to the raid as a "reprisal action," concluding "that the intolerable escalation of terrorism has led to a reprisal action which itself relaunches the chain of violence." On April 22, however, French officials acknowledged that the government had in fact favored stronger military action against Libya. But as Prime Minister Chirac suggested, France was piqued at not being consulted prior to the raid. West German Foreign Minister Hans-Dietrich Genscher expressed his government's preference for "political efforts." "The government of the Federal Republic [of Germany] always has rejected force," Helmut Kohl said, but suggested that the United States had acted in self-defense. "Whoever continually preaches and practices violence, as Qaddafi does, must count on the victims defending themselves." Kohl also indicated that his own government held conclusive evidence of its own that Libya bore responsibility for the La Belle bombing.

The United Kingdom, Israel, and South Africa alone issued statements in support of the attack. The Thatcher government, however, was criticized by the opposition Labour Party for an apparent shift in position. Three months before, Prime Minister Thatcher had said that she did "not believe in retaliatory strikes that are against international law."[76] British polls indicated that two-thirds of those questioned opposed the raid. Canada's support was qualified by its concern for the loss of innocent life.

Arab condemnation was less equivocal. The governments of Syria, Iran, Algeria, Egypt, Jordan, and Saudi Arabia, and other Gulf States all criticized the raid. A Kuwaiti statement referred to the strike as "an act of terrorism and flagrant aggression." OPEC condemned the raid, but rejected a Libyan request for an oil embargo against the United States. Iraq was silent. The secretary-general of the Arab League condemned the raid.

The Arab reaction, however, was not unanimous. Journalists reported that members of the Shi'a Moslem community in southern Lebanon were pleased with the attack.[77] One U.S. news source reported that an unnamed Arab diplomat "told reporters in Washington that some Arab countries might have favored a covert plan to assassinate Qaddafi but that none would support overt U.S. military action against another Arab state."[78]

At a meeting of the Non-Aligned Movement in India, twenty-one foreign ministers voted to endorse Rajiv Gandhi's statement calling the raid "a dastardly, blatant and unprovoked act of aggression." The strike also provoked an outpouring of popular reaction across the globe. Demonstrations were reported in West Berlin, Rome, Madrid, Vienna, London, Manila, Pakistan, and a number of Arab cities.

An official Soviet statement issued on April 15 called the raid "a brutal violation of international law." In protest Moscow canceled Foreign Minister Shevardnadze's May visit to Washington. In addition, a note was delivered to the British ambassador protesting the British role in the raid.

Secretary-General Javier Perez de Cuellar condemned both Libyan terrorism and the United States raid. A Security Council draft Resolution condemning the raid was vetoed by the United States, the United Kingdom, and France, but nine council members voted in favor of it. In addition, the General Assembly "[c]ondemn[ed] the military attack perpetrated against the Socialist People's Libyan Arab Jamahiriya on 15 April 1986, which constitutes a violation of the Charter of the United Nations and of international law" by passing a resolution whose title, citing "the aerial and naval attack . . . by the present United States Administration," suggested the personal as well as politico-military nature of the conflict between Libya and the United States.[79]

As Mahnoush Arsanjani has suggested,[80] and the French government was quick to assert, the United States raid might more accurately be depicted as an act of reprisal than an act of self-defense. The language of President Reagan's April 15 statement is the language of reprisal, not self-defense. The statement, for example, refers to the four commonly cited criteria for exercise of a lawful reprisal: a prior wrongful act, absence or exhaustion of alternative remedial measures, notification to the wrongdoer, and proportionality. Moreover, the statement makes clear that the raid was both retaliatory and preemptive, two classic purposes of reprisals. By the same token, self-defense requires some sense of immediate harm or threat. Some authors go so far as to suggest that the survival of the state itself must be at risk.[81]

Nevertheless, the United States justified the raid on the basis of self-defense. This choice of legal rationales reflects confusion concerning the parameters of self-defense and perhaps uncertainty regarding the validity of reprisal or countermeasures. The Charter, after all, allows for self-defense in certain circumstances, whereas "reprisal" by name is, if not expressly prohibited, hardly authorized by implication.

What does the international reaction to the raid tell us about elite expectations about military countermeasures? First, most official responses were expressed in terms of political and moral outrage or solidarity with the Libyan people and not in terms of international law. The Canadian response was in part grounded on concern about proportionality (that is, the loss of innocent life) whereas the unnamed Arab diplomat suggested that a more discreet covert operation might have received support or at least silence.

Second, although the Libyan raid was precipitated by the bombing of a Berlin nightclub and President Reagan and the media inextricably linked the two incidents, the raid was also the culmination of a spiraling series of incidents, of action and reaction, overt and covert, between Libya and the United States over the preceding year, including the December terrorist attacks at Rome and Vienna airports and the disclosure of United States efforts to covertly overthrow Qaddafi.[82] Any legal assessment of the Libyan raid must therefore take these other incidents into account. Against what earlier incident, if any, for example, should proportionality be assessed? Indeed the cycle continued after the raid. Although no single episode in the confrontation provoked as much world reaction as the United States raid, we can not be certain that international reaction was responding alone to that event.

Third, the initial covert nature of the raid does not appear to have figured in the reactions. The French response alone appears grounded in the covert and unilateral nature of the incident. But its motivation appears to be political and not legal. The French were piqued at not being informed of the operation at an earlier date and were concerned at protecting an independent foreign policy. In addition, the Mitterand government was concerned for the safety of its hostages in Lebanon. That concern proved to be well founded.

### Response to Mines in the Persian Gulf, 1987

In January 1987, Kuwait formally requested United States protection for its vessels transiting the Persian Gulf that were subject to attack as a result of the Iran-Iraq war. The United States initially balked, citing a six-month time delay for the reflagging of foreign vessels. When Kuwait approached the Soviet Union with a similar request, however, the United States responded by offering to escort Kuwaiti tankers consistent with an expedited reflagging program. In July, U.S. Navy vessels entered the Gulf and began escort duty.

During the night of September 21, 1987, a U.S. helicopter tracking an Iranian vessel in the Persian Gulf discovered the Iranian ship laying mines beyond Iranian territorial waters. Iran had not given notice of this mining. Such an act, according to the navy's rules of engagement in the Gulf, warranted an armed response. The United States had warned Iran that it would respond forcefully to mine laying. After receiving clearance from the commander of the U.S. Gulf fleet, the helicopter fired on the Iranian vessel with rockets and machine guns. Three Iranian crew members were killed. Twenty-six other crew members were taken captive by U.S. forces the next morning. The navy believed it located the six or seven mines it believed the Iranian vessel had placed.

A spokesman for the Department of Defense stated that the United States had acted in self-defense, characterizing the laying of mines as a "hostile act." A spokeswoman for the Department of State also justified the incident as an act of self-defense, noting that a state has a right to use "reasonable and proportionate force" in such a case.[83] The United States Senate agreed and on October 6 passed an amendment by voice vote which stated in relevant part: "(2) the use of force by the United States Navy to terminate that Iranian mining was justified under international law; (3) international law offers a framework for such positive action."[84]

### Aviation Boycott of Polish Airline, 1981

In chapter 3, we described the events of, and initial international reaction to, the imposition of martial law in Poland. The United States responded to these events with, among other things, imposition of political and economic sanctions against Poland and against the Soviet Union. On December 30, 1981, for example, the Civil Aeronautics Board suspended landing rights in the United States for Poland's national airline, Lot. Aeroflot flights to the United States were also suspended. The United Kingdom, Belgium, Canada, and Japan also imposed a variety of sanctions against Poland.

Unilateral United States suspension of landing rights was contrary to the terms of a 1972 Air Transport Agreement[85] between the two nations that among other things required one-year notice prior to suspension or termination. Nor did Lot meet any of the three designated grounds for suspension in the agreement. Moreover, the agreement provided for consultation prior to arbitration in the event of disputes. Poland brought the matter to arbitration in compliance with the terms of the agreement, but prior to decision the ban was lifted and the arbitration was suspended.[86]

### European Boycott of Ariana
### Afghanistan Airlines, 1981

On March 2, 1981, three Pakistani dissidents hijacked a domestic Pakistan International Airline flight to Kabul. The aircraft spent the next seven days on the runway in Kabul. During this time a Pakistani diplomat was killed. Pakistan alleged that the terrorists received food and additional arms from Afghan authorities. The United States charged Soviet complicity. The plane flew to Syria where the hostages were released after continued negotiations. The three hijackers returned to Afghanistan, where one was soon apprehended along the Pakistani border. Pakistan requested extradition of the other two hijackers pursuant to the Hague and Montreal conventions. Kabul declined to extradite, nor did it prosecute the hijackers.

Citing Kabul's failure to comply with the Hague Convention, the leaders of the G-7 decided, in July 1981, to denounce their air service agreements with

Ariana Afghan Airlines. The suspension, however, did not take effect until November 30, 1981, after expiration of the notice requirement provided in the relevant bilateral aviation treaties and nine months after the precipitating event.[87] The suspension was lifted in 1986.

Neither airline boycott nor the tactical events in the Persian Gulf evoked much international response. Silence is eloquently ambiguous. It could be interpreted as a sign of silent consent or affirmation of an expanding right of response. It is more likely, however, that the incidents were viewed in the contexts of the broader political struggles within which they occurred, or simply did not meet what was deemed to be a threshold requiring neutral state response. Whatever the motives of the jury, unprotested acts such as these are generative of new legal expectations. The Persian Gulf incident also illustrates the untested limits and vagaries of the doctrine in the area of physically coercive countermeasures falling somewhere between self-defense and coercive self-help or self-protection.[88]

### UNRESOLVED ISSUES:
### COVERT COUNTERMEASURES

It is still too early to tell whether the doctrine of countermeasures will be more widely pleaded by government elites and accepted by legal scholars and juridical bodies. Nor, as *Nicaragua* and the pleadings in *Air Services* suggest, has the doctrine gained an identity distinct from that of reprisal, which is largely associated with armed retaliation. To the extent that *Nicaragua* limits a state's right of self-defense, states may more frequently plead a right of counter-measure, at least in the alternative. This, however, depends on whether the doctrine continues to develop and what shape it takes.

Two issues will largely determine the direction and vitality of the doctrine in noncommercial settings, particularly in areas like law enforcement and counter-terrorism. First, does the doctrine allow for a state unilaterally to determine the gravity of the triggering wrongful act and thus the proportionality of the response? And, should proportionality be measured against the original act or the purpose of the reprisal? Rephrased, in institutional terms, can counter-measures extend to overt military action absent United Nations authorization? Second, is advanced notification of the act of reprisal required of nonbelligerent reprisals as it is of belligerent reprisals? If so, what form must this notification take? Would otherwise lawful countermeasures, whether using military or nonmilitary modalities, become unlawful when accomplished in covert fashion?

To date, international decision, doctrine, and state practice have accepted the use of economic and political countermeasures by injured states in response to the internationally wrongful acts of defendant states. *Air Services, Nicaragua,* and part 2 of the Draft Articles on State Responsibility do not explicitly preclude more forceful forms of countermeasures, but they do make them subject to the Charter principles governing the use of force which, as we have seen, are themselves controversial. Formal international agencies associated with the United Nations have condemned military reprisals and by extension military countermeasures. It is, as yet, uncertain whether these law-making and law-applying efforts have succeeded in installing an international prescription.

*Nicaragua* now presents one very clear version of law on this matter. It suggests that armed countermeasures could only meet the international legal requirement of proportionality in response to an armed attack. But that, of course, would also trigger a right of self-defense and make resort to countermeasures redundant. The reactive use of military coercion is thus prohibited by formal international bodies, except in cases of actual armed attack.

More difficult to assess is the relative standing of the right to countermeasures with regard to other international norms. For example, what about countermeasures using force of a "lesser degree of gravity than armed attack," but which might still be categorized as intervention? Or countermeasures using the modes of low-intensity conflict?

Imagine the following: a hijacker seizes an aircraft carrying the nationals of country Y. After the aircraft lands to refuel, the hijacker holds the passengers hostage before fleeing and receiving sanctuary in country Z. Z is a signatory of the Tokyo, Hague, and Montreal conventions.[89] As a result, the government of Y demands that Z honor its obligation under these conventions to submit the hijacker for the purposes of prosecution or to extradite her to Y. No action is taken. Moreover, Z refuses to submit to the arbitration clauses of the conventions. So far, this is similar to the Pakistan International Airlines hijacking, but what if the victim state wishes to pursue more aggressive countermeasures. May Y take legitimate countermeasures against Z? May Y seize the hijacker to stand trial?

The answers to both questions are not necessarily negative. Z has committed a wrongful international act by not honoring its obligation to "extradite or prosecute" the suspect. Moreover, Y has demanded redress (were it required in such an instance). Finally, though the notion of "proportionality" is not susceptible to precision in cases like these, the seizure of the hijacker could be claimed to be proportional to state Z's wrongful action. Possibilities such as these have raised concern about the potential mischievousness of this doctrine, as currently conceived.

Countermeasures, like reprisals, authorize the party initiating them to do something that would otherwise be unlawful in response to the unlawful act of the target. But the doctrine of countermeasures, as it has developed to date, does not indicate whether certain norms are so important that countermeasures may not violate them. Other than the general demand that uses of coercion meet tests of proportionality, it would appear that there are, as yet, no other limitations. This could be a serious oversight in the work of the International Law Commission and may have to be addressed in the future.

The sabotage of Pan Am flight no. 103 over Lockerbie, Scotland, suggests just how far the ill-defined notion of countermeasures may be pushed.[90] The agents and principals behind this event have not yet been conclusively identified. It is now believed that Libya was the culprit, but, assume, for purposes of discussion, that Iran was the principal and that the action was undertaken as a countermeasure or reprisal against the United States for the downing of the Iranian AirBus by U.S. forces some months earlier. If Iran made some statements that might qualify as a warning, e.g., "We will respond in an appropriate fashion, at a time of our choosing," and then restricted its countermeasure to one civilian airliner, would such an action have been lawful under the emerging doctrine? The tests of proportionality and discrimination would have been achieved with a macabre precision. The sanctioning and deterrent effect of the reprisal or countermeasure would have been achieved even if the matter had been conducted covertly and the United States were unable to prove Iran's responsibility. The suspicion alone would serve to make U.S. forces more careful in the future.

Does the international system want a doctrine of countermeasures that extends to such covert actions? Does the United States want such a doctrine?

At this time, there is no explicit prohibition against covert countermeasures. Although there is a generally recognized duty to seek reparation, or make a prior demand (necessity) before undertaking countermeasures, nowhere in current case law and commentary is there found a corollary requirement that the victim state provide prior notice of the specific countermeasure itself. In some cases, such a requirement would undermine the effectiveness of the mission. In other cases, however, prior warning may be possible. Thus, for example, when U.S. naval forces were instructed to destroy Iranian oil platforms in the Persian Gulf in response to Iranian targeting of merchant vessels and mining of the Gulf, U.S. forces notified the people on the platforms that they were about to be destroyed and allowed them to leave. One may imagine situations in which such humanitarian considerations might not operate. Given the general requirement of notification and demand, however, we submit that countermeasures that are not preceded by a warning would be considered unlawful.

# Chapter 6

## United States
## Internal Procedures

In conducting its foreign relations, the United States employs, in varying combinations, the four basic modalities or strategies (the diplomatic, the economic, the ideological, and the military). Each modality is susceptible to overt and covert use. More often than not, United States covert operations appear to be tactical phases of broader ideological, economic, political, and military strategies, not all of which, themselves, are necessarily covert.

Like all issues at the interface between constitutional law and foreign affairs, the constitutional problem presented by covert operations is how to achieve an appropriate accommodation of interests in efficiency, economy, power sharing, and responsibility in ways consistent with historic national values. The mechanism used is the device of formal or informal oversight of the executive branch by the legislative branch. The postwar history of this issue has been one of successive efforts at regulation and accommodation in a context of increasingly aggravated relations between the executive and Congress. The particular pattern of interbranch accommodation has usually been shaped by popular perceptions of the level of crisis: the graver the perceived crisis, the more leeway allowed the executive. Not infrequently, a key part of the public debate has centered on what that level of crisis actually is, the assumption often being that intelligence agencies in the executive have an incentive in exaggerating it. None of the interbranch accommodations, as we shall see, has proved durable.

In this chapter, we will briefly review the arrangements and limitations imposed by the internal constitutive process on the design and performance of covert activities. As in our previous chapters, our purpose is to set out trends in broad outlines and to forecast possible future directions in order to facilitate policy appraisal and recommendation.[1]

In 1954, the Doolittle Committee concluded:

> It is now clear that we are facing an implacable enemy whose avowed objective is world domination by whatever means at whatever cost. There are no rules in such a game. Hitherto acceptable norms of human conduct do not apply.[2]

These were extraordinary words, all the more since the United States was not in a formal state of war. Although it would be easy to emphasize their near hysteria and hysteria-sowing character, one should avoid anachronism and remember that the adversary the Doolittle Committee referred to was a Stalinist regime, ruling an expanding totalitarian empire, resting on force and a Gulag archipelago and not Mikhail Gorbachev, presiding over a decomposing one. One of the consequences of this extreme vision was to justify operations that even Congress and the U.S. public might not be fully aware of and to limit, if not obviate, oversight.

At this time, there were few domestic laws governing covert action. Key congressmen were kept informed as a matter of politics, if not law, as was the case with Senator Fulbright prior to the U.S.–supported invasion of the Bay of Pigs. Not until the mid 1970s, however, were formal domestic mechanisms governing the authorization, oversight, and conduct of covert actions enacted.[3] These mechanisms, however, were often intentionally ambiguous or obscure, a reflection of tensions between interests in executive efficiency in the conduct of covert operations and the accountability key to the democratic process. Totalitarian and authoritarian regimes, of course, are not presented with this problem.

### CONSTITUTIONAL AUTHORITY

The executive's constitutional authority to conduct covert action independent of legislative authorization or notification has been the subject of separation of powers debate since the beginning of the Republic. Justice Jackson noted in *Youngstown,* "A Hamilton may be matched against a Madison."[4] Advocates of independent executive power argue that "the President is the sole organ of the nation in its external affairs."[5] Moreover, the Constitution grants the executive an enumerated power to ". . . appoint Ambassadors, other public Ministers, and Consuls"[6] and "he shall receive Ambassadors and other public Ministers."[7] In addition, the president, it is argued, possesses whatever inherent powers are necessary to protect the nation from foreign attack[8] as well as his constitutional powers as commander-in-chief,[9] not to speak of his executive mandate to take care that the laws be faithfully executed.[10] It has also been argued that covert foreign operations may be a part of "the executive Power" vested in a president.[11] In this vein, the Supreme Court has noted that "a systematic, unbroken, executive practice, long pursued to the knowledge of the Congress and never before questioned . . . may be treated as a gloss on 'executive Power.'"[12] As a matter of practice, at least since President Jefferson, the executive has conducted covert action without specific congressional authorization, and at other times has gone beyond whatever authorization was given.[13]

On the other hand, Congress has the constitutionally assigned power "[t]o declare War, grant Letters of Marque and Reprisal," and "[t]o make Rules for the Government and Regulation of the land and naval Forces."[14] Congress also retains the power of the purse[15] and with it, proponents of congressional power contend, an implied power to oversee appropriated expenditures. Finally, Congress is "[t]o make all Laws which shall be necessary and proper for carrying into Execution the foregoing Powers, and *all* other Powers vested by this Constitution in the Government of the United States, or in any Department or Officer thereof (emphasis supplied)."[16]

The full constitutional arguments are better engaged elsewhere. As in debates about most fundamental issues, they are inconclusive.[17] What is clear, and indeed common ground, is that any executive power to conduct covert action insofar as it exists, absent statutory authority, arises from an implied constitutional power and not an explicit enumerated power.

### STATUTORY AUTHORITY

Statutory authority for covert action is found in section 102(d)(5) of the National Security Act of 1947 which states in relevant part "it shall be the duty of the Agency, under the direction of the National Security Council . . . (5) to perform such other functions and duties related to intelligence affecting the national security as the National Security Council may from time to time direct."[18] With little dissent,[19] this language was soon understood to authorize the executive to conduct covert action. Congressional acquiescence in subsequent presidential covert action did not suggest otherwise. Implied legislative authority for covert action is arguably also found in statutes dealing with specific scenarios such as the Hostage Act of 1868.[20] If there was any doubt regarding the statutory basis for covert action, the Hughes-Ryan Amendment (1974) to the Foreign Assistance Act of 1961[21] and the Intelligence Oversight Act of 1980[22] removed it. Moreover, intelligence authorization and appropriation acts, at least since the formation of the congressional intelligence commit-tees, have provided line item authorization for covert actions abroad.

If the National Security Act of 1947 sparked little debate over the statutory authorization of covert action, it had just the opposite effect regarding who would conduct those activities and what scope they would take. The act itself implied, and subsequent National Security Council (NSC) directives dictated, that it was necessary "in time of peace to place the responsibility for them within the structure of the Central Intelligence Agency and correlate them with espionage and counter-espionage operations under the over-all control of the Director of Central Intelligence."[23] But "[i]n time of war, or when the President directs, all plans for covert operations shall be coordinated with the Joint Chiefs of Staff. In active theaters of war where American forces are engaged, covert operations will be conducted under the direct command of the American The-ater Commander. . . ." In fact, the services resisted the CIA's claim to a preeminent position. Moreover, the covert operations role was not embraced by all elements of the agency itself.[24]

The Hughes Ryan Amendment of 1974 and the Intelligence Oversight Act of 1980, among other things, statutorily clarified what was by then already ac-cepted in practice: the Central Intelligence Agency was to be the lead govern-ment entity for the conduct of covert activity. Moreover, Executive Order 12,333 (1981) provides that

> No agency except the CIA (or Armed Forces of the United States in time of war declared by Congress or during any period covered by a report from the President to the Congress under the War Powers Resolution (87 Stat. 855)) may conduct any special activity unless the President determines that another agency is more likely to achieve a particular objective.[25]

Note that the initial clarity of the executive order is bled by the "unless" clause which effectively leaves the matter up to the president. In general, the statutory and executive language is not exclusive.[26] As the Iran-Contra affair illustrates, *which* executive entities are authorized or exclusively authorized to conduct covert operations is not always certain.[27] The Drug Enforcement Administra-tion (DEA) and Federal Bureau of Investigation have both, apparently, under-taken peacetime covert operations.[28] In times of conflict or in preparation for potential overt missions, elements within the Department of Defense also con-duct special activities.[29] Overt and covert foreign military assistance, for exam-ple, is largely administered through the Department of Defense under the "general direction" of the secretary of state.[30] Moreover, some tasks formally conducted by the CIA on a covert basis are now conducted overtly by quasi-public entities such as the National Endowment for Democracy.[31]

### ACCOUNTABILITY

Whether called covert action, covert operations, covert intervention, or special activities, most covert operations require presidential approval in the form of a "Finding,"[32] that is, a presidential determination that an activity "is necessary to support identifiable foreign policy objectives" and "is important to the national security of the United States."[33] Before the president sees a covert action proposal, however, the matter undergoes internal review within the executive branch. The process is the product of executive direction, not statutory arrangement, and therefore is subject to unilateral and secret alteration. The names of the committees and the dramatis personae seem to change from administration to administration,[34] but the contours of the process are necessary for understanding at what points international and domestic legal concerns are considered, or could be considered.

In the case of a covert action initiative originating within the Directorate of Operations, the proposal is initially reviewed by a covert action review group[35] comprised of senior CIA officers, including the associate deputy director of operations, the general counsel and representatives of the Directorate of Intelligence. From this review group, the proposal goes to the deputy director, then on to the director.

Should the director approve, the proposal is transmitted to a staff working group at the NSC. This group is comprised of the deputies to the National Security Planning Group (NSPG) and, perhaps, the NSC's legal adviser, but its membership has varied over the years. The proposal then goes to the NSPG, the NSC committee charged with advising the president on special activities.

NSPG members have included the vice president, the secretaries of state and defense, the director of central intelligence and the national security adviser. Because the president has discretion to designate members of this committee, membership has varied over the years.[36]

Executive Order 12,036, the Carter administration order governing "United States Foreign Intelligence Activities," (effective January 24, 1978 to December 4, 1981) dictated that any meeting of the committee to consider special activities "*shall* include" (emphasis supplied) designated members of the Administration including the Attorney General. Its successor, however, Executive Order 12,333, specifies only that "a committee . . . shall consider and submit to the President a policy recommendation, including dissents, on each special activity." The NSPG either returns the proposal to the director of central intelligence for rework, terminates it, or sends it to the president for approval.

If the president authorizes a covert action, a signed finding (and in most cases a memorandum of notification and a national security adviser's memorandum) are then sent to the director of central intelligence, the members of the

NSPG, and the head of any executive department or entity instructed to engage in or support a special activity. At this point, the president, the director of central intelligence, or the relevant department or agency head will inform the Senate Select Committee on Intelligence and House Permanent Select Committee on Intelligence of the Finding.[37] In "extraordinary circumstances" only select members of the congressional leadership are briefed.[38] The Intelligence Oversight Act of 1980, as amended, however, also provides that the president "shall fully inform the intelligence committees in a timely fashion" of covert actions for which prior notice was *not* given.[39] The president and director of central intelligence have on occasion "agreed" with the committees not to withhold notification beyond a time certain.[40] On the other hand, a 1986 opinion by the Office of Legal Counsel concluded that "a number of factors combine to support the conclusion that the 'timely fashion' language should be read to leave the president with virtually unfettered discretion to choose the right moment for making the required notification."[41] In turn, the Joint Explanatory Statement Vice Conference Report to the 1991 Intelligence Authorization Act rejected this opinion but did note congressional intent that the "timely fashion" provision "be interpreted in a manner consistent with whatever authority the Constitution may provide."

Members of Congress receive prior notice of covert activities pursuant to the oversight and notification provisions of Title V of the National Security Act of 1947, rather than by a constitutional right of operational pre-sight.[42] Thus Title V, as amended, provides that "Nothing in this title shall be construed as requiring the approval of the intelligence committees as a condition precedent to the initiation of any significant anticipated intelligence activity," a euphemism for covert action. Should a covert action implicate the War Powers, however, Congress might claim a broader constitutional right to preview a covert action. Congress might also invoke the consultation and reporting provisions of the War Powers Resolution if covert operations place U.S. personnel "into situations where imminent involvement in hostilities is clearly indicated by the circumstances . . . " The resolution's applicability to covert action conducted by elements outside the armed forces, however, is questionable in light of the bill's legislative history.[43] Were the War Powers Resolution invoked, the executive would likely notify Congress, but only as a matter of comity, for every successive administration has contested the constitutionality of the resolution.

In practice, members of Congress in their oversight roles have objected to covert action findings and brought their objections to the attention of the president (and less often the press) prior to initiation.[44] And, on occasion, the president has changed course.[45] In addition, the Congress can seek to nullify or curtail initiatives through passage of legislative prohibitions, such as the Boland and Clark amendments. Even then, however, the executive could theoretically insist upon the unconstitutionality of that exercise as well. However, as a practical matter, a strongly held view by a majority of Congress can be ignored only at great political cost.

Congressional oversight does not stop upon approval and initiation of a covert program. The Senate Intelligence Committee, for example, reviews all covert action programs on a quarterly basis.[46] Each program is evaluated according to eleven criteria first promulgated in 1985. The criteria include:

> 6. What is the character of those whom we support? Do they support democratic processes and human rights?
> 11. How important is it that this program be covert, and how likely is it to remain secret? If it were to become known, could it be justified under international law?[47]

In addition, an audit and investigations staff was added to the oversight process in 1988.[48] The audit staff is composed of a certified public accountant, a government auditor/investigator and a research assistant. The audit staff reviews covert action programs, surveys the audit coverage in the intelligence agencies, reviews compliance with regulations, and conducts financial management and internal control audits of special access projects. In comparison, no other system of legislative oversight is as open or thorough.[49]

The president's Intelligence Oversight Board (IOB) and the president's Foreign Intelligence Advisory Board may also play a peripheral role in covert action mechanisms. The IOB is composed of three members, one of whom is selected from the membership of the president's Foreign Intelligence Advisory Board and serves as chairman. The IOB is charged with among other things "inform[ing] the President of intelligence activities that any member . . . believes are in violation of the Constitution or laws of the United States, Executive Orders, or Presidential directives."[50] In at least one publicized instance, however, the IOB's general counsel rendered an opinion on the legality of an ongoing covert operation.[51]

The president's Foreign Intelligence Advisory Board was initially established by President Eisenhower (as the Board of Consultants on Foreign Intelligence Activities), disbanded by President Carter, and reconstituted during the Reagan administration. According to Executive Order No. 12,537, the board "shall assess the quality, quantity, and adequacy of intelligence collection, of analysis and estimates, of counterintelligence, and other intelligence activities."[52] The board reports directly to the president and is required to do so at least semiannually. The president's Foreign Intelligence Advisory Board has been a sometime board with an uncertain mission. In July 1990, however, President Bush reduced membership on the board from fourteen to six. The reduction in size and the character of the Bush administration's appointments,[53] suggests that the board will play a more active role in shaping United States intelligence policy. What impact this will have on covert action policies has yet to be seen. The current board is endowed with both technical and scientific expertise and foreign policy and intelligence experience.

Executive orders do not explicitly provide either the president's IOB or the president's Foreign Intelligence Advisory Board a role in the immediate mechanics of covert action finding and oversight, although in the longer run they may review covert actions after the fact. Their influence appears to be limited. Although the heads of departments and agencies are required to provide the boards with all "necessary" information, they need do so only "to the extent permitted by law."[54] Most commentators suggest the Foreign Intelligence Advisory Board has been ineffectual to date. Perhaps because of its smaller size the IOB has been somewhat more influential in matters outside the scope of oversight and covert action, such as independent studies of intelligence issues or postmortem reports on intelligence failures. Indeed, the IOB's record during the Iran-Contra affair was dismal.

## CONDUCT

Covert operations include a wide range of actors and actions. Statutory language and executive orders, however, have not been explicit concerning what is included in covert action. Executive Order 12,333, for example, defines special activities, a euphemism for covert action, as

> . . . activities conducted in support of national foreign policy objectives abroad which are planned and executed so that the role of the United States Government is not apparent or acknowledged publicly, and functions in support of such activities, but which are not intended to influence United States political processes, public opinion, policies, or media and do not include diplomatic activities or the collection and production of intelligence or related support functions.

The Intelligence Authorization Act for Fiscal Year 1991, included the first statutory definition of "covert action," which is intended to supersede the definition of "special activities" in Executive Order 12,333. The Act defines covert action as

> . . . an activity or activities of the United States Government to influence political, economic, or military conditions abroad where it is intended that the role of the United States Government will not be apparent or acknowledged publicly, but does not include—
> (1) activities the primary purpose of which is to acquire intelligence, traditional counterintelligence activities, traditional activities to improve or maintain the

operational security of United States Government programs, or administrative activities;

(2) traditional diplomatic or military activities or routine support to such activities;
(3) traditional law enforcement activities conducted by United States Government law enforcement agencies or routine support to such activities; or
(4) activities to provide routine support to the overt activities (other than activities described in paragraph (1), (2), or (3)) of other United States Government agencies abroad.

From the perspective of international politics and law, however, these executive and legislative definitions are underinclusive and, as we suggest at the end of this chapter, this new statutory exercise in clarification includes hidden ambiguity. A secret diplomatic mission, for example, may still be covert, even if internal United States mechanisms for covert action *may* not apply (see table 1 in chapter 1). In fact, the scope of United States covert operations includes not only "special activities" executed so that the identity of the United States as sponsor is not apparent, but also clandestine operations that, by their nature, require concealment of the operation itself, such as supply of intelligence to an ally, or seizure of a fugitive overseas. Thus, the statutory language of the Hughes-Ryan Amendment may still come closest to the range of covert action by defining what it is not, that is, "activities intended solely for obtaining necessary intelligence."[55] The point, however, may be largely academic, as the Senate Intelligence Committee has concluded that "neither the Central Intelligence Agency or the Congress have actually applied the sole-purpose test [of the Hughes-Ryan Amendment] since enactment of the Hughes-Ryan Amendment."[56]

Covert operations that include political action and intrigue, propaganda, and military and paramilitary operations[57] are conducted in accord with the general principles of the president's Executive Order on United States Intelligence Activities as well as other relevant executive orders and presidential directives. These orders are subsequently implemented by national security decision directives, National Security Council intelligence directives, and most importantly, agency and departmental directives.[58] By direction of Executive Order 12,333 these implementing procedures are reviewed by the attorney general[59] and as a matter of practice and agreement by the congressional committees.[60]

Political action and intrigue options range from the informal provision of advice, to covert efforts to influence elections, to direct intervention in the machinations of a coup or change in government. United States financial support for the Christian Democrats in postwar Italy designed to defeat Italian communism at the ballot box and the secret financing of Eduardo Frei and others to defeat the presidential aspirations of Salvador Allende in Chile (1964–

1973) are two of the CIA's better known "election projects." In conjunction with electoral efforts such as these, operations designed to support and influence foreign media were undertaken in Italy, Chile and, more recently, in Nicaragua (among other places). Operations in Guatemala (1954), the 1953 coup in Iran, and Chile all illustrate a second more active category of political action. We would surmise, however, that political funding will increasingly be administered overtly through public entities like the National Endowment for Democracy.[61] This trend may reflect renewed confidence in the message as well as the practical realization that covert assistance to a candidate may do more harm than good.

Propaganda, as stated earlier, refers to communications in support of national objectives designed to influence the opinions and behavior of any outside audience in order to achieve preferred outcomes. Whereas diplomatic strategy aims at communicating with an elite audience, an ideological or propaganda strategy targets the wider body politic, the rank and file. Although the word *propaganda* is often linked to internal efforts to control and direct populations with bald lies and incantation, as Goebbels did in Germany, in its broader and more pharisaical form, it is an effort to convey selected, but not necessarily false, information to a foreign audience through various media so that attitudes will be produced that would not have been produced, if all the information had been made available. United States doctrine recognizes three shades of propaganda. Black propaganda refers to communications that purport to originate from somebody other than the true source, for example, a radio broadcast under a "false flag." Gray propaganda is communication that does not specifically identify a source. White propaganda is information disseminated and acknowledged by its true source.[62]

The principal arms of the United States ideological instrument have been Radio Free Europe, Radio Liberty, and the Voice of America.[63] Although all three stations are now operated overtly, at one point Radio Free Europe and Radio Liberty were funded covertly through the CIA while Voice of America was utilized for covert military and psychological operations. Therefore, the stations warrant brief mention in any discussion of United States covert action.

Radio Free Europe is a quasi-public entity run by the Board for International Broadcasting. Radio Free Europe broadcasts throughout Eastern Europe; its companion service, Radio Liberty, broadcasts to the Soviet Union. The stations' mission has been to encourage the development of democracy in Eastern Europe and the Soviet Union through the broadcast medium. Radio Free Europe was established in 1949 as a private corporation with funding provided covertly by the CIA through dummy foundations. Radio Liberty was incorporated in 1951 with a similar arrangement for funding. In 1973, the two stations merged, the Board for International Broadcasting was established, and covert funding terminated in favor of direct congressional appropriations. A similar service directed at China, Voice of Asia, was initiated in 1951 and discontinued in 1965.

The Voice of America is a United States government station operated by the United States Information Agency. Voice of America broadcasts throughout the world from relay stations in Greece, Spain, Portugal, Germany, Liberia, and Manila among other places. The Voice of America recently announced plans to continue with development of a $300 million transmitter in Israel's Negev desert.[64] The service was initiated in 1942 as the Foreign Information Service in order to provide information to occupied Europe and Germany and to counter German propaganda in Latin America. In addition, the broadcasts were used to transmit messages to resistance units in Europe. More recently, Voice of America was used to transmit messages from the United States government and private persons for U.S. citizens trapped or held hostage in Kuwait and Iraq.

Radio Marti was created in 1985 by congressional mandate for the purpose of broadcasting to Cuba. Although the station is prohibited from "inciting its audience to revolution or violence," the station is used in part to broadcast white propaganda. In 1988, for example, Radio Marti carried special reports on Acquired Immune Deficiency Syndrome (AIDS) in Cuba, Cuban troops in Angola, and human rights abuses in Cuba, in addition to the regular news and entertainment programming. The station operates on AM and shortwave frequencies under the direction of Voice of America.[65]

Television Marti was funded for the first time in 1990 as a pilot program. The initial broadcasts were vigorously protested by the Cuban government as an unlawful intervention. Whereas Radio Marti operates on a Florida frequency, Television Marti functions on a frequency allocated by the International Telecommunications Union to Cuba. Cuba jams all the television broadcasts.

Although Radio Free Europe has received praise from both European and United States sources for its contribution to political change in Eastern Europe,[66] its fate, along with that of Radio Liberty and to a lesser extent Radio Marti, is uncertain in a post–Cold War world. In May 1990, a bipartisan presidential advisory board, the Advisory Commission on Public Diplomacy, recommended the gradual phasing out of the broadcasts and eventual transfer of Radio Free Europe's assets to Voice of America. Congressional legislation to this effect will likely be introduced in 1991.

As described in chapter 3, the United States has engaged in more direct forms of political action than broadcast, including support for coups. Executive Order 12,333, however, delimits the scope of such support. Among the order's more controversial sections is that prohibiting assassination, which states: "No person employed by or acting on behalf of the United States Government shall engage in, or conspire to engage in assassination."[67] This language is generally understood to mean that the United States does not engage in "selective or individual assassination," either directly or by hiring surrogates.[68] The definition of assassination, however, remains unclear and has been susceptible to some bending. Is, for example, a bombing raid, with a leader's residence as a target, assassination? Not, apparently, if that leader's location is also considered a legitimate military target, for example, a headquarters, and the leader's death might be construed even prospectively as collateral damage.

In a rather cavalier fashion, President Reagan made clear that the killing of Colonel Qaddafi was an objective of the Libyan raid. He was not criticized for it. That may have signaled the beginning of a change in policy. The issue arose again in the context of the build-up to the 1991 war with Iraq when Air Force Chief of Staff General Dugan was relieved from duty after telling reporters that

> Israeli sources have advised that "the best way to hurt Saddam" is to target his family, his personal guard and his mistress. Because Saddam is a "one-man show" in Iraq, Dugan said, "if and when we choose violence he ought to be at the focus of our efforts"—a military strategy known as decapitation.[69]

Secretary of Defense Cheney's subsequent statements, however, suggest that Dugan may not have been fired because he advocated war plans which might violate the prohibition on assassination, but because his remarks were public and suggested Israeli involvement in U.S. planning. In addition to the diplomatic embarrassment, Dugan's remarks appeared to eliminate any room for "plausible deniability" were Hussein, or his family, to become casualties of an air raid.

The Dugan incident sheds light on the evolution in executive branch thinking on assassination since Libya. It may signal an end to the United States prohibition on direct participation in assassination, by whatever name, within the context of military operations or war. The degree to which the conspiracy prohibition will henceforth be interpreted to bar United States personnel from assisting groups or individuals who may independently engage in assassination may also be in flux. United States reluctance to support the October 1989 Giroldi coup against Noriega suggests that the prohibition was interpreted at that time to extend to such events. But in the wake of the failed coup and the recriminations that followed, Judge Webster, then director of central intelligence, called on the president and Congress to clarify and relax the regulation on conspiring to engage in assassination.[70]

Another area of United States covert activity employs the military instrument. Covert military and paramilitary options have historically included: sabotage; anti-sabotage; demolition; subversion against hostile states, including assistance to underground resistance movements and to guerrillas and refugee liberation groups; and support of indigenous elements in threatened countries of the free world.[71] This area of covert activity also includes covert assistance to friendly governments who wish such assistance, as in arms transfers, to remain secret. Moreover, covert military activities are not always discrete events distinct from overt military strategies, but are rather secret phases of broader overt strategies, for example, reconnaissance prior to a raid or landing.[72]

The visibility of some covert military activities should not, however, confuse us concerning the broader trends. Although there can be little doubt that paramilitary operations like Afghanistan, Nicaragua, Cambodia, and Angola account for the majority of recent covert action spending, as a percentage of findings and actual operations undertaken, paramilitary operations account for a relatively small part of the total number of covert operations. In addition, covert action as a percentage of the total intelligence budget, and in real terms, declined sharply at the end of the Vietnam conflict before beginning a gradual incline at the end of the Carter presidency. It continued to climb through the Reagan administration. In addition, spending on the Defense Department portion of the intelligence budget known as the Tactical Intelligence and Related Activities program has regularly exceeded funding for the National Foreign Intelligence Program. These trends reflect a commitment to technical intelligence collection and processing, and perhaps, a decline in use of at least some covert action options.[73]

Numbers and relative percentages should not, of course, be used to minimize the public policy significance of even a few activities. In any case, the numbers are often confusing, as it is not always clear what part of the budget public disclosures refer to. On the other hand, the available numbers do provide some sense of the relative contributions of different types of activities and underscore in addition to the paramilitary the gamut of covert diplomatic and political activities that are being supported.

Future covert military and paramilitary operations by the United States may center on *indirect* support and sponsorship of insurgency by nongovernmental parties and aid to governments countering insurgency, as well as on efforts to extend the territorial reach of United States laws targeting terrorism and the drug trade.

Apprehension of fugitives overseas is usually accomplished through bilateral extradition treaties or through formal or informal methods of deportation where an operable treaty either does not exist or publicity is to be avoided. In cases where extradition is refused (or impossible as in Lebanon), deportation is denied, or permission to apprehend a fugitive is denied, Executive orders have, apparently, prohibited forcible extradition of fugitives. *Yunis,* however, suggests at least one exception to United States policy: those occasions when the suspect can be lured from the safe haven of foreign soil into international waters or air space. United States policy on nonconsensual extraterritorial arrests, or rendition as it is also known, is currently under review.[74]

In 1989 the Office of Legal Counsel reversed a 1980 O.L.C. opinion which concluded that "U.S. agents have no law enforcement authority in another nation unless it is the product of that nation's consent."[75] In contrast, the 1989 opinion found that, as a matter of United States law, a controlling executive act could authorize executive officials to violate the territorial sovereignty of other states in contravention of customary international law.[76] The opinion did not address the separate issue of executive orders that might violate treaty obligations. "Where, as here," then Assistant Attorney General Barr argued before Congress, "the President's constitutional authority to enforce the laws intersects with his foreign affairs power, we believe that he retains the constitutional authority to order enforcement actions in addition to those permitted by statute . . . this authority carries with it the power to direct Executive Branch agents to carry out arrests that contravene customary international law and other international law principles which our legislature has not acted upon to make part of our domestic law." This ruling, Barr continued, is "consistent with the very nature of customary international law," which evolves by states departing from existing practice. States, however, are liable for breaches under international law until a new rule of customary law develops.

Then Department of State Legal Adviser Abraham Sofaer argued that such arrests might even be lawful under international law as a legitimate exercise in self-defense. "Arrests in foreign States," Sofaer wrote, "without their consent have no legal justification under international law aside from self-defense. But where criminal organization grows to a point where it can and does perpetrate violent attacks against the United States, it can become a proper object of measures in self-defense." Some subsequent proposals have aroused foreign governmental concern.

Notwithstanding executive regulations and international norms against extraterritorial kidnapping,[77] federal courts, until now, have followed the so-called Ker-Frisbie rule,[78] which holds that once custody is obtained, the Court will not examine how a defendant was brought to the dock unless it involved conduct that "shocks the conscience."[79] Apparently, violation of foreign or international law in this regard is not necessarily "shocking" to the American judicial conscience. In case the conscience is shocked, the *Toscanino* exception applies and the defendant is returned to his *status quo ante*.[80] *Toscanino,* however, sets a very high threshold of shocking conduct to warrant dismissal.[81]

Indeed, Toscanino did not meet the test and no subsequent case has ever been found to satisfy the *Toscanino* requirement.[82] However, in July 1991, the Ninth Circuit Court of Appeals reversed and remanded the district court's decision in *U.S. v. Verdugo-Urquidez,* which arose from the murder in Mexico of Enrique Camarena, a DEA agent. The court ruled that "should the district court conclude on the basis of the evidentiary hearing that the United States authorized or sponsored Verdugo's kidnapping, it shall order the United States to tender Verdugo to the Mexican authorities," provided the Mexican government does not first withdraw their protest.[83]

An August 1990 district court decision in *Alvarez,* however, could also serve as a new benchmark. Dr. Humberto Alvarez-Machain was indicted in Los Angeles for the same 1986 felony-murder. When negotiations broke down with Mexican officials for the extradition of Alvarez, Alvarez was abducted in Guadalajara by Mexican citizens who turned him over to United States authorities in Texas. The Mexican agents were paid $20,000. In addition, seven of the abductors and their families were relocated to the United States. Alvarez was the third of seven Camarena defendants brought to court by covert forcible abduction.[84]

Alvarez filed a motion to dismiss arguing that his abduction violated due process of law, the U.S.-Mexican extradition treaty, and the charters of the United Nations and OAS. In addition, Alvarez urged the court to exercise its supervisory power and dismiss the indictment. The court denied Alvarez's motion to dismiss for outrageous government conduct,[85] and chose not to reach Alvarez's challenge that his abduction violated the United Nations Charter and OAS Charter.[86] The court, however, found that the United States had violated its extradition treaty with Mexico. As remedy, the court ordered the defendant discharged and the government to repatriate Alvarez to Mexico.[87]

In so ruling, Judge Rafeedie distinguished Alvarez from other abduction cases, where courts had found jurisdiction, on the grounds that "the United States acted unilaterally, without the participation or consent of the Mexican government." "The United States is responsible for the actions of its paid agents, and a unilateral abduction . . . when combined with an official protest . . . constitutes a violation of the extradition treaty. . . ." Thus, although the court held "that it is for the state, and not the individual, to initially protest and thereby raise a claim that the method of securing a person's presence violates an extradition treaty . . . Mexico has expressly and adequately protested and thereby vested Dr. Machain with its rights under the extradition treaty."

The United States government has appealed. The Supreme Court, which recently held that the Fourth Amendment does not apply to the property of foreigners overseas,[88] would appear unlikely to uphold Judge Rafeedie's ruling should it reach the Court.

## LOOKING AHEAD

Until the 1970s, United States commitment to peacetime covert activity remained relatively constant in personnel and funding. Since that time, however, United States covert action programs have undergone a series of pendulum swings marked by congressional investigations and the Reagan Doctrine. However, despite these spikes on the graph, there appears an underlying national consensus for both a strong intelligence process, with covert capacity, and effective oversight. Continued tensions and the war in the Persian Gulf will, we believe, reinforce this consensus.

The separation of powers issue has, of late, dominated the domestic debate on oversight. At times, this debate has left the national security community with uncertain direction. Solemn invocations of Supreme Court decisions such as *Curtiss-Wright* or *Youngstown* have not helped to clarify issues, for there is more at stake than institutional prerogatives founded on inconclusive constitutional claims. The urgent policy question is which emerging legal and administrative arrangements best equip the United States for its world role while preserving its democratic values.

The national debate must assume from the outset that both Congress and the executive have legitimate but different responsibilities over intelligence and foreign affairs. This requires some accommodation by each side. If the executive claims to need the flexibility to conduct some covert operations free from immediate congressional scrutiny, it must also realize that only policies founded on congressional and ultimately public support can succeed in the long run. On the other hand, congressional desire for improved accountability and shared power should not develop into congressional micro-management that obviates the executive and impedes or frustrates intelligence operations and oversight itself.

The Iran-Contra Affair revived the call for a comprehensive national security statute or charter.[89] Although appealing to a sense of legal order, one should remember that the charter approach was tried in the 1970s but found impractical. Until the Intelligence Authorization Act of 1991, the various remedial measures that were stimulated by the Iran-Contra affair proceeded largely on a piecemeal and patchwork basis. Each was the product of careful compromise between the executive and legislative branches reflecting as much the political as the constitutional realities involved. But they were not integrated into any larger coherent conception. The only significant innovation to emerge from this process was the post of statutory inspector general at the CIA.[90] Less formal arrangements, however, emerged in the form of letters between the president and the Intelligence Committees.

The Intelligence Authorization Act of 1991 would shift away from informal mechanisms of oversight to formal mechanisms designed to assure the legislative branch an expanded and meaningful role. In fact, this shift began in 1984, before Iran-Contra.

In 1984, in the wake of the mining of Nicaraguan harbors, Director of Central Intelligence William Casey signed an informal agreement with the chairman and vice chairman of the Senate Select Committee on Intelligence providing procedures "governing" reporting of covert actions. An addendum to this "accord" was signed in 1986 at which time the committee principals and the director of central intelligence agreed that "the Procedures have worked well and that they have aided the Committee and the DCI in the fulfillment of their respective responsibilities." It was further agreed that the Committee would receive prior notification if "significant military equipment actually is to be supplied for the first time in an ongoing operation . . . even if there is no requirement for separate higher authority or Presidential approval." This occurred five months *after* the president signed the January 17, 1986, Iran Finding authorizing the secret transfer of tube-launched, optically tracked, wire-command-link (TOW) antitank/assault missiles to Iran.

National Security Decision Directive 286, a 1987 presidential directive on special activities, was drafted in the wake of Iran-Contra after "extensive consultations" between then National Security Advisor Carlucci and the congressional intelligence committees.[91] The directive incorporates provisions of congressional legislation that initially failed to become law, such as a prohibition against retroactive findings and a requirement that findings be written. Unlike a statute, however, a national security decision directive is subject to executive revision or revocation without congressional consent.

The Intelligence Authorization Act of 1991 overhauled the existing oversight framework by codifying elements of the "Casey Accords," National Security Decision Directive 286, and independent legislative proposals aimed at plugging loopholes exposed by the Iran-Contra affair. The president initially pocket vetoed the measure on the grounds that "the Act's definition of covert action included any 'request' by the United States to a foreign government or a private citizen to conduct a covert action on behalf of the United States," thus making such activities subject to the reporting procedures of the National Security Act. "This provision purports to regulate diplomacy by the President and other members of the executive branch," the President argued. "[T]he very possibility of a broad construction of this term could have a chilling effect on the ability of our diplomats to conduct highly sensitive discussions concerning projects that are vital to our national security."[92] The president also argued that language contained in the Joint Explanatory Statement accompanying the Conference Report which purported to limit the president's authority to withhold prior notification to "exigent circumstances" and interpreted "timely fashion" as meaning "within a few days," infringed on the president's constitutional authorities. The act, however, also included, in its initial form and as revised, provisions which, arguably, are favorable to the executive. The statutory definition of "covert action," for example, excludes "traditional diplomatic or military activities or routine support of such activities," language that could be read to give the president considerable discretion to act outside of the procedures for covert action oversight.[93]

If there is no more legislation to be passed, it is still important to keep in focus the larger lessons of the unhappy Iran-Contra affair. Presidential optimism notwithstanding, we would surmise that points of contention will emerge in the current oversight regime as they have in previous regimes to oversee the executive use of covert action. Where these pressure points surface will reflect the content of existing law and the personalities and policies of the individuals entrusted with the process. A Carter, for example, offers a different leadership style than a Reagan, a Wright a different vision of oversight than a Moynihan, and a Turner a different statutory interpretation than a Casey.[94]

Clearer allocations of competence and arrangements for oversight should also address the *how* and *when* of covert action. The debate should keep long-term goals in sight and not focus solely on current crises and perceived fiascoes. The Giroldi coup in Panama is a case in point. Although Congress and the press criticized the administration's decision not to aid Major Giroldi (the decision-making process may well have been flawed), they might also have noted the executive's good faith compliance with existing prohibitions. Instead, "plausible deniability" assumed new meaning. If Congress did have a hand in reviewing and implementing the executive order on intelligence activities, as administration spokesmen alleged, it was a hidden hand whose presence could be revealed or concealed after the fact.

Less than one year after the Panama invasion, the United States again faced the prospect of war to remove a ruthless dictator. Although it is yet to be seen how postmortems will assess the adequacy of United States intelligence prior to Iraq's invasion of Kuwait, the invasion raised again the ethical dilemma of what to do about the ruthless dictator. Should the United States have considered covert action in advance of the crisis? Should the United Nations consider it? Is it possible to have an internationally sanctioned, and lawful, covert action without Security Council consent? In this context, John Stuart Mill's observation from 1857 is still apt:

> The doctrine of nonintervention to be a legitimate principle of morality, must be accepted by all governments. The despots must be bound by it as well as the free

States. Unless they do, the profession of it by free countries comes but to this miserable issue, that the wrong side may help the wrong, but the right must not help the right.[95]

Hindsight vision that is 20–20 is no great achievement. What was appropriate yesterday, for example, a Noriega on the payroll, is questioned today. So too, what was prohibited yesterday may be appropriate tomorrow, such as support for a coup whose members, their assurances notwithstanding, might in the process independently engage in assassination. The "threat" will also change. It already has. Certainly, the hypothetical situation we posited in chapter 1 regarding the mapping of the genome would not have been imaginable ten or fifteen years ago. Politics, and not just covert actions, require constant reappraisal of policies and their consequences in different contexts. Therefore, a good argument can be made for allowing the executive to retain a certain case-by-case discretion over the conduct of covert action and dissemination of information consistent with congressional oversight and general normative policies. Whatever regime is established, subsequent appraisers should never overlook the importance of "real-time" context in decision making.

This does not mean that the United States should or must maintain a capacity for covert action or keep the threshold of such action at the same level at which it is now. It is difficult to imagine circumstances in which the United State's political existence or security would be directly threatened and a covert action the only means of deflecting the threat. If such a danger materialized, responses would be conceived in a military paradigm and the legal and moral quandaries that covert action provoke would not arise. It is true that individual Americans, particularly those abroad, may be endangered in ways that could have been deflected or reduced by anticipatory or retaliatory covert actions, but policymakers and the public may conclude that the political and moral costs of covert action outweigh the gains for a handful of Americans. When Americans were held hostage in Lebanon, a majority of Americans appeared content to ignore the matter.

Shared power means shared responsibility. The executive branch has signalled that United States policies on extraterritorial law enforcement and assassination are in transition. Although many statutes already provide domestic law exemptions for intelligence activities,[96] the Congress should affirmatively consider whether assassination, in whatever guise, shall be a part of United States policy, and in what manner the nation should enforce its laws overseas. Does the Senate, for example, intend to authorize, or acquiesce in, operations like the Alvarez-Machain seizure when it reports that

[t]raditional law enforcement activities include activities such as those of the FBI to apprehend, or otherwise cooperate with foreign law enforcement authorities

in the apprehension of those who have violated U.S. laws or the laws of other nations.[97]

Consideration of issues like these must occur in advance of the next crisis when the long-term equities are in balance with shorter-term political and security expedients.

No long-term goal is more at risk in the face of national security expediency than international law. At least in public posture, Congress has shown more concern that intelligence operations are conducted within the parameters of international law than the executive branch has. On at least one public occasion, for example, objection was made to a covert operation on the basis of international law.[98] Moreover, congressional criteria for the annual review of covert action programs includes consideration of international law. In contrast, the Office of Legal Counsel's 1989 opinion on extraterritorial law enforcement only addresses domestic legal issues. What occurs in secret executive and congressional deliberations, however, cannot be ascertained, for it is not reported.

# Chapter 7

**Covert Operations
in the Future:
Projections and
Some Modest Guidelines**

The covert use of the various instruments of strategy, whether proactively or reactively (for self-defense or as a countermeasure), with the intention of inducing a target to modulate its behavior in ways that henceforth discriminate in favor of the state using the strategy, will, we believe, continue to be used, on various occasions and at varying levels of intensity, against other entities with whom varying degrees of amity or hostility obtain. They appear, alas, to be part of contemporary international politics. Such actions may be far from the relatively tranquil domestic politics of many of our citizens, but it would be unrealistic and incautious on the part of United States decision makers to believe that American facilities and American citizens will not occasionally be targets.

The United States may, as a moral matter, simply decide to eschew all covert action of certain kinds. But this would not, we believe, lead all other actors, whether from weakness, desperation, or rational calculations, to refrain similarly from such actions. On the contrary, the absence of a manifest retaliatory capacity might even encourage adventurism. Like the strategy of maintaining an arsenal of hideous weapons to deter others from using them, a covert capacity may deter noxious covert activities, pending universal, effective agreement to outlaw them.

We predict that, as in the past, rather than blanket condemnations of all such covert uses, international decision-making processes will assess lawfulness not simply by reference to the property of secrecy, which accompanies the execution of different phases of many policy instruments, but by reference to the many different policies engaged in the particular case, the options available, the aggregate consequences likely to attend each of the options, and so on. When such criteria are applied, not all covert operations will be condemned. We believe that, on balance, the United States has no choice but to continue to maintain a capacity and to develop means and procedures, at the very least, for countering hostile covert actions. The maintenance of a capacity does not necessarily mean a commitment to proactive uses.

For many of the reasons considered above, covert actions of different types that many may consider in particular cases to be justified will continue to be controversial precisely because they collide with so many important democratic ideals and, democracy aside, because they are susceptible to organizational pathologies that more overt operations resist. Even when covert actions appear to promise economical success, they will have a political price, both domestically and internationally. Though they may be romanticized, the nasty manipulative, exploitative, and necessarily deceitful character of most such actions will always arouse revulsion.

Ironically, these various costs will multiply the value of secrecy and increase the efforts to maintain it. At the same time, the media, whose role in modern life, indeed, whose constitutive function in modern consciousness, cannot be overstated, will redouble efforts to expose such secrecy. Exposures of secret actions will be newsworthy because when a popular government is caught trying to do something secretive, the media, by exposing that action validate themselves as the indispensable check on those who would wield power. These efforts will sometimes be assisted by domestic and external political opponents who may be able to use the fact of a secret operation to unseat the incumbents or, at least, to increase their own power.

The target and design of covert operations may change. It is clear that the use of the strategy in the postwar period was profoundly affected by the Cold War and a global power process in which free market democracies were arrayed against an expansive totalitarian order. Part of that context is disappearing. The possible disintegration of the tsarist-Soviet empire will certainly precipitate major changes. The finding of the Doolittle Committee of the Hoover Commission in 1954, which we cited in chapter 6, may have been cogent at the time it was expressed, but the context has changed to the point where it now appears to be and even to have been an expression of a Manichean hysteria.

But predictions often gang aglay. The fundamental structure of world politics of the last fifty years may not change so rapidly or, indeed, so substantively. A Russia shorn of all of its territories with the exception of Siberia (and it is likely to retain much more) would still continue to be a superpower. If the so-called end of the Cold War is, like co-existence and *détente,* only one more U.S.-Soviet effort, this time at Moscow's initiative, to fashion a mutually convenient readjustment of the global system, then the fundamental structure of the world power process will continue. In this interpretation, the Soviets, economically exhausted and unable to sustain the next phase of weapons development, have sought respite by proposing a moratorium on some weapons, reducing the military balance to drastically lower levels of parity, suspending and possibly terminating certain unfruitful conflicts in a number of subarenas, and promising to cooperate in addressing some nonsecurity problems. In return, according to this interpretation, Moscow is offering to relax controls over some buffer states and to open its own internal political processes to the extent that it induces economic development without threatening elite control. The continuation of the system is all the more likely if the United States and NATO accommodate President Gorbachev's initiative and, by making appropriate reductions, maintain the fundamental superpower parity between the United States and the Soviet Union.

Even if this construct of the future comes to pass, it is unlikely that the idiosyncratic style of covert warfare (and the intermittent but still remarkable public tolerance of it) that prevailed throughout the Cold War will persist. But some form is likely to continue, driven by the dynamic of political and economic competition and the emergence of new competing versions of public order, for example, some strains of Islamic fundamentalism which endorse covert terror as a legitimate political instrument.[1]

Key parts of the focus of covert operations may change. It is apparent that external threats to national public order are increasingly being redefined in terms of a number of nongovernmental operations: terrorism, broadly and often inconsistently defined; organized crime and narcotics; and, to a lesser degree, transnational white-collar crime. The apprehension of those engaged in these activities must be international and, as the examples we posed in the first chapter suggest, many police actions will incorporate a number of covert phases, which will increasingly take place abroad. In addition, the geographical focus may change. We would anticipate that the diversion of disposable development funds from the Third World to Eastern Europe, finally and lamentably effecting a genuine North-South division, will exacerbate instability in key Third World regions and make them fertile ground for covert actions, by regional and global actors.

With the change of mood in the international political arena, however, the international legal tolerance for covert operations may decline precipitously. Although state elites may continue to hold views comparable to those in the past, more popular characterizations, increasingly important in contemporary international law, may issue broad condemnations of such activities. In this regard, the split reaction to the *Rainbow Warrior* incident, considered in chapter 3, may foreshadow future reactions.

But not all international elites are likely to be willing to surrender the short-term advantages to be gained from different types of covert operations. It is no surprise that the warming of political relationships between the East and West has been reported to be marked by an increase in a wide range of political and industrial espionage activities. Intelligence agencies may simply be searching for a new raison d'être or they may take longer views and assume that when a cycle has run and interstate hostility increases, they will be in a better position to perform their functions.

In the United States, however, fundamental changes in the domestic constitutive process signal significant changes in the way covert activities will be planned and implemented. Congress' increasingly effective demand to play a role in the *conduct* of foreign affairs will mean that more cooks will be trying to make each covert stew. The media, in an intense and competitive search for dramatic news in their industry, will increasingly seek out revelations about secret operations. The media crusades describing violations of formal norms will become an increasing feature of domestic politics.

Yet we would predict that the overall popular reaction will be one of unstable ambivalence. Covert operations bear a certain resemblance, in terms of popular attitudes, to the use of police informers in domestic criminal justice systems.[2] People in the so-called criminal world who serve as confidential informants in return for money or remission of prosecutions or sentences are part of a widely used and probably indispensable criminal justice practice. But the practice of confidential informants is popularly distasteful and generally ignored. From time to time, the public discovers what is happening and a popular outcry may result. Though this sometimes leads to new legislation, the practice itself continues. It would obviously be better if either a clear public rejection or a clear public acceptance of the need for such types of social "dirty work" were to occur. But, given the mix of utility and disgust, such clarity is unlikely. Hence our prognosis of a repetitive series of sequences: practice, crusade against the practice, resumption of the practice.[3]

The cohesion and self-confidence of the national elite, an important factor in undertaking covert operations, may continue to decline. All of these factors could limit the possibilities of keeping the plans no less than the implementation of covert operations secret. They could, as a result, limit the use of the strategy.

Even when there appear to be compelling reasons to resort to covert operations, the basic tension in democratic politics between the need for openness as a way of assuring power sharing and the need for secrecy as a way of assuring efficiency will (and in our view should) continue. We would predict that there will be a series of efforts to achieve a workable balance between these two interests, each surviving only until a covert operation implemented under it fails or proves politically costly. Thereafter, it will be succeeded by another, designed to correct the now demonstrated failings of its predecessor. None of these efforts will prove to be very durable.

Nonetheless, there will be moments when key segments of the elite will conclude that covert operations or covert phases of some sort are a necessary and economic method of achieving a legitimate national objective. When covert operations appear to be necessary, we would suggest a decalogue of executive guidelines for planning and implementing particular covert operations. They are all guidelines. None is proposed as a hard and fast rule.

1. **Try, as far as possible, to accomplish overtly what subordinates propose to do covertly.** This recommendation is subject to a broad margin of appreciation, for the property of being "covert" is slippery and can be achieved in many ways, for example, a very "general" statement of plans to an oversight agency may be claimed after the fact as full revelation despite the fact that at the time its effect was to shroud in secrecy whatever was on the drawing boards. By "overt," here, we mean overt, first, in terms of disclosure to the appropriate oversight agency; second, in terms of disclosure to the international community; third, in terms of disclosure to the target. The *specificity* of disclosure will necessarily be a function of many variables and will involve democratic considerations, efficiency considerations, and international political considerations.

2. **Never say that you will never do things covertly.** It may be very tempting to take the "moral high ground" and to favor diplomacy, mutual understanding, accommodation, and economic sanctions. But there may come a time when reasonableness will have been exhausted and philosophy and poetry manifestly will not prevail over a grave evil or danger. Poverty may be at the root of all political instability. But there are moments of crisis calling for resolute action when talk of poverty as the root of evil and the need for economic and developmental assistance is escapism and may border on madness. At certain levels and for certain phases of operations, secrecy will continue to be required and will be a part of governmental operations in the foreign policy area. When secrecy is exposed after public promises of "never," the net effect will be to damage public confidence in governmental operations, in general, and the credibility of the incumbents in particular. It is best to acknowledge beforehand that this is one of the lawful tools at the disposal of the executive, that it has been authorized by legislation, that appropriate procedures have been prescribed, but that because of the special costs of its use in a democracy, it will be resorted to no more than

necessary. In short, the responsible executive official should be on record that there are instances when its use may be lawful and appropriate and that not to use it then would be wrong.

3. **Do not confuse covert actions or phases of actions with coercive actions or phases of actions.** Though some may find some philosophical cogency or rhetorical mileage in arguments that concealing anything from another, under any circumstances, constitutes an act of violence against that other, we think it is more sensible to assume that concealing one's motives, preparatory actions, or implementation from someone else, although not necessarily nice or ethically optimal and hence not generally desirable, nevertheless is not the same as an act of coercion against another and that its lawfulness or morality may turn on many contextual factors.

4. **But all executives should eschew secrecy for its own sake.** The political advantages of secrecy are obvious. It enhances the power of the party using it, and where power sharing is called for, secrecy circumvents it. The costs of secrecy in a democracy should rule it out in all but those cases in which other compelling democratic values would be lost if secrecy were not used.

5. **An act accomplished covertly should be overtly lawful.** Assuming that secrecy is not per se unlawful (in some legislative contexts, it may be), the action or phase of action that is being accomplished secretly should itself be lawful. In other words, secrecy should not be used to evade the requirements of law or to conceal unlawful actions. Covert actions and, in particular, interstate collaborative covert actions should be tested by international standards as if they were actions to enforce international obligations. The outcome of that inquiry should be a critical factor in deciding whether to proceed with the action. But the test should be conducted honestly and not evaded by the use of euphemisms. Earlier we indicated why we think state-sponsored assassination is bad policy, though we acknowledged that tyrannicide has been a morally difficult issue through the ages. But, apart from that, any operation may lead to the deaths of people. In any instance where a politically motivated killing is a possible or probable outcome of United States action or inaction, we would argue that democratic values oblige decision makers to express policy preferences with clarity and specificity, not with such obfuscating terms as *personal defense weapons, remove,* and *neutralize,* terms that appeared during the Trujillo and Chilean episodes and that seem to recur with some regularity in secret government documents.[4] The use of such terms subverts personal moral examination and critical political review.

6. **In determining what is lawful under international law, it is important to use contextual and consequential methods of inquiry rather than methods of textual and logical derivation.** Two points are noteworthy. First, inter-

national law is structurally different from developed domestic systems and perforce uses a different method for assessing lawfulness. Hence the consequentialist mode, based on a thorough contextual examination, rather than a textual and rule-oriented approach should be employed. Second, not everything that is permitted in international law should be automatically deemed permissible in particular cases. One should not pretend that the defects of international law are a virtue. The low-level of regulation in many strategic modes is lamentable because it does not serve world order. A state actor that refrains from some theretofore licit practices may contribute, by its own abstinence, to the formation and installation of a more appropriate norm.

The implementation of this recommendation requires that lawyers who have the necessary background, but who are not in the direct chain of command have an opportunity to submit their written views, which become part of the record.

7. One of the costs of secrecy is that a vigorous and open examination of reasons for, and likelihood of success of, an operation will not take place. Instead, a process characterized by what Janis has called "groupthink" may operate.[5] Hence the need in a nonpublic decision-making process contemplating covert action to **structure internally an examination process as vigorous and critical as would be the public debate were it to occur. In particular, if you think circumstances require departure from national law and procedure, carefully review your motives to be sure that irrational factors are not operating.**

8. **When the educative or informative function of a strategy is important, the ultimate implementation of the strategy should not be covert.** This recommendation is driven, obviously, by efficiency considerations. Many particularly coercive strategies are designed to inform and deter and not simply to inflict some deprivation or punishment on the target. If adequate information about the message, the messenger, and the sender is not available, the real purpose of the strategic operation is frustrated. Equally obviously, the overt quality of the operation may make it more costly to the initiating party.

In discussion with other scholars in the initial presentation of our views in the Institute of Peace, this guideline raised many questions. Secrecy and "untraceability" may be useful when the object is to destroy a target after persuasive means have failed. The elimination of a target such as the reported chemical weapons factory at Rabta is not an informative or educative project. Since its purpose is destruction, untraceability may be desirable, especially because the target government will predictably seek to avenge itself, perhaps by terrorism. But when the United States, after protests about mining and targetting of shipping in the Persian Gulf, decided to punish Iran by destroying general oil installations, a covert destruction that could have been interpreted as an accident would have been far less educational than an overt operation in which the identity of the actors, the demonstration of their capacity, and the reasons were unmistakable. In addition, overt action could incorporate warnings to personnel in the targetted facilities and minimize loss of life.

9. **We strongly endorse the refinement of methods of congressional oversight, though we would think that the oversight, for reasons of both executive and congressional efficiency, should be retrospective and judgmental rather than prospective and executive.** There is a tendency to view executive branches as monarchical vestiges. As a wide range of organizational phenomena indicate, specialized agencies for policy implementation are required in all but the simplest organizations. Hence the recurring development of separate institutions designed to make (including to appraise the fulfillment of policy objectives) and implement policy.

Covert actions, in our view, require an executive. If there is a national decision to have a capacity for such action, it should not be frustrated by an inefficient system of implementation. But democracies also require that executive actions be subjected to oversight and appraisal. If those charged with these functions have also been involved in the actions, they are unlikely to appraise themselves very vigorously. Hence, in the interests of the national community, we recommend a clean division and specialization of function in the various successive oversight regimes we anticipate.

10. **In contemplating any covert operation, whether from the standpoint of the operator or those providing oversight, assume that it will become public knowledge much sooner than you would like and decide if you can live with the consequences before you discover you have to.** The illusion of secrecy can provide a false and treacherous sense of security. A game-theory proposition may be a useful *vade mecum* for the political operator: always assume your adversary knows everything you are doing so that when he does find out, you will already have discounted the cost.

# Appendix

## Twenty Years of Alleged Covert Aggression Brought to the Attention of the Security Council

This appendix lists in chronological order Security Council *Agenda* items from 1969–1988 that we judge to have involved covert coercion. Thus, this is by definition a subjective listing based on the authors' definition of covert coercion and not a United Nations definition. It is only a brief and suggestive exercise.

Some of the items we include might also be classified as episodes of direct aggression, for example, "Complaint by Democratic Kampuchea" (1979 regarding Vietnamese aggression). A large proportion of the alleged covert operations reaching the agenda of the Security Council involve border incursions, covert and overt support for insurgents, and incidents related to broader regional and overt conflicts, for example, an alleged violation of Pakistani airspace by Afghanistan. To reflect these variances, we have compiled two separate results: (1) agenda items involving any alleged or reported instance of coercion that arguably included covert phases and (2) agenda items specifically addressing single instances of covert action, not within a larger politico-military conflict or action, for example, "Complaint by Benin" regarding a coup attempt. These latter matters are marked with an asterix.

Once a matter is included on the agenda it remains there until the Security Council agrees to its removal. To avoid double-counting, we have only cited and counted specific instances of alleged coercion once, for example, Iraq's complaint against Israel involving the 1981 air raid on an Iraqi nuclear reactor, which has appeared on the agenda every year since. Where separate allegations have appeared under a recurring item, e.g., Middle East Situation, we repeat the heading.

Finally, the list is not exhaustive of claims asserting alleged covert actions. Other instances of alleged covert coercion, for example, may be brought to the attention of the

Security Council in the form of a letter, yet not be included on the agenda, for example, S/15734 Colombia letter Apr. 26, 1982, "transmitting note to Libyan Arab Jamahiraya [*sic*] concerning an intended overflight of Colombian territory by four Libyan commercial aircraft presumably carrying medical assistance for Nicaragua, and which were ascertained to be carrying munitions and war materiel." And, of course, many if not most instances of covert activity are not brought to the attention of the Security Council at all.

*Matters considered by, or brought to the attention of, the Security Council during 1969*

Relations between Cambodia and the Republic of Vietnam [concerning aggressive actions by United States and South Vietnamese forces]

Relations between Cambodia and Thailand [concerning alleged territorial infiltrations at sea]

Complaint by Zambia against Portugal [territorial incursions]

Complaint by Equatorial Guinea against Spain [colonial war]

Complaint by the United States concerning the attack by North Korea against a reconnaissance aircraft of the United States

The situation in Haiti [attacks by unidentified aircraft]

Relations between El Salvador and Honduras [frontier incidents]

Complaint by Guinea against Portugal

Complaint by Senegal against Portugal [violations of airspace and attacks]

*Matters considered by, or brought to the attention of, the Security Council during 1970*

Relations between Cambodia and Thailand [intrusions into territorial waters by Thai fishing junks and aggressive acts against a Thai village]

The declaration on the Prohibition or Military, Political or Economic Coercion in the Conclusion of Treaties

Complaint by Guyana against Venezuela [alleged armed attack]

The situation in Southern Yemen [territorial violations by British and Saudi forces]

Relations between El Salvador and Honduras

Relations between Portugal and Senegal [violations of territorial sovereignty]

Relations between Guinea and Portugal [armed attacks against Guinea]

*Matters considered by, or brought to the attention of, the Security Council during 1971*

The situation in the Middle East [terrorism and occupation of territories]

The situation in Laos

Guinea and Portugal

Portugal and Senegal

Relations between Portugal and Zambia [blockade]

Relations between South Africa and Zambia

*Matters considered by, or brought to the attention of, the Security Council during 1972*

The situation in the Middle East

The situation in Laos [attacks by North Vietnamese troops]

Relations between Iran and Iraq [border incidents]

Relations between Democratic Yemen and Oman [alleged aggressive acts by British military forces in Oman against Yemen and by Yemen against Oman]

Portugal and Senegal

Occupation of Persian Gulf Islands by Iranian armed forces

Relations between Equatorial Guinea and Gabon [requesting intervention by Security Council concerning withdrawal of Gabonese force from territorial waters]

*Matters considered by, or brought to the attention of, the Security Council during 1973*

The situation in the Middle East

Complaint by Zambia against Southern Rhodesia [acts of aggression]

Complaint by Libyan Arab Republic against United States [concerning presence of Sixth Fleet in Mediterranean Sea and violations of Libyan airspace]

Relations between Chile and Cuba [aggressive acts by Chile against Cuban Embassy during and after overthrow of Allende government]

Relations between Guinea and Senegal

Illegal occupation by Portuguese military forces of certain sectors of the Republic of Guinea-Bissau and acts of aggression committed by them against the people of the Republic

Relations between Democratic Yemen and Oman [violations of Omani airspace]

*Matters considered by, or brought to the attention of, the Security Council during 1974*

Middle East situation [Israeli aggression against six villages in southern Lebanon]

Complaint by Iraq concerning incidents on its frontier with Iran

Relations between Congo and Portugal [incursions by Portuguese fighter planes]

*Matters considered by, or brought to the attention of, the Security Council during 1975*

Middle East situation [series of aggressive acts by PLO against Israel and aggressive acts by Israel against Lebanon]

Relations between Greece and Turkey [violations of Greek airspace over Aegean Islands]

The situation in Cambodia [concerning seizure of Mayaquez]

The situation concerning western Sahara [invasion announced by Morocco]

Relations between Democratic Yemen and Oman

*Matters considered by, or brought to the attention of, the Security Council during 1976*

The situation in the Middle East

Relations between Algeria and Mauritania* [mercenary and military operations against Mauritania]

Relations between Guinea and Ivory Coast* [alleged act of aggression by mercenaries organized against Guinea from within borders of Senegal and Ivory Coast]

Relations between Libyan Arab Republic and Sudan* [concerning acts of aggression against Sudan and counter-claim that "events that took place in Sudan were an internal uprising carried out by Sudanese people."]

Relations between Israel and Uganda* [Entebbe raid]

*Matters considered by the Security Council during 1977*

Complaint of the Government of Botswana against the illegal regime in Southern Rhodesia [concerning violations of its territorial sovereignty]

Complaint by Benin* [concerning coup attempt by French mercenaries January 16, 1977, with alleged foreign complicity]

The situation in the Middle East

Complaint by Mozambique [concerning attacks by Southern Rhodesia]

*Other matters brought to the attention of the Security Council during 1977*

Relations between Algeria and Mauritania [concerning aggressive acts by mercenaries against Mauritania, acts of terrorism and the occupation of Western Sahara]

Complaint by Kenya, on behalf of the African group of states at the United Nations, concerning the act of aggression committed by South Africa against the People's Republic of Angola

Relations between Egypt and Libyan Arab Jamahiriya [concerning aerial raids by Egyptian aircraft]

*Matters considered by the Security Council during 1978*

Complaint by Chad [frontier dispute with Libya]

Complaint by Zambia [invasion of Zambian territory by Rhodesian forces]

Complaint by Angola against South Africa [invasion of territory]

*Other matters brought to the attention of the Security Council during 1978*

Relations between Algeria and Morocco* [concerning alleged attack by an armed band from Algeria against Moroccan lorries]

Question of the territorial waters and airspace of Sao Tome and Principe [concerning violations of territorial waters and airspace by unidentified boats and reconnaissance aircraft]

Complaint by Zambia against South Africa [concerning act of aggression against town of Sesheke by Security Forces of South Africa and concerning attacks against South African military bases launched from Zambia]

*Matters considered by the Security Council during 1979*

Complaint by Democratic Kampuchea [Vietnamese aggression]

Complaint by Angola against South Africa [incursions and air attack]

Complaint by Morocco against Algeria* [concerning alleged Moroccan parachute drop of weapons in Algeria, and Moroccan claims of Algerian ambush and sabotage in Morocco]

Complaint by Zambia [against Rhodesian incursions]

Relations between Iran and the United States [embassy situation]

*Other matters brought to the attention of the Security Council during 1979*

The situation in Nicaragua [concerning normalization of frontier traffic with Costa Rica]

Relations between Ethiopia and Somalia [reconnaissance flights, 151 major Ethiopian air violations alleged]

Relations between Uganda and United Republic of Tanzania [Tanzanian invasion]

Relations between China and Lao People's Democratic Republic [concentrating troops on border, false charges]

Relations between Botswana and Southern Rhodesia [armed intervention]

Relations between South Africa and Zambia [violations of airspace, bombing attack]

The situation in Afghanistan [Soviet "invasion"]

*Matters considered by the Security Council during 1980*

Complaint by Malta against Libyan Arab Jamahiriya [dispute over continental shelf, alleged threats by Libyan warships against Maltese offshore activities]

Relations between Iran and Iraq [Iran-Iraq war]

The situation in Afghanistan

Iran and United States* [note concerning action by Canadian embassy to evacuate U.S. diplomats; statement concerning rescue mission, note verbale concerning "military aggression of U.S. against Iran."]

Complaint by Zambia [against South Africa; South African incursions to attack insurgents]

Relations between Angola and South Africa

*Other matters brought to the attention of the Security Council during 1980*

Relations between China and Viet Nam

Complaint by Bahamas (against Cuba) [violation of airspace and sovereignty]

Relations between Egypt and Libyan Arab Jamahiriya* [alleged Libyan attempts to infiltrate subversive elements across border and general border tension]

Relations between Libyan Arab Jamahiriya and United States [alleged violations of Libyan airspace]

*Matters considered by the Security Council during 1981*

Complaint by Iraq* [Israeli raid on nuclear reactor June 7, 1981]

Complaint by Angola against South Africa

Complaint by Seychelles* [concerning attack by mercenaries, of alleged South African origin; Kenya rejects allegations of complicity.]

Relations between Libya and Malta [dispute over continental shelf and allegations of Libyan use of force to advance position regarding dispute]

*Other matters brought to the attention of the Security Council during 1981*

Relations between Ecuador and Peru ["aggressive acts against Ecuador by Peruvian armed forces"]

Relations between Lao People's Democratic Republic and Thailand

The situation in Chad [Libyan invasion]

Relations between Mauritania and Morocco* [alleged attacks by commandos under Moroccan authority March 16, 1981]

Relations between Mozambique and South Africa [incident near Punta do Duro]

Relations between Chad and Sudan [charge and countercharge of aggression and efforts at destabilization]

Relations between Libyan Arab Jamahiriya and Sudan

The situation in El Salvador

Relations between Guatemala and United Kingdom [alleged violation of Guetemalan airspace by reconnaissance plane]

The situation in Kampuchea [frontier violations]

Relations between China and Vietnam [hostile actions; intrusions]

Relations between Iran and Iraq

The situation in Afghanistan [alleged incursions and violations of Pakistani airspace by Afghanistan and of Afghani airspace by Pakistan]

Relations between Egypt and Libya [propaganda: alleged hostile attitude and statements by President Sadat]

Relations between Libya and United States

The situation in Nicaragua

*Matters considered by the Security Council during 1982*

The situation in Central America

Disputes between Argentina and the United Kingdom over Falkland Islands (Malvinas)

Complaint by Lesotho against South Africa [mortar attack]

Relations between Iran and Iraq

*Other matters brought to the attention of the Security Council during 1982*

Relations between Nicaragua and United States

Complaint by Angola against South Africa

Relations between Guyana and Venezuela [incursions by Venezuelan troops into mainland Guyana]

Relations between Costa Rica and Nicaragua

Relations between Honduras and Nicaragua

Relations between Thailand and Viet Nam

The situation in Kampuchea

Relations between China and Viet Nam

Relations between Libya and United States

The situation in Afghanistan

*Matters considered by the Security Council during 1983*
   The situation in Grenada [United States invasion]
   Relations between Libya and United States
   The situation in Chad
   Relations between Honduras and Nicaragua [contras, incursions]
   Relations between Lesotho and South Africa
   Relations between Iran and Iraq
   Relations between Angola and South Africa
   The situation in Lebanon [Syrian air strikes]

*Other matters brought to the attention of the Security Council during 1983*
   Relations between Libyan Arab Jamahiriya and Somalia
   Relations between El Salvador and Nicaragua
   Relations between China and Viet Nam
   The situation in Afghanistan
   Relations between Libya and Sudan
   Korean question [alleged propaganda by both sides]
   Relations between Egypt and Libya* [propaganda and incitement]
   The situation in the Seychelles
   Relations between Mozambique and South Africa
   Relations between Costa Rica and Nicaragua [contra activities]
   The situation in Nicaragua

*Matters considered by the Security Council during 1984*
   Freedom of Navigation in the Persian Gulf
   Relations between Nicaragua and the United States [including complaint concerning Tayacan manual]
   Relations between Lao People's Democratic Republic and Thailand
   Relations between Angola and South Africa
   Relations between Honduras and Nicaragua
   Relations between Libya and Sudan
   Relations between Iran and Iraq
   The situation in Lebanon

*Other matters brought to the attention of the Security Council during 1984*
   The situation in Afghanistan
   Falkland Islands [alleged acts of provocation against Argentine fishing vessels]
   Relations between China and Viet Nam
   Relations between Lesotho and South Africa
   Relations between Libya and United States
   Relations between Mozambique and South Africa
   Relations between Costa Rica and Nicaragua
   Relations between Thailand and Viet Nam

*Matters considered by the Security Council during 1985*
    The situation created by hostage taking and abduction
    The situation in Nicaragua
    Relations between Iran and Iraq
    Relations between Angola and South Africa [sabotage of oil refinery]
    Relations between Botswana and South Africa [commando attack on Gabarone]
    The situation in Chad
    Relations between Lesotho and South Africa

*Other matters brought to the attention of the Security Council during 1985*
    The situation in Central America
    The situation in Afghanistan
    The situation in the Falklands [contacts between air forces]
    Relations between Thailand and Viet Nam
    Relations between China and Viet Nam
    Relations between Laos and Thailand
    Relations between Libya and United States

*Matters considered by the Security Council during 1986*
    The situation in Nicaragua
    Relations between Iran and Iraq
    The situation in Central America
    Relations between Libya and United States* [concerning Rome and Vienna airport attacks and United States air raid on Libya]

*Other matters brought to the attention of the Security Council during 1986*
    Relations between Angola and the United States
    Incidents involving attacks on aircraft, airports, and other public areas* [terrorism]
    Security of diplomatic personnel
    The situation in Afghanistan* [allegations regarding incursions and booklet suggesting Chinese interference in internal affairs of Afghanistan]
    Relations between Thailand and Viet Nam
    Relations between China and Viet Nam
    Relations between Laos and Thailand
    Relations between Angola and South Africa
    Apartheid [South African aggression against front line states]

*Matters considered by the Security Council during 1987*
    Relations between Iran and Iraq
    Relations between Angola and South Africa

*Other matters brought to the attention of the Security Council during 1987*
    Relations between Chad and Libyan Arab Jamahiriya
    Relations between Israel and Lebanon
    The situation in Afghanistan

The situation in Central America
Relations between Israel and Lebanon
Relations between Laos and Thailand
Relations between Libya and United States
The situation in Nicaragua
Relations between Thailand and Vietnam

*Matters considered by the Security Council during 1988*
The abduction of Lieutenant-Colonel William R. Higgins*
Relations between Israel and Tunisia* [assassination of Khalil al-Wazir, April 16, 1988]
The situation in Afghanistan
Relations between Iran and Iraq [war, chemical weapons, Gulf incidents]
Relations between Israel and Lebanon [alleged attacks and abduction of Lebanese citizens by Israeli intelligence agents]
The situation in Nicaragua

*Other matters brought to the attention of the Security Council during 1988*
Relations between Chad and the Libyan Arab Jamahiriya
Concern of China regarding international relations (China - sovereignty)* [concerning allegations that Taiwan authorities were trying to develop "official relations" with some countries having diplomatic relations with PRC]
Relations between Panama and the United States
Relations between Angola and South Africa
The situation in Central America
Relations between China and Viet Nam
Relations between Laos and Thailand
Relations between Libya and United States [including complaint concerning Voice of America broadcast]
Relations between Thailand and Viet Nam
The situation in Cyprus [alleged Turkish violation of airspace and waters]

*Summary*
Total matters cited: 208
Matters involving allegations of discrete instances of covert coercion: 19

# Notes

## INTRODUCTION

1. Lasswell and McDougal, *Legal Education and Public Policy: Professional Training in the Public Interest,* 52 Yale L. J. 203, 266 (1943).


## CHAPTER 1: THE PROBLEM

1. For discussion of the legal significance of the term *armed attack,* see chapter 4.
2. One may substitute biological or nuclear weapons production, as the case may be.
3. Pub. Papers, Gerald R. Ford, 156 (Sept. 16, 1974); for excerpts from President Ford's response to Seymour Rubin, see M. McDougal and W. Reisman, International Law in Contemporary Perspective 1022 (1981).
4. N.Y. Times, Oct. 23, 1983, at 19.
5. For a discussion of foreign legislative oversight, see chapter 6, note 49.
6. Beitz, *Covert Intervention as a Moral Problem,* 3 Ethics and International Affairs 45 (1989).
7. Reisman, *Private Armies in a Global War System: Prologue to Decision,* 14 Va. J. Int'l. L. 1 (1973).
8. *See, e.g.,* Report of the Department of Defense Commission on Beirut International Airport Terrorist Act, Oct. 23, 1983 (Long Commission) 63–66, 136 (Dec. 20, 1983); R. Spector, Eagle against the Sun (1985); R. Wohlstetter, Pearl Harbor: Warning and Decision (1962).
9. Brandeis, *What Publicity Can Do,* Other People's Money 92 (1932) (first published in Harper's Weekly, Dec. 20, 1913).

**CHAPTER 2: THE CONSTITUTIVE PROCESS
OF INTERNATIONAL LAW**

1. Reisman, *International Law-making: A Process of Communication*, Lasswell Memorial Lecture, American Society of International Law, Apr. 24, 1981. Proceedings of the A.S.I.L. 101 (1981).
2. Article 38 states:
   1. The Court, whose function is to decide in accordance with international law such disputes as are submitted to it, shall apply:
      a. international conventions, whether general or particular, establishing rules expressly recognized by the contesting states;
      b. international custom, as evidence of a general practice accepted as law;
      c. the general principles of law recognized by civilized nations;
      d. subject to the provisions of Article 59, judicial decisions and the teachings of the most highly qualified publicists of the various nations, as subsidiary means for the determination of rules of law.
   2. This provision shall not prejudice the power of the Court to decide a case *ex aequo et bono,* if the parties agree thereto.
3. W. Reisman and A. Willard, International Incidents (1988).
4. Reisman, *supra* note 1.
5. McDougal, Lasswell, and Reisman, *The World Constitutive Process of Authoritative Decision,* 19 J. Legal Ed. 253 (1967) (reprinted in M. McDougal and W. Reisman, International Law Essays 191 (1981).
6. Fisheries Jurisdiction (U.K. v. Ice.), 1974 I.C.J. 3 (Judgment).
7. *See* Declaration on Fundamental Principles concerning the Contribution of the Mass Media to Strengthening Peace and International Understanding to the Promotion of Human Rights and to Countering War Propaganda, Racialism, Apartheid and Incitement to War, 20 UNESCO GCOF, Resolutions 100, UNESCO Doc. 20C/Resolution 3/3.1/2 (1978); *Many Voices One World* (Report of the International Commission for the Study of Communication Problems, (MacBride Commission) UNESCO (1980); B. Murty, The International Law of Propaganda xvii–lxx (1989).
8. *See* Declaration on the Establishment of a New International Economic Order, G.A. Res. 3201 (xxix 1974); Charter of Economic Rights and Duties of States, Dec. 12, 1974, G.A. Res. 3281 (xxix), 29 U.N. GAOR, Supp. (No. 31) 50, U.N. Doc. A/9631 (1974); M. Bedjaoui, Towards a New International Economic Order (1979); O. Schachter, Sharing the World's Resources (1977); M. Arsanjani, Internal Resources in World Public Order (1981); B. Weston, The New International Economic Order and the Deprivation of Foreign Proprietary Wealth: Some Reflections Upon the Contemporary International Law Debate (1983).
9. Protocol Additional to the Geneva Conventions of 12 August 1949, and Relating to the Protection of Victims of International Armed Conflicts (Protocol I), 1125 U.N.T.S. 3, 16 I.L.M. 1391 (1977); Protocol Additional to the Geneva Conven-

tions of 12 August 1949, and Relating to the Protection of Victims of Non-International Armed Conflicts (Protocol II), 1125 U.N.T.S. 609, 16 I.L.M. 1442 (1977).

10. *See* Vienna Convention on Diplomatic Relations, Apr. 18, 1961, 23 U.S.T. 3227, T.I.A.S. No. 7502, 500 U.N.T.S. 95; Vienna Convention on Consular Relations, Apr. 24, 1963, 21 U.S.T. 77, T.I.A.S. No. 6820, 596 U.N.T.S. 261; Convention on the Law of the Sea, Dec. 10, 1982, 21 I.L.M. 1261.

11. Reisman, et al., *The Formulation of General International Law,* 2 Am. U. J. Int'l L. & Pol'y, 448–54 (1987).

12. For further discussion, see W. Reisman and A. Schreiber, Jurisprudence: Understanding and Shaping Law, chaps. 1 and 12 (1987).

13. Article 2(4) reads as follows: "All Members shall refrain in their international relations from the threat or use of force against the territorial integrity or political independence of any state, or in any other manner inconsistent with the Purposes of the United Nations."

14. Article 18 reads as follows: "The American States bind themselves in their international relations not to have recourse to the use of force, except in the case of self-defense in accordance with existing treaties or in fulfillment thereof."

15. W. Reisman, Folded Lies: Bribery, Crusades and Reforms 15–16 (1979).

16. M. McDougal and F. Feliciano, Law and Minimum World Public Order (1961); McDougal, *The Soviet-Cuban Quarantine and Self-Defense,* 57 Am. J. Int'l. L. 597 (1963); Reisman, *Private Armies in a Global War System: Prologue to Decision,* 14 Va. J. Int'l. L. 1 (1973).

## CHAPTER 3: INTERNATIONAL
## LEGAL REGULATION OF
## PROACTIVE COVERT OPERATIONS

1. *See* G. Hufbauer, J. Schott, and K. Elliott, Economic Sanctions Reconsidered: History and Current Policy (1985), an excellent study of lessons drawn from 103 case abstracts of economic sanctions imposed to achieve foreign policy goals.

2. Seidl-Hohenveldern, *The United Nations and Economic Coercion,* 18 Belgian Rev. Int'l L. 9, 12 (1984–1985).

3. A Brazilian amendment to Article 2(4) would have read "All Members shall refrain . . . from the threat or use of force *and from the threat or use of economic measures in any way inconsistent* . . . (emphasis supplied)" The amendment, however, was defeated at San Francisco by a vote of 26–2. *Id.* at 10.

4. The General Assembly, for example, condemned the U.S. economic embargo against Nicaragua both before and after the International Court's decision on the merits in Nicaragua v. U.S., 1986 I.C.J. 1. *See, e.g.,* G.A. Res. 185, Trade Embargo against Nicaragua, 43 U.N. GAOR Supp. (No. 49) at 139, U.N. Doc. A/43/49 (1988)(89-2-50)("Deplores the continuation of the trade embargo contrary to its resolutions 40/188, 41/164, 42/176 and the judgment of the Interna-

tional Court of Justice."). Other resolutions address economic coercion in more general and aspirational terms. *See* G.A. Res. 173, Economic Measures as a Means of Political and Economic Coercion against Developing Countries, 42 U.N. GAOR Supp. (No. 49) at 130, U.N. Doc. A/42/49 (1987)(128-21-5)(indicative of resolutions passed in conjunction with the annual agenda item titled "Development and International Economic Co-operation"); *See also* G.A. Res. 2625, (Friendly Relations), 25 U.N. GAOR, Supp. (No. 28) 121, 123, U.N. Doc. A/8028 (1970); G.A. Res. 3281 (xxix), Charter of Economic Rights and Duties of States, 29 U.N. GAOR Supp. (No. 31), 50 U.N. Doc. A/9631 (1975).

5. *E.g.,* S.C. Res. 333, 28 U.N. SCOR, Resolutions and Decisions 14, U.N. Doc. S/INF/29 (1973)(sanctions against Rhodesia); G.A. Res. 35/206, 25 U.N. GAOR Supp. (No. 48) at 29, U.N. Doc. A/35/L.13 (1980); G.A. Res. 1761, 167 U.N. GAOR Supp. (No. 17) at 9, U.N. Doc. A/5276 (1962)(sanctions against South Africa). *See also,* Case Concerning United States Diplomatic and Consular Staff in Iran, (U.S. v. Iran), 1980 I.C.J. 3, at 16–17, 27–28, 54 (Op. Diss. Morozov).

6. Charter of the Organization of American States (OAS), 2 U.S.T. 2394, T.I.A.S. 2361, 119 U.N.T.S. 3. See in particular articles 15, 16, and 17. Art. 16 states: "No State may use or encourage the use of coercive measures of an economic or political character in order to force the sovereign will of another State and obtain from it advantages of any kind." Articles 15 and 17, however, must be read in light of Article 19 which provides that "Measures adopted for the maintenance of peace and security in accordance with existing treaties do not constitute a violation of the principles set forth in Articles 15 and 17."

7. For a recent review of U.S. citizens convicted of accepting foreign bribes in exchange for national security information, see *Meeting the Espionage Challenge,* Report of the Select Committee on Intelligence, United States Senate, S. Rep. No. 522, 99th Cong., 2d Sess. 12–15 (1986).

8. 15 U.S.C. secs. 78dd-1, 78dd-2, 78ff (1982)(amended by P.L. 100–418 Title V, sec. 5003(a), 102 Stat. 1415 (1988) (substituting inter alia "Prohibited Foreign Trade" for "Foreign Corrupt" in the chapter title).

9. W. Reisman, Folded Lies (1979); Iga and Auerbach, *Political Corruption and Social Structure in Japan,* 17 Asian Survey 556 (1977); *Bribery: A Shocker in U.S., but a Tradition Overseas,* U.S. News & World Report, Apr. 19, 1976, at 33.

10. Retorsions are unfriendly, but not unlawful acts taken in response to prior unfriendly but lawful acts by another party. F. Kalshoven, Belligerent Reprisals 27–28 (1971). Zoller also includes within the scope of retorsions "acts as a response to international wrongful acts." E. Zoller, Peacetime Unilateral Remedies 5 (1984). For further discussion of retorsions see chap. 5.

11. *See* Hufbauer, Schott, and Elliott, Economic Sanctions Reconsidered. For a collection of documents, commentary, and treaties regarding the 1973 embargo, *see* J. Paust and A. Blaustein, The Arab Oil Weapon (1977); *see also* Paust and Blaustein, *The Arab Oil Weapon—A Threat to International Peace,* 68 Am. J.

Int'l. L. 410 (1974); *contra* Shihata, *Destination Embargo of Arab Oil: Its Legality Under International Law,* 68 Am. J. Int'l. L. 591 (1974).

12. *See supra* note 4.

13. J. Paust and A. Blaustein, "The Arab Oil Weapon—A Threat to International Peace," in Paust and Blaustein, The Arab Oil Weapon 67 (1977); Parry, *Defining Economic Coercion in International Law,* 12 Tex. Int'l. L.J. 3 (1977); Comment, *Use of Nonviolent Coercion: A Study in Legality under Article 2(4) of the Charter of the United Nations,* 122 U. Pa. L. Rev. 983 (1974).

14. Seidl-Hohenveldern, *supra* note 2, at 14.

15. *See, e.g,.* E. Herman, Demonstration Elections: U.S. Staged Elections in the Dominican Republic, Vietnam, and El Salvador (1984). Regarding the election in Nicaragua see, Sec. 104, Intelligence Authorization Act, FY 1990 (prohibiting covert assistance to opposition parties or candidates without specific approval from Intelligence and Appropriations Committees.)

16. For background, see B. Murty, The International Law of Propaganda (1989); J. Whitton and A. Larson, Propaganda: Towards Disarmament in the War of Words (1963); W. Davison, International Political Communication (1965); S. Neumann, Permanent Revolution: Totalitarianism in the Age of International Civil War (2d ed. 1965).

17. International Convention concerning the Use of Broadcasting in the Cause of Peace, 186 U.N.T.S. 301, 32 A.J.I.L. Supp. 113 (29 Parties). The United States did not participate in the conference and is not a signatory to the convention.

18. Convention on the Prevention and Punishment of the Crime of Genocide, entered into force for the U.S. Feb. 23, 1989. 78 U.N.T.S. 277, 45 A.J.I.L. Supp. 7.

19. The Trial of German Major War Criminals: Proceedings of the International Military Tribunal Sitting at Nuremberg Germany, Part 22, 501–2 (1950). Streicher was publisher of *Der Stürmer,* an anti-Semitic weekly newspaper, from 1923 to 1945. According to the Tribunal, "Streicher was widely known as 'Jew-Baiter Number One.' . . . As early as 1938 Streicher began to call for the annihilation of the Jewish race. Twenty-three different articles of *Der Stürmer* between 1938 and 1941 were produced in evidence, in which extermination 'root and branch' was preached." Streicher was found not guilty on Count One (common plan or conspiracy), but guilty on Count Four (crimes against humanity).

20. Murty, *supra* note 16, at 143–47.

21. The word *propaganda* is derived from the *College of the Propaganda* a committee of Cardinals of the Roman Catholic Church founded in 1622 with responsibility for the oversight of foreign missions, hence, the modern Latin title *Congregatio de propaganda fide* (congregation for propagating the faith). Oxford English Dictionary 632 (2d ed. 1989).

22. G.A. Res. 110(II), Yearbook of the United Nations 1947–1948, 88–93 (1949).

23. Murty, *supra* note 16, at 3–4; Wright, *The Crime of "War-Mongering",* Editorial Comment, 42 Am. J. Int'l. L. 128 (1948).

24. *E.g.,* Declaration on the Inadmissibility of Intervention and Interference in the

Internal Affairs of States, II(j); G.A. Res. 2625 (Declaration on Friendly Relations).

25. 999 U.N.T.S. 171, 6 I.L.M. 368 (1967) (G.A. Res. 2200A, 21 U.N. GAOR, Supp. [No. 16] 49, 55, U.N. Doc. 6316 [1966]).

26. 26 U.N. GAOR, Annexes (Agenda Item 51) 1, U.N. Doc. A/8340 (1971).

27. G.A. Res. 2200A, 3(b), *supra* note 25.

28. Declaration on Fundamental Principles concerning the Contribution of the Mass Media to Strengthening Peace and International Understanding to the Promotion of Human Rights and to Countering War Propaganda, Racialism, Apartheid and Incitement to War, 20 UNESCO GCOF, Resolutions 100, UNESCO Doc. 20C/Resolution 3/3.1/2 (1978).

29. 37 U.N. GAOR, Supp. 51 (No. 51) 98, U.N. Doc. A/37/51 (1983). *See also,* Gorove, *The Geostationary Orbit: Issues of Law and Policy,* 73 Am. J. Int'l. L. 444 (1979).

30. Murty, *supra* note 16, at lxi. For a recent example involving television broadcasts from the United States to Cuba, *see* French, "Cuba Fights New Telecast from U.S.," N.Y. Times, Mar. 17, 1990, at 3, col. 2.

31. International Telecommunication Convention (Nairobi, 1982), United States Senate, Treaty, Doc. 99-6, 99th Cong., 1st sess. (1985). The 1982 convention replaces the convention adopted at Malaga-Torremolinos Oct. 25, 1973, 28 U.S.T. 2495, T.I.A.S. 8572.

32. 634 U.N.T.S. 239, 59 A.J.I.L. 715, 62 A.J.I.L. 814.

33. Opened for signature, Dec. 10, 1982. U.N. Doc. A/CONF 62/122, reprinted in 21 I.L.M. 1261 (1982). The convention will enter into force and replace the 1958 conventions twelve months after the sixtieth acceptance. As of this writing there are forty-two parties to the convention.

34. *The Goddess of Democracy* was chartered by a coalition of worldwide publications in the wake of the "Tienanmen Spring" for the purpose of serving as a private platform to broadcast prodemocracy programs into the People's Republic of China from international waters. The vessel, however, was refused permission to dock at Hong Kong; Taiwan said it would initially let the ship dock but would not allow the ship to return to the Republic of China if it engaged in unauthorized broadcasts. Citing the 1982 Law of the Sea Convention, Taiwan's chief spokesman said, "As a member of the international community, we do not support the ship's unauthorized broadcasts in international waters." As a result of these actions, the ship's mission was ultimately aborted. Kristoff, N.Y. Times, May 12, 1990, at A7.

35. *E.g.,* "Radio Truth," "The Voice of the Broad Masses of Eritrea," "The Voice of the Resistance of the Black Cockerel," "Radio Namibia," "The Voice of the Mozambique National Resistance" and so on. C. Mitchell, "Insults, Songs, Heroic Victories," Proprietary to the UPI, Sept. 16, 1984.

36. J. Barron, KGB 225 (1974). Shultz and Godson define covert disinformation as "a non-attributed or falsely attributed communication, written or oral, containing

intentionally false, incomplete, or misleading information (frequently combined with true information), which seeks to deceive, misinform, and/or mislead the target." R. Shultz and R. Godson, Dezinformatsiya: Active Measures in Soviet Strategy 194 (1984).

37. The Joint Chiefs define psychological operations as "[p]lanned operations to convey selected information and indicators to foreign audiences to influence their emotions, motives, objective reasoning, and ultimately the behavior of foreign government[s], organizations, groups, and individuals. The purpose of psychological operations is to induce or reinforce foreign attitudes and behavior favorable to the originator's objectives." JCS Pub 1, 292 (1987). For a vivid example, see the discussion of the CIA's 1954 Guatemala operation in G. Treverton, Covert Action (1987).

38. Protocol Additional to the Geneva Conventions of 12 August 1949, and Relating to the Protection of Victims of International Armed Conflicts, Art. 37.2 (Protocol I) (1977), 16 I.L.M. 1391 (1977).

39. Service A of the First Chief Directorate, KGB. *See,* Meeting the Espionage Challenge, Report of the Select Committee on Intelligence, United States Senate, S. Rep. No. 99–522, 99th Cong., 2d Sess. 30–33 and appendix F (1986); Soviet Active Measures, Hearings before the Subcommittee on European Affairs, Committee on Foreign Relations, United States Senate, Sept. 12–13, 1985 (1985); Soviet Active Measures, Hearings before the Permanent Select Committee on Intelligence, House of Representatives, July 13–14, 1982 (1982). R. Shultz and R. Godson, Dezinformatsiya (1984). Soviet doctrine groups disinformation with political influence operations under the rubric of "active measures."

40. *See, e.g.,* "Moynihan Assails India-C.I.A. Charge," N.Y. Times, Nov. 21, 1989, at 10; "Britain Tells of 70s Anti-I.R.A. Drive," N.Y. Times, Feb. 1, 1990, at 3; "Of British Smears in 1970s, and a Mess in 1990," N.Y. Times, Feb. 4, 1990, at 8; Article 19 World Report 1988 300 (1988, K. Boyle ed.).

41. *E.g.,* the Soviet campaign to associate the AIDS virus with U.S. biological weapons research. L.A. Times, Apr. 19, 1987, at 2; W. Post, Nov. 3, 1987, at 27. The SSCI cites among other recent Soviet efforts at disinformation a program to discredit safety at the Los Angeles Olympic Games and a forged letter from an official of USIA to Sen. Durenberger concerning exploitation of the Chernobyl disaster for the purposes of propaganda.

For recent examples of alleged United States disinformation see J. Richelson, Foreign Intelligence Organizations 339 (1988), and B. Woodward, Veil: The Secret Wars of the CIA 1981–1987, 471–77 (1987) (re: Muammar Qaddafi). Gregory Treverton reports that Claire Sterling's 1981 book *The Terror Network,* documenting inter alia Soviet support for international terrorism, was largely and unwittingly based on CIA disinformation, an illustration of the problem of so-called blow-back. Covert Action, *supra* note 37, at 165. Roy Godson, however, challenges this assertion in the absence of supporting evidence "not even a footnote." "Conditions Affecting Present Trends: Activities Destructive of World

Order by Intelligence Services," at 13, United States Institute of Peace, Conference, Oct. 14, 1989.

42. *See, e.g.*, Foreign Agents Registration Act, 22 U.S.C. secs. 611–21, excerpted in bibliography.

43. 435 U.N.T.S. 191 (Aug. 24, 1962). Within five days of notification, the contracting state, regardless of its opinion concerning the facts in question, is supposed to submit the correction to the correspondents and information agencies regularly operating in its territory and to the information agency whose correspondent was responsible for the original material. If the contracting state fails to do so, the aggrieved state may submit the correction to the secretary-general who shall "give appropriate publicity through the information channels at his disposal." There are currently twelve parties to the convention, the most recent addition being Burkina Faso in 1987.

44. *Many Voices One World* (Report of the International Commission for the Study of Communication Problems, (MacBride Commission) UNESCO 249 (1980).

45. Case concerning Right of Passage over Indian Territory (merits) (India v. Portugal), 1960 I.C.J. 6; See also Tribunal Arbitral Pour La Détermination de La Frontière Maritime (Guinea-Bissau v. Senegal), 1990 Affaire Relative a la Sentence Arbitrale du 31 Juillet 1989, Annexe 23 Août 1989.

46. 23 U.S.T. 3227, T.I.A.S. No. 7502, 500 U.N.T.S. 95 (Apr. 18, 1961). Entered into force with respect to the United States on Dec. 13, 1972. For U.S. statutory implementation, see Diplomatic Relations Act, 22 U.S.C. sec. 254a (1988).

47. *E.g.*, U.N. Charter Art. 2(4); OAS Charter, Articles 15, 16, 17.

48. G. McClanahan, Diplomatic Immunity 27–34 (1989).

49. *See also*, Art. 22 (premises), Art. 24 (archives), Art. 26 (freedom of movement), Art. 27 (communications), Art. 30 (private residence and papers), Art. 37 (application to members of family). For articles applicable to acts of coercion *by* diplomats see Art. 3 (functions of a diplomatic mission), Art. 4 (*agreement* of receiving state for person proposed as head of mission of sending state), Art. 9 (*persona non grata* power), Art. 31 (immunity of diplomatic agent from criminal and administrative jurisdiction), Art. 32 (waiver of immunity), and Art. 41 (duty to respect laws and not interfere in the internal affairs of the state).

50. 21 U.S.T. 77, T.I.A.S. No. 6820, 596 U.N.T.S. 261 (1963).

51. Convention on Prevention and Punishment of Crimes against Internationally Protected Persons, Including Diplomatic Agents, Dec. 14, 1973, 28 U.S.T. 1975, T.I.A.S. No. 8532, 1035 U.N.T.S. 167.

52. Article 2 requires each state party to the convention to make certain intentional acts crimes under its internal law, including the murder, kidnapping, or violent attack on the transportation of an internationally protected person, or any threat, attempt, or participation in an act to do so. *See, e.g.*, "Act for the Prevention and Punishment of Crimes against Internationally Protected Persons," P.L. 94–467, Oct. 8, 1976, 90 Stat. 1997, 18 U.S.C. secs. 1116, 112, 878, 1201 (1988). The state in

whose territory an alleged offender is found shall either extradite the suspect or submit him for the purposes of prosecution. Art. 7.

53. *E.g.* Agreement relating to the Privileges and Immunities of all Members of the Soviet and American Embassies and Their Families, with Agreed Minute. 30 U.S.T. 2341, T.I.A.S. 9340.

54. *See, e.g.,* Convention on the Privileges and Immunities of the United Nations, 21 U.S.T. 1418, T.I.A.S. No. 6900, 1 U.N.T.S. 15 (1946); International Organizations Immunities Act, 59 Stat. 669 (1945), 22 U.S.C.A. Sec. 288 et seq. (1976).

55. *E.g.,* the Iraqi denial of food, necessities, and freedom of movement to foreign embassies in Kuwait, 1990; the hostage case; the storming of the British embassy in China during the Cultural Revolution 1967; five U.S. ambassadors have been murdered at their posts since 1968; four British ambassadors have been murdered since 1976. McClanahan, *supra* note 49, at 142–53.

56. U.S. troops in Panama were accused of violating the Vienna Convention by establishing security perimeters around the diplomatic facilities of Cuba, Libya, Nicaragua, Peru, and the Vatican. In addition, on Dec. 29, 1989, U.S. troops forcefully entered the residence of the Nicaraguan ambassador, seizing a quantity of arms in the process. As a result, the OAS passed a resolution declaring the action a violation of international law (19-0-6). President Bush termed the intrusion a "screw-up," and the State Department sent a note of "regret" to the Nicaraguan Foreign Ministry and returned the captured weapons. Nicaragua responded by ordering the U.S. mission in Managua reduced by two-thirds. Diplomats in Kuwait City were denied food, water, and other necessities and were denied all freedom of movement, but were not physically evicted from embassy compounds.

57. 1980 I.C.J. 3, at 30–33, 35–41.

58. For a discussion of the abuse of diplomatic immunity for the purpose of state sponsored terrorism and an incident report on the 1984 Libyan People's Bureau shootings in London see G. Levitt, Democracies against Terror (1988). On the subject of diplomatic drug smuggling see McClanahan, *supra* note 48, 155–59 (1989). For examples of U.S. use of the diplomatic channel for purposes of aiding a coup, see discussion of the Trujillo assassination and the 1973 coup in Chile.

59. Vienna Convention, *supra* note 46, Art. 27. The I.C.J. in the hostages case describes the rules of diplomatic law as "a self-contained regime." 1980 I.C.J. 40.

60. C. Hyde, International Law 1686 (2d ed. 1945).

61. The International Military Tribunal in Nuremberg did not and indeed could not condemn all unilateral resort to force. What it held in its judgment was that "[t]o initiate a *war of aggression* is therefore not only an international crime; it is the supreme international crime" (italics supplied).

62. G.A. Res. 2734 (xxv), 25 U.N. GAOR, Supp. (No. 28) 22, U.N. Doc. A/8028 (1970).

63. G.A. Res. 103, 36 U.N. GAOR, Supp. (No. 51) 78, U.N. Doc. A/36/51 (1981).

64. Holmes, *The Path of the Law,* 10 Harv. L. Rev. 457, 461 (1897), reprinted in O. W. Holmes, Collected Legal Papers 167 (1920).

65. International Convention against the Taking of Hostages, 34 U.N. GAOR Supp. (No. 39) at 23, U.N. Doc. A/34/39 (1979).

66. Protocol Additional to the Geneva Conventions of 12 August 1949, and Relating to the Protection of Victims of International Armed Conflicts (Protocol I) (1977), 16 I.L.M. 1391 (1977) (78 Parties).

67. *See,* Feith, *Law in the Service of Terror: The Strange Case of the Additional Protocol,* The National Interest 36 (Fall 1985); Roberts, *The New Rules for Waging War: The Case against Ratification of Additional Protocol I,* 26 Va. J. Int'l L. 109 (1985). For a different perspective see Gasser, *An Appeal for Ratification by the United States,* 81 A.J.I.L. 910 (1987); see generally Armed Conflict and the New Law (M. Meyer, ed. 1989).

68. Article 37 states:
    1. It is prohibited to kill, injure or capture an adversary by resort to perfidy. Acts inviting the confidence of an adversary to lead him to believe that he is entitled to, or is obliged to accord, protection under the rules of international law applicable in armed conflict, with intent to betray that confidence, shall constitute perfidy. The following acts are examples of perfidy:
        a. the feigning of an intent to negotiate under a flag of truce or of a surrender;
        b. the feigning of an incapacitation by wounds or sickness;
        c. the feigning of civilian, non-combatant status; and
        d. the feigning of protected status by the use of signs, emblems or uniforms of the United Nations or of neutral or other States not Parties to the conflict.
    2. Ruses of war are not prohibited. Such ruses are acts which are intended to mislead an adversary or to induce him to act recklessly but which infringe no rule of international law applicable in armed conflict and which are not perfidious because they do not invite the confidence of an adversary with respect to protection under the law. The following are examples of such ruses: the use of camouflage, decoys, mock operations, and misinformation.

69. I.e., the United Nations Special Committee authorized to determine which peoples fall under the provisions of the Declaration on Granting Independence to Colonial Countries and Peoples, which declares inter alia that "All peoples have the right to self-determination; . . . All armed action or repressive measures of all kinds directed against dependent peoples shall cease in order to enable them to exercise peacefully and freely their right to complete independence, and the integrity of their national territory shall be respected." G.A. Res. 1514 (xv) (89-0-9), reprinted in Yearbook of the United Nations 1960 48; G.A. Res. 1654 (xvi) (97-0-4), reprinted in Yearbook of the United Nations 1961 56 (establishing a special committee, initially of seventeen members, to examine application of the Declaration on Granting Independence).

70. Kovalev, *Sovereignty and the Internationalist Obligations of Socialist Countries,*

Pravda, Sept. 26, 1968, *trans. in* 20 CDSP, No. 39. *But see,* "Warsaw Pact Condemns '68 Prague Invasion," N.Y. Times, Dec. 5, 1989, at 1, col. 4; Soviet statement, N.Y. Times, Dec. 5, 1989, at 15, col. 1:

. . . In 1968, the Soviet leadership of that time supported the stand of one side in an internal dispute in Czechoslovakia regarding objective pressing tasks.

The justification for such an unbalanced, inadequate approach, an interference in the affairs of a friendly country, was then seen in an acute East-West confrontation.

We share the view of the Presidium of the Central Committee of the Communist Party of Czechoslovakia and the Czechoslovak Government that the bringing of armies of five socialist countries into Czechoslovak territory in 1968 was unfounded, and that decision, in light of all the presently known facts, was erroneous.

71. Remarks at the Conservative Political Action Conference's Twelfth Annual Dinner, 21 Weekly Comp. Pres. Doc. 243 (Mar. 8, 1985).
72. E.g., Truman (Eastern Europe, Ukraine), Eisenhower (Guatemala, Tibet), Kennedy (Cuba, Tibet), Johnson (Laos), Nixon (Southeast Asia), Ford (Angola), Carter (South Yemen, Afghanistan), Bush (Afghanistan, Cambodia). *See* J. Prados, President's Secret Wars: CIA and Pentagon Covert Operations since World War II (1986); W. Blum, The CIA, A Forgotten History (1986).
73. *See* Franck and Rodley, *After Bangladesh: The Law of Humanitarian Intervention by Military Force,* 67 A.J.I.L. 275 (1973); Brownlie, *Humanitarian Intervention,* in Law and Civil War in the Modern World 218 (J. Moore ed. 1974).
74. L. Oppenheim and H. Lauterpacht, International Law: A Treatise, vol. 2, 280 (7th ed. 1948); M. Ganji, International Protection of Human Rights (1962); F. Teson, Humanitarian Intervention: An Inquiry into Law and Morality (1988); Bayzelr, *Reexamining the Doctrine of Humanitarian Intervention in Light of the Atrocities in Kampuchea and Ethiopia,* 23 Stan. J. Int'l. L. 547 (1987); Lillich, *Forcible Self Help under International Law,* 62 Readings in International Law from the Naval War College Review 134–37 (1988); see generally, Humanitarian Intervention and the United Nations (R. Lillich ed. 1973).
75. Nov. 3, 1950, G.A. Res. 377A(v), 5 U.N. GAOR Supp. (No. 20) 10, U.N. Doc. A/1755 (1951).
76. *Response by Professors McDougal and Reisman,* 3 Int'l Law. 438, 444 (1969).
77. Digest of United States Practice in International Law 1979, 16–25, 122–23 (M. Nash ed. 1983).
78. For a more detailed discussion of this argument see Reisman, *Old Wine in New Bottles: The Reagan and Brezhnev Doctrines in Contemporary International Law and Practice,* 13 Y. J. Int'l L. 171 (1988).
79. *Id.* at 178–79. *See also* The State of the Union, 16 Weekly Comp. Pres. Doc. (Jan. 23, 1980) (Carter Doctrine); Transcript of President's News Conference on Foreign and Domestic Matters, N.Y. Times, Oct. 2, 1981, at A26, col. 5.
80. Friedman, "Baker Gives U.S. Approval if Soviets Act on Rumania," N.Y. Times,

Dec. 25, 1989, at 13, col. 5. For French Foreign Minister Roland Dumas's comments see L.A. Times, Dec. 25, 1989, at 14, col. 1 (inter alia "I let the Soviet authorities know yesterday that if they judge it necessary to intervene, France would not see this as inconvenient, but would support that action.").

81. Hufford and Malley, "The War in Lebanon: The Waxing and Waning of International Norms," in W. Reisman and A. Willard, International Incidents 144 (1988).

82. One author has gone so far as to suggest that the absence of information on Soviet covert operations implies an absence of Soviet covert operations. ". . . of KGB covert action there is almost no hard evidence at all. Not a single major KGB covert action—comparable, say, to the Bay of Pigs or the Chile de-stabilization—has been uncovered. . . . The novel exception seems to be Poland. . . . No intelligence service is that good or that lucky for forty years on the trot, so one is forced to the conclusion that the KGB employs covert action sparingly, if at all." Johnson, *Making Things Happen,* London Review of Books, 6–19 Sept. 1984, at 14.

83. This factual summary is largely drawn from Facts on File 1953. *See also,* G. Treverton, Covert Action (1987) for a discussion of the United States covert operation.

84. Kermit Roosevelt's own account of the coup, Countercoup: The Struggle for the Control of Iran, was published in 1979.

85. Both letters are reproduced in the ICJ's opinion. Case concerning United States Diplomatic and Consular Staff (U.S. v. Iran), 1980 I.C.J. 3, at 19.

86. 1980 I.C.J. 3, at 38.

87. Keesing's Contemporary Archives 1959–1960, at 17489. *See also,* Facts on File 1960; M. Whiteman, Digest of United States Practice in International Law, Department of State, vol. 5, 208–14 (1965). For a description of the operation from the Israeli perspective see P. Malkin and H. Stein, Eichmann in My Hands (1990); D. Raviv and Y. Melman, Every Spy a Prince (1989); and I. Harel, The House on Garibaldi Street (1975).

Eichmann directed the deportation and extermination of millions of Jews from German-occupied countries while chief of "Section IV 4b" of the Reich Security Head Office of the S.S. In 1944, Eichmann was alleged to have offered to exchange 1,000,000 Jews to the Allies for 10,000 trucks and 1,000 tons of coffee and tea. For a summary of the fifteen-count indictment against Eichmann see Facts on File 1961, at 127. Eichmann's "Memoirs" were published in *Life,* Nov. 23 and 30, 1961.

88. Israel and Argentina had signed an extradition treaty on May 9. The treaty exempted extradition in cases of "military, political, or related crimes." Keesing's, *supra* note 87, at 17490.

89. 15 U.N. SCOR (865th mtg. at 4), U.N. Doc. S/4349 (1960).

90. *See* Joint Communique of the Governments of Israel and Argentina of Aug. 3, 1960 (quoted at 36 Int'l L.Rep. 59).

91. Attorney General of Israel v. Eichmann, Israel Supreme Ct. (1962), 36 Int'l L. Rep. 277 (1968).
92. *See generally* Facts on File 1961; Keesing's Contemporary Archives (1961–1962); Bissell, *Reflections on the Bay of Pigs,* 8 Strategic Review 66 (Fall 1984); G. Treverton, Covert Action (1987); P. Wyden, Bay of Pigs (1979). Kennedy administration memoirs include A. Schlesinger, A Thousand Days (1965), T. Sorensen, Kennedy (1965). For an analysis of the decision-making process see I. Janis, Groupthink (2d ed. 1982).
93. Schlesinger, *supra* note 92, at 242.
94. Sorensen, *supra* note 92, at 303.
95. 15 U.N. GAOR Annex XV (Agenda Item 90) at 5, U.N. Doc. A/4708 (1960–1961).
96. By presidential direction, United States personnel were prohibited from playing a direct role in the assault. This prohibition was in fact violated, it would appear, by overzealous operatives in the area of operations rather than as a matter of covert policy. At least one U.S. frogman took part in the initial landing. Four contract pilots from the Alabama National Guard were killed flying close air support in the exiles' B-26s on the final day of operations.
97. Facts on File 1961, at 146.
98. Sorensen, *supra* note 92, at 534.
99. Schlesinger discounts these demonstrations as "brief, communist-inspired and not very serious." *Supra* note 92, at 290–91.
100. Facts on File 1961, at 138.
101. Schlesinger, *supra* note 92, at 291. Neither Schlesinger nor Sorensen, however, report any backchannel criticism.
102. Complaint by the Revolutionary Government of Cuba regarding various plans of aggression and acts of intervention being executed by the Government of the United States of America against the Republic of Cuba, constituting a manifest violation of its territorial integrity, sovereignty and independence, and a clear threat to international peace and security, 15 U.N. GAOR Annex XV, (Agenda Item 90) at 2, U.N. Doc. A/4543 (1960).
103. *See,* Report of the First Committee, 15 U.N. GAOR Annex XV, (Agenda Item 90) at 7–11, U.N. Doc. A/4744 (1961).
104. *Id.,* at 7.
105. Schlesinger, *supra* note 92, at 292.
106. I. Janis, Groupthink, 35 (2d ed. 1982).
107. Treverton, *supra* note 83, at 84–98.
108. The Bay of Pigs invasion has been uniformly criticized by legal scholars. *See, e.g.,* Falk, *American Intervention in Cuba and the Rule of Law,* 22 Ohio St. L. J. 546 (1961); J. Moore, Law and the Indo-China War, 215–16 (1972); Wright, *Intervention and Cuba in 1961,* 55 Am. Soc. Int. L. Proc. 2 (1961).
109. For Arthur Schlesinger, a Kennedy adviser at the time and a participant at many White House conferences on the subject, "The rigid nonintervention argument had

never deeply impressed me . . . in a world shadowed by communism, the pure theory had even less force." Schlesinger, quoting John Stuart Mill continues "The doctrine of nonintervention to be a legitimate principle of morality, must be accepted by all governments. The despots must consent to be bound by it as well as the free States. Unless they do, the profession of it by free countries comes but to this miserable issue, that the wrong side may help the wrong, but the right must not help the right." (The quotation is from Mill's essay *A Few Words on Non-Intervention,* Fraser's Magazine, Dec. 1859 (republished among other places in Falk, ed. The Vietnam War and International Law, Am. Soc'y Int'l. L. [1968]).

110. Pub. Papers, John F. Kennedy, 286–87 (Apr. 19, 1961).

111. Schlesinger, *supra* note 92, at 246–47. Schlesinger and Sorensen provide valuable insight into the internal mechanisms of the Kennedy administration. As with other memoirs, however, their conclusions should be tempered by any suggestion of bias. Schlesinger's analysis, for example, emphasizes the role of the experts behind the operation while downplaying Kennedy's own decisions before and during the operation.

112. 18 U.S.C. secs. 958–962.

113. M. Whiteman, Digest of International Law, Department of States, vol. 5, 275–76 (1965).

114. Facts on File 1961, at 67.

115. Facts on File 1960, at 314; Facts on File 1961, at 8.

116. *Alleged Assassination Plots Involving Foreign Leaders,* An Interim Report of the Select Committee to Study Governmental Operations with Respect to Intelligence Activities 191 (1976) [hereinafter *Alleged Assassination Plots*].

117. *Alleged Assassination Plots,* at 192.

118. *Id.* at 195 (quoting letter from Deputy Chief of Mission Dearborn to Assistant Secretary of State Inter-American Affairs Robottom, 7/14/60).

119. *Id.* at 195 (quoting letter from Dearborn to Assistant Secretary of State for Inter-American Affairs Thomas Mann, 10/27/60).

120. *Id.* at 198.

121. *Id.* at 206.

122. *Id.* at 211.

123. *Id.* at 211 (quoting cable, Department to Dearborn 5/29/61).

124. Following the assassination of Trujillo the State Department directed the CIA station to destroy all records of contacts with the dissidents except the contingency plans and the May 29, 1961, cable. All CIA personnel and the consul general were withdrawn. *Id.* at 214.

125. *Id.* at 210.

126. Facts on File 1961, at 189, 209–10. The Senate investigation was not able to determine whether U.S.-supplied weapons were in fact used during the assassination. The committee concluded that "there is no direct evidence that the weapons which were passed were used in the assassination." *Alleged Assassination Plots,* at 191.

127. Facts on File 1961, at 210.
128. Hearings Before the Select Committee to Study Governmental Operations with Respect to Intelligence Activities (Dec. 4–5, 1975), vol. 7, Covert Action 154 (1976) [hereinafter Church Report](this document includes Covert Action in Chile, 1963–1973, Staff Report of the Select Committee to Study Governmental Operations with Respect to Intelligence Activities, Dec. 18, 1975.)

    This factual summary is drawn from the Church Committee Report; Facts on File 1973 and 1974; M. McDougal and W. Reisman, International Law in Contemporary Perspective 1022–26 (1981); Treverton, *supra* note 83.
129. Church Report at 10, 11, 156. The report notes that "By CIA estimates, the Cubans provided about $350,000 to Allende's [1970] campaign, with the Soviets adding an additional, undetermined amount." At 167.
130. *Alleged Assassination Plots,* at 225.
131. *See Alleged Assassination Plots,* at 225.
132. For a discussion of the economic measures taken see G. Hufbauer, J. Schott, and K. Elliott, Economic Sanctions Reconsidered: History and Current Policy 439-44 (1985); Church Report at 180.
133. The Staff Report of the Select Committee would eventually conclude that: "There is no hard evidence of direct U.S. assistance to the coup, despite frequent allegations of such aid. Rather the United States . . . probably gave the impression that it would not look with disfavor on a military coup. And U.S. officials in the years before 1973 may not always have succeeded in walking the thin line between monitoring indigenous coup plotting and actually stimulating it." Church Report, at 175. *See also Alleged Assassination Plots,* at 226.

    The committee also found that no direct support for the Chilean truck drivers was authorized, but that money provided to private sector organizations may have been passed on to the striking truck drivers. *Id.* at 178.
134. *See* chapter 1, U.S. Policy; Church Report, at 6–7, 54.
135. 28 U.N. GAOR (2148th mtg.) at 23–25, vol. 1.
136. *Id.* at 41.
137. In June 1973, the Senate Foreign Relations Committee had issued its own report on ITT's intervention in Chile during 1970 and 1971. The report concluded, among other things, that the ITT had offered the CIA $1 million to prevent Allende's election.
138. Thirteen hostages were released in November 1979, pursuant to a decree by the Ayatollah Khomeini to "hand over the blacks and the women, if it is proven they did not spy, to the Ministry of Foreign Affairs so that they may be immediately expelled from Iran." 1980 I.C.J. 3, at 13. Six other Americans were secretly withdrawn through the Canadian embassy. One hostage was released because of illness. The remaining fifty-two hostages were held for 444 days.
139. 1980 I.C.J. 3, at 12, 13. *See also* Reisman and Freedman, *The Plaintiff's Dilemma: Illegally Obtained Evidence and Admissibility in International Adjudication,* 76 Am. J. Int'l L. 739 (1982).

140. Sec. Res. 457, Dec. 4, 1979, (Unam.), Resolutions and Decisions of the Security Council 1979 24 (1980).
141. Sec. Res. 461, (11–0–4), Resolutions and Decisions of the Security Council 1979 24–25 (1980).
142. 1980 I.C.J. 3, at 35.
143. 50 U.S.C. secs. 1701–5 (1982 & Supp. V 1987).
144. U.S.C. sec. 1732 (1988). *See* Dames & Moore v. Regan, 453 U.S. 654, 675–79 (1981); American Int'l Group, Inc. v. Islamic Republic of Iran, 657 F.2d 430, 452 (U.S. App. D.C. 1981) (Mikva, J., separate statement) (for legislative history and argument that, in the words of Justice Rehnquist, "the moniker 'Hostage Act' was newly coined for purposes of this litigation"); M. Reisman, "Should We Just Write off Hostages?" N.Y. Times, Dec. 3, 1986, at 31.
145. Facts on File 1980, at 281.
146. *Id.* at 298.
147. As reported in Facts on File 1980, at 378.
148. Within ten days Britain announced that it would only impose a trade ban on new contracts and then only on firms not currently doing business with Iran. British trade with Iran at the time was over $100 million a month. A government spokesman stated, "This way the Americans get their sanctions . . . and our exporters will still be able to do business." Facts on File 1980, at 378, 393.
149. At an earlier emergency session in January 1980, the Conference of Islamic States condemned the Soviet invasion of Afghanistan as well as Iran for holding the hostages.
150. 1980 I.C.J. 3, at 18. The ICJ's discussion of the operation is found in paragraphs 32, 93, and 94.
151. *Id.* at 43.
152. *Id.* at 43–44.
153. The Declaration of Martial Law was apparently preprinted in the Soviet Union. R. Johnson, "Making Things Happen," London Review of Books, Sept. 6–9, 1984, at 14. Colonel Wladyslaw Kuklinski, a U.S. source on the Polish general staff, furnished the CIA with a copy of the operations order in advance of the declaration. J. Richelson, The U.S. Intelligence Community 240 (2d ed. 1989).
154. Conference on Security and Co-operation in Europe, Final Act (Helsinki Accords), Dep't of State Publication 8826, Gen. Foreign Policy series 298 (Aug. 1975), 14 I.L.M. 1292 (1975). There is perhaps no more emphatic textual statement of the doctrine of nonintervention in the internal affairs of other states or prohibition against the use of force in international relations. The Declaration on Principles Guiding Relations between Participating States, for example, includes ten articles titled: Sovereign Equality; Respect for the Rights Inherent in Sovereignty; Refraining from the Threat of Use of Force; Inviolability of Frontiers; Territorial Integrity of States; Peaceful Settlement of Disputes; Non-intervention in Internal Affairs; Respect for Human Rights and Fundamental Freedoms, Including the Freedom of Thought, Conscience, Religion or Belief; Equal Rights and

Self-Determination of Peoples; Co-Operation among States; and, Fulfillment in Good Faith of Obligations under International Law. Article 6 states inter alia:

> They [the participating States] will likewise in all circumstances refrain from any other act of military, or of political, economic or other coercion designed to subordinate to their own interest the exercise by another participating State of the rights inherent in its sovereignty and thus to secure advantages of any kind.

155. Facts on File 1981, at 945, 961.

156. *Id.* at 961.

157. *Id.* at 961, 962.

158. *Id.*

159. Greece was the only one of fifteen members not to endorse the communique in full. A Greek spokesman indicated that Greece was not willing to "participate in a campaign led by the United States." Facts on File 1982, at 10.

160. *See* G.A. Res. 103, Declaration on the Inadmissibility of Intervention and Interference in the Internal Affairs of States, 36 U.N. GAOR Supp. (No. 51) at 78, U.N. Doc. A/36/51 (1981) (Dec. 9, 120–22–6); G.A. Res. 27, Armed Israeli Aggression against the Iraqi Nuclear Installations and Its Grave Consequences for the Established International System concerning the Peaceful Uses of Nuclear Energy, the Non-Proliferation of Nuclear Weapons and International Peace and Security, 36 U.N. GAOR Supp. (No. 51) at 130, U.N. Doc. A/36/51 (1981) (Nov. 13, 109–2–34); G.A. Res. 34, The Situation in Afghanistan and Its Implications for International Peace and Security, 36 U.N. GAOR Supp. (No. 51) at 26, U.N. Doc. A/36/L.15 (1981) (116–23–12); G.A. Res. 172C, Acts of Aggression by the *Apartheid* Regime against Angola and Other Independent African States, 36 U.N. GAOR Supp. (No. 51) at 40, U.N. Doc. A/36/51 (1981) (17 Dec., 136–1–3).

161. In contrast, in 1981 alone, the Security Council considered twenty instances of alleged coercion or covert action including: complaint by Iraq [against Israel]; complaint by Malta against Libyan Arab Jamahiriya; complaint by Angola against South Africa; complaint by Seychelles; relations between Lao People's Democratic Republic and Thailand; the situation in Chad; relations between Mozambique and South Africa; the situation in Afghanistan; relations between Chad and Sudan; relations between Egypt and Libyan Arab Jamahiriya; relations between Libyan Arab Jamahiriya and Sudan; relations between Libyan Arab Jamahiriya and United States; and the situation in Nicaragua. Index to the Proceedings of the Security Council Thirty-Sixth Year—1981, ST/LIB/SER.B/S.18 (1982).

162. Facts on File 1982, at 704.

163. The facts in this section are adapted from an unpublished student paper, E. Eisold, The Rainbow Warrior Incident (1989). The analysis and conclusions, however, are our own. For background on France's nuclear testing program in the South Pacific see Nuclear Tests Case (Australia v. France), 1973 I.C.J. 98 (Request for the Indication of Interim Measures Protection); Nuclear Tests Case (Australia v.

France) 1974 I.C.J. 252 (Judgment). *See also,* New Zealand v. France, International Arbitration Award of the Tribunal, Apr. 30, 1990.

164. Eisold, *supra* note 163, at 11–12 (quoting U.N. secretary-general's "Ruling Pertaining to the Differences between France and New Zealand Arising from the Rainbow Warrior Affair," July 9, 1986, 1361, 1358, reprinted in part in 26 I.L.M. 1349 [1987]).

165. Note, *The Rainbow Warrior Affair: State and Agent Responsibility for Authorized Violations of International Law,* 5 B.U. Int'l. L. J. 398, 411 (1987).

166. For a discussion of the context and legality of the French actions see New Zealand v. France, International Arbitration Award of the Tribunal (Apr. 30, 1990). The government of New Zealand alleged that France had breached an earlier agreement not to withdraw the officers without mutual consent. An international arbitral tribunal subsequently "declare[d] that the condemnation of the French Republic for its breaches of its treaty obligations to New Zealand, made public by the decision of the Tribunal, constitutes in the circumstances appropriate satisfaction for the legal and moral damage caused to New Zealand."

167. N.Y. Times, Oct. 23, 1983, at 19.

168. And by comparison, it was Czechoslovakia and Mongolia that introduced U.N. resolutions in response to the 1961 agenda item no. 78 "Complaint by Cuba of threats to international peace and security arising from new plans of aggression and acts of intervention being executed by the Government of the United States of America against the Revolutionary Government of Cuba." The milder Mongolian draft resolution (A/L.385/Rev.1) "reaffirming [that] respect for non-interference in the internal affairs of States is a permanent aim of the United Nations," was not adopted at the 1105th meeting of the General Assembly having failed to obtain a two-thirds majority. More recently, Nicaragua requested inclusion of "the Situation in Grenada" as an agenda item for the 38th General Assembly. Oct. 31, 1983, letter, Gen. Docs. A/38/245.

169. 28 U.S.T. 1975, T.I.A.S. 8352.

170. 27 U.S.T. 3949, T.I.A.S. 8413.

171. Convention concerning the Laws and Customs of War on Land, Oct. 18, 1907, 36 Stat 2277, TS 539.

172. Res. 611, Apr. 25, 1988, 43 U.N. SCOR (2810th mtg.) at 15 (1988) (the United States abstained).

173. *Alleged Assassination Plots,* at xix (Introduction by Sen. Frank Church). Assassination and U.S. law is discussed further in chapter 6, "Conduct."

174. Reisman, *The Tormented Conscience: Applying and Appraising Unauthorized Coercion,* 32 Emory L. J. 499, 520 (1983); Paust, *Aggression against Authority,* 18 Case W. Res. J. Int'l Law. 283 (1986).

175. *Alleged Assassination Plots,* at 256. *See also* Hufbauer and Schott, at 302–7.

176. Moreover, tensions in the Middle East seem to have triggered a wave of assassinations, or perhaps just made existing state practice more visible. In March 1990, arms architect and merchant Gerald Bull was killed in Brussels. At the time, Bull

was alleged to be designing a nuclear biological chemical (NBC) capable "super-gun" for Iraq. The speaker of the Egyptian Parliament, Rifaat Al-Mahgoub, was gunned down in Cairo on October 12. And, on October 21 Lebanese Christian leader, Danny Chamoun was killed in Beirut, along with his wife and two children.

177. United States v. Toscanino, 500 F.2d 267 (2d Cir. 1974). The Toscanino court writes: "That international kidnappings such as the one alleged here violate the U.N. Charter was settled as a result of the Security Council debates following the illegal kidnapping in 1960 of Adolf Eichmann."

178. For citation to United States cases see chapter 6, "Conduct."

179. L.A. Times, Feb. 16, 1988, at 1, col. 3.

180. *See* Letelier v. Republic of Chile, 488 F.Supp. 665 (1980).

181. Former DCI Stansfield Turner provides three such examples in "Covert Common Sense: Don't Throw the CIA Out with the Ayatollah," Wash. Post, Nov. 23, 1986 (CIA person sent into Tehran to facilitate rescue of six Americans from the Canadian embassy; light aircraft flight to desert landing zone to take soil samples; repeated missions into Tehran to conduct rescue force reconnaissance and purchase trucks).

182. Secretary of State Daniel Webster's famous (and inaccurate) qualification on the right of self-defense in the context of the *Caroline* incident concerned the destruction of an American steamboat in U.S. territory by British forces during the Canadian rebellion of 1837. Use of force in self-defense, Webster argued, was justified only when "necessity of self-defence, [was] instant, overwhelming, leaving no choice of means, and no moment of deliberation."

The incident arose out of private efforts by U.S. citizens to assist the Canadian insurgents. In December 1837, this assistance took the form of active involvement when a force of U.S. volunteers from upstate New York invaded and took possession of Navy Island, a British possession in the Niagara River, where they undertook to establish a provisional Canadian government. The men on the island were supplied by the steamboat *Caroline* which also offered the rebels access to the Canadian shore.

On the night of December 29, a British force crossed the river and captured the *Caroline* docked at Fort Schlosser, New York. Two Americans were killed during the raid. The *Caroline* was set on fire, cut loose, and towed into the current of the river where it was soon swept over Niagara Falls. The United States demanded redress. The British government, however, defended the raid citing "[t]he piratical character of the steam boat 'Caroline' and the necessity of self-defence and self-preservation." Secretary of State Daniel Webster responded with a note (July 27, 1842) challenging Special Minister Lord Ashburton to show "a necessity for all this."

"Necessity . . . arose from altered circumstances at the moment of execution," Ashburton wrote back. The British force had expected to find the *Caroline* at mooring off Navy Island and only in the course of the raid decided to continue into

American territory to capture the vessel. Ashburton did, however, express regret that the raid had occurred in American territory. This apology was accepted and the incident closed. See, Jennings, *The Caroline and McLeod Cases,* 32 Am. J. Int'l L. 82 (1938).

183. Suzuki, *Extraconstitutional Change and World Public Order: A Prologue to Decision-Making,* 15 Hous. L. R. 23, 78 (1977). *See also* Singer, *Commitments, Capabilities and US Security Policies in the 1980s,* IX Parameters 27, 29 (No. 2, 1979).

184. *Id.* at 78.

### CHAPTER 4: INTERNATIONAL LEGAL REGULATION OF REACTIONS TO COVERT ACTIVITY

1. Low-Intensity Conflict (LIC) is defined by the Joint Chiefs of Staff as

A limited politico-military struggle to achieve political, social, economic, or psychological objectives. It is often protracted and ranges from diplomatic, economic and psychological pressures through terrorism and insurgency. Low-intensity is generally confined to a geographic area and is often characterized by constraints on the weaponry, tactics, and the level of violence (JCS Pub 1, Department of Defense Dictionary of Military and Associated Terms 214–15 [1987]).

The concept is not a new one, although it has received extraordinary attention in the U.S. military in the past ten years, paralleling an equally extraordinary growth in private armies and terrorism. Recall Justice Washington's distinction in Bas v. Tingy, 4 U.S. (4 Dall.) 37, 1 L.Ed. 731 (1800), between war "of the perfect kind" and "*imperfect* war":

If it be declared in form, . . . and is of the perfect kind; because one whole nation is at war with another whole nation; and all the members of the nation declaring war, are authorized to commit hostilities against all the members of the other, in every place, and under every circumstance. . . . But hostilities may subsist between two nations more confined in its nature and extent; being limited as to places, persons, and things; and this is more properly termed *imperfect* war.

2. Declaration on Principles of International Law concerning Friendly Relations and Co-Operation among States in Accordance with the Charter of the United Nations, Oct. 24, 1970, G.A. Res. 2625, 25 U.N. GAOR, Supp. (No. 28) 121, U.N. Doc. A/8028 (1971).

3. G.A. Res. 2734 (XXV), 25 U.N. GAOR, Supp. (No. 28) 22, U.N. Doc. A/8028 (1970).

4. G.A. Res. 3314, 29 U.N. GAOR, Supp. (No. 31) 142, U.N. Doc. A/9631 (1974).

5. For a discussion of whether Article 51 sets out the totality of circumstances in which self defense is authorized see MacDonald, *The Nicaragua Case: New Answers to Old Questions?* 24 Can. Y.B. Int'l L. 127, 143–46 (1986).

6. See Report of the Special Committee on the Question of Defining Aggression, 11 Mar.-12 Apr. 1974, 29 U.N. GAOR, Supp. (No. 19) 14–40, U.N. Doc. A/9619, (1974). *E.g.,* statements of Mr. Iguchi (Japan) "it being understood that the struggle for self-determination by peoples forcibly deprived of that right and the efforts to support their struggle must be in conformity with the principles of the Charter and the Declaration on Friendly Relations . . . his delegation had always maintained that an act of aggression which was not part of a war of aggression gave rise only to State responsibility"; Mr. Ceausu (Romania), "One of the essential aims of the definition of aggression was to help the victim defend himself against the aggressor. Any act of aggression automatically brought into play the right of self-defense"; Mr. Correa (Mexico) "Article 3(g) could under no circumstances be interpreted as adding to the number of situations in which the right of self-defense in accordance with the Charter could be invoked. It would be counterproductive if a State could use that provision to invoke the right of self-defense if it used armed force against another State when acts of subversion or terrorism took place in its territory"; Mr. Wang (Canada) "Article 3 (g), . . . reflected acceptance of the thesis that the distinction between direct and indirect aggression was artificial. The determining criterion had been and was whether or not a sufficient degree of armed force had been used to amount to an act of aggression by the State to which such acts could be attributed."

   Lobel argues that the Charter's prohibition on the use of force makes no distinction between direct and indirect uses of force. Lobel, *Covert War and Congressional Authority: Hidden War and Forgotten Power,* 134 U. Pa. L. Rev. 1035, 1054 n. 28 (1986).
7. B. Ferencz, Defining International Aggression, vol. 2, 28 (1975).
8. *Id.* at 40.
9. G.A. Res. 103, 36 U.N. GAOR Supp. (No. 51) at 78, U.N. Doc. A/36/51 (1981).
10. *See, e.g.,* General Assembly agenda items "Good Neighborliness" and "International Security Declarations" made pursuant to implementation of the Declaration on the Strengthening of International Security. The majority of complaints/allegations during the past ten sessions (34th-43rd, 1979–1988) allege territorial incursions and armed attacks between Afghanistan and Pakistan and between Laos and Thailand. Other complaints, however, include: China and Vietnam concerning uses of force involving a dispute over possession of the Spratly Islands; Mozambique concerning the attack on Maputo; Somalia concerning attacks by Ethiopian air and land forces; South African troops in Angola; Nicaragua concerning introduction of the Tayacan manual as well as subversive activities sponsored by the United States inside Nicaragua; National Fatherland Front (Afghanistan) alleging U.S. interference in the internal affairs of Afghanistan; Libya concerning U.S. forces in Egypt.

   During this same period specific instances of alleged covert coercion were considered as separate agenda items by the General Assembly including: the situation in Central America; Kampuchea; Southeast Asia; the U.S. raid on Libya;

Afghanistan; the 1981 Israeli raid on Iraq; military and nuclear collaboration with South Africa; South African acts of aggression against Angola; Grenada; and the U.S. embargo against Nicaragua. In addition, the Afghanistan situation was the subject of the General Assembly's Sixth Emergency Special Session (10–14 Jan. 1980).

The Security Council's agenda during this same period included 144 items that arguably entailed some use of covert coercion, and in most instances overt coercion. And 10 of these agenda items arguably dealt exclusively with allegations of discrete covert actions and their aftermath. These instances are listed in the Appendix by agenda item.

11. The section is adapted from Reisman, *No Man's Land: International Legal Regulation of Coercive Responses to Protracted and Low Level Conflict,* 11 Hous. J. Int'l L. 317 (1989).

### CHAPTER 5: COUNTERMEASURES AND COVERT ACTIONS

1. See Bowett, *Reprisals Involving Recourse to Armed Force,* 66 Am. J. Int'l. L. 1 (1972); F. Kalshoven, Belligerent Reprisals (1971); I. Brownlie, International Law and the Use of Force by States (1963); E. Zoller, Peacetime Unilateral Remedies: An Analysis of Countermeasures (1984) ; G. von Glahn, Law among Nations 494– 501 (1976).

2. Reprisals within the context of already existing armed conflicts are called "belligerent reprisals." See Greenwood, *Reprisals and Reciprocity in the New Law of Armed Conflict,* in Armed Conflict and the New Law (M. Meyer, ed. 1989); F. Kalshoven, Belligerent Reprisals Revisited (1990) (on file with the authors); M. McDougal and F. Feliciano, Law and Minimum World Public Order, 689 (1967).

Articles 51–56 of Protocol I would extend existing prohibitions against reprisals contained in the Hague and Geneva Conventions to civilians, civilian objects, historic monuments, works of art or places of worship which constitute the cultural or spiritual heritage of peoples, objects indispensable to the survival of the civilian population, and attacks against the natural environment. In addition, Protocol I would prohibit reprisals against works or installations containing dangerous forces, namely dams, dykes, and nuclear electrical generating stations. The 1980 Protocol on Prohibitions or Restrictions on the Use of Mines, Booby-Traps and Other Devices would prohibit the use of mines, booby-traps, and other manually emplaced devices designed to kill or injure, "either in offense, defence or by way of reprisals, against the civilian population as such or against individual civilians." Article 3. In contrast, Protocol II relating to noninternational armed conflicts makes no reference to reprisals.

Greenwood argues that although the restrictions in Protocol I are commendable on humanitarian grounds, the protocol does not provide for alternative sanctions. "Since the provisions on reprisal in the Protocol, unlike their counterparts in the

1949 Conventions, are concerned with activities which may have a significant effect upon the military balance between the belligerents, it is likely that they will come under considerable strain in any conflict in which one of the parties is prepared to violate its obligations under the Protocol." At 246.

3. I. Brownlie, International Law and the Use of Force by States 281 (1963); L. Oppenheim and H. Lauterpacht, International Law: A Treatise, vol. 2, at 152–53 8th ed. (1948); P. Jessup, A Modern Law of Nations 175 (1948); D. Bowett, Self-Defence in International Law 13 (1958); V. Brierly, The Law of Nations, 5th ed., 324–25 (1963); Paust, *Responding Lawfully to International Terrorism: The Use of Force Abroad,* 8 Whittier L. Rev. 711 (1986); Schachter, *The Right of States to Use Armed Force,* 82 Mich. L. Rev. 1620 (1984). *Contra* Zoller, *supra* note 1, at 62; Von Glahn, *supra* note 1, at 500.

4. Bowett, *Reprisals Involving Recourse to Armed Force,* 66 A.J.I.L. 1 (1972).

5. 1986 I.C.J. 1.

6. Case concerning the Air Service Agreement of 27 March 1946 between the United States of America and France (U.S. v. France), 18 R. Int'l Arb. Awards 417 (1978).

7. Zoller, *supra* note 1, at xvi.

8. Responsibility of Germany for damage caused in the Portuguese colonies in the South of Africa (Naulilaa Incident), 2 R. Int'l Arb. Awards 1011 (1928).

9. Responsibility of Germany for acts committed subsequent to 31 July 1914 and before Portugal entered into the war ("Cysne" case), 2 R. Int'l Arb. Awards 1035 (1930).

10. *Report of the International Law Commission on the Work of its Thirty-first Session: State Responsibility,* [1980] 2 Y.B. Int'l L. Comm'n 117, (1980) (quoting R. Int'l Arb. Awards, vol. 2, at 1025–26).

11. *Id.* at 120–21 (quoting R. Int'l Arb. Awards, vol. 2, at 1056–57).

12. The Corfu Channel Case (United Kingdom v. Albania) 1949 I.C.J. 4.

13. See discussion this chapter, "Response to Mines in the Persian Gulf, 1987."

14. 3 U.N. SCOR (1948).

15. 19 U.N. SCOR (1964). Resolution of Apr. 9, 1964. Adopted by nine votes to none with two abstentions (United Kingdom and United States).

16. 21 U.N. SCOR (1966).

17. France alleged that Pan Am's change of gauge in London (747 to 727) prior to continuing service to Paris from the West Coast violated an exchange of notes in 1960 that authorized the United States to designate a carrier to operate air service to and from the West Coast to Paris via London (without traffic rights between London and Paris). That same note authorized a carrier designated by the French government to provide service to and from Paris to Los Angeles via Montreal (without traffic rights between Montreal and Los Angeles). In accordance with a *compromis* of arbitration, the change of gauge issue was submitted for binding arbitration, whereas the dispute over U.S. reactive measures was submitted for an advisory opinion.

18. Article 10 of the Air Services Agreement provides in pertinent part:

    Except as otherwise provided in this Agreement or its Annex, any dispute between the Contracting Parties relative to the interpretation or application of this Agreement or its Annex which can not be settled through consultation shall be submitted for an advisory report to a tribunal of three arbitrators . . .

19. Air Services, at 426–28.
20. *Id.* at 428.
21. *Id.* at 427.
22. *Id.* at 443.
23. *Id.* at 444.
24. *Id.* at 445.
25. *Id.* at 445–46. See Damrosch, *Retaliation or Arbitration—or Both? The 1978 United States-France Aviation Dispute,* 74 A.J.I.L. 785 (1980). Damrosch, Deputy agent for the United States in the case, argues that under the traditional doctrine of retaliation "the legality of a retaliatory breach of treaty is judged by whether it is a proportional response to a prior material breach." Moreover, "states should refrain from implementing countermeasures until a tribunal rules on the existence of a breach, at least when there is a preexisting commitment to third-party dispute settlement."

    That view is not based on authority or policy. First, the tribunal held that a material breach was not required in order to implement countermeasures, in apparent contradiction to Article 60 of the Vienna Convention on the Law of Treaties. Second, the decision "permits states to apply countermeasures that would be disproportionate in an economic sense, in order to enforce a principle." Moreover, in determining proportionality the reaction of third countries to the decision may be considered by the tribunal, particularly in an aviation context. Finally, on the timing of countermeasures, the tribunal concluded "that the presence of an arbitration clause in the Agreement did not preclude the United States from implementing countermeasures during the period until the tribunal was constituted and in a position to indicate interim measures of protection."

    The second half of the Damrosch article addresses two issues in light of the tribunal's ruling, (1) does retaliation undercut or facilitate arbitration? and, (2) should states be permitted to engage in countermeasures when third-party remedies are available or pending? Not surprisingly, Damrosch supports the tribunal's decision, arguing among other things that retaliation prior to arbitration facilitates arbitration by creating motivation for the parties to negotiate and then compromise on the issues to present to a tribunal. This is so especially when only one party is injured by the original breach.

26. Air Services, at 441, 447. The tribunal did not decide on the lawfulness of countermeasures taken in response to an alleged wrongful act in a case where in fact a tribunal subsequently found that the alleged wrongful act was lawful. In other words, must the initial breach be found unlawful before resort to countermeasures?

Damrosch questions the assumption "that only an underlying breach can justify a retaliatory breach," arguing instead for a good faith standard whereby states may undertake countermeasures if they believe in good faith that a prior breach of an international obligation has occurred. In so arguing, Damrosch identifies three possible approaches to the question: (1) countermeasures are unlawful until after an arbitral panel identifies a prior breach; (2) countermeasures may be implemented prior to judgment but at the risk of liability; and (3) countermeasures implemented pending arbitration will be evaluated on the basis of the implementing party's good faith belief in a prior breach rather than in accordance with the tribunal's decision. Damrosch's good faith standard is commensurate with this third approach. The right to retaliate, however, should be subject to the authority of the tribunal to take effective measures once it is in a position to act. Moreover, "responsive counter-measures must be proportional and must cease either when its purpose is achieved or when its continuation would be inconsistent with actions of a functioning tribunal." In support of this standard, she cites state practice, the need to maintain a balance of equities, and the Hostage case. Damrosch, *supra* note 24, at 792–97.

Zoller takes exception to this analysis. "The *Air Services* Award," she argues, "can by no means be interpreted as a departure from the classical theory according to which only an underlying breach can justify retaliation and especially counter-measures." The tribunal did not intend to depart from this principle first enunciated by the Naulilaa Tribunal. Zoller's argument relies on the distinction between the English "alleged" meaning "'so declared,' but 'without proof'" and the French *allegué* meaning "to quote as an authority, to refer to." "In other words there was no possibility to resort to countermeasures and *a fortiori* to sanctions against lawful conduct." Zoller, *supra* note 1, at 95–96.

27. 1980 I.C.J. 3, at 27–28.
28. *Id.* at 43.
29. 1980 I.C.J. 3, at 54 (Diss. Op. Morozov).
30. The International Law Commission is comprised of fifteen rotating members representative of "the World's great legal traditions." See 2 U.N. GAOR, (Agenda Item No. 117), U.N. Doc. A/505 (1947). Among the conventions drafted by the ILC are the Vienna Convention on the Law of Treaties and the Vienna Convention on Diplomatic Relations.
31. The ILC has worked since 1963 on codifying the law of state responsibility. Part 1 of the Draft Articles addressing the origin of international responsibility were adopted by the ILC in 1980. *Report of the International Law Commission on its Thirty-first Session, supra* note 9, at 91. Part 2 of the Draft Articles address the form, content, and degrees of international responsibility (Articles 1–5 provisionally adopted by the ILC, Articles 6–16 referred to the Drafting Committee). *Sixth Report on the Content, Forms and Degrees of International Responsibility (Part 2 of the Draft Articles; and "Implementation" (mise en oeuvre) of International Responsibility and the Settlement of Disputes (Part 3 of the Draft Articles, by Mr. Willem Riphagen, Special Rapporteur,* [1985] 2 Y.B. Int'l L. Comm'n (part 1) at 3, U.N.

Doc. A/CN.4/389/SER. A/1985. Part 3, in the process of being drafted, deals with implementation (*mise en ouvre*) of international responsibility and the settlement of disputes. *Seventh Report on State responsibility by Mr. Willem Riphagen, Special Rapporteur,* [1986] 2 Y.B. Int'l Comm'n (part 1) at 1, U.N. Doc. A/CN.4/397 and Add. 1/1986.

32. Draft Articles (Part 2), 2 Y.B. Int'l L. Comm'n 1985, at 11.
33. *Id.* at 12.
34. Nicaragua v. United States, *supra* note 5, at 127.
35. *Id.* at 350 (Diss. Op. Schwebel).
36. Judge Schwebel, in dissent, also interchanges counter-intervention with counter-measures. *Id.* at 349.
37. Restatement (Third) of Foreign Relations Law of the United States Sec. 905 (1987).
38. *Id.* at 381.
39. Draft Articles (Part 1), at 106, Art. 30, Commentary (1).
40. Draft Articles (Part 2), at 10, Art. 8, Commentary (2).
41. Draft Articles (Part 1), at 121, Art. 30, Commentary (22).
42. Draft Articles (Part 2), at 10, Art. 8, Commentary (3).
43. Draft Articles (Part 1), at 121, Art. 30, Commentary (22).
44. M. Nash, Digest of United States Practice in International Law 1979, Department of State, Office of the Legal Adviser, 1749–52 (1983).
45. A. Rovine, Digest of United States Practice in International Law 1974, Department of State, Office of the Legal Adviser, 700 (1975).
46. Other incidents, such as the Falkland Islands conflict, (Reisman, *The Struggle for the Falklands,* 93 Yale L.J. 287, 311–14 (1983), the Pueblo incident, (Butler, *The Pueblo Crisis: Some Critical Reflections,* 63 Proc. Am. Soc'y Int'l L. 7 (1969)), and the provision of assistance to the Mujahidin in Afghanistan might also warrant countermeasures analysis but require a factual discussion beyond the purposes of this chapter.

    Some scholars have recognized a doctrine of counterintervention in response to a prior illegal use of force against another state, provided such response is proportional. *E.g.,* "I would distinguish the support of the opposition in Afghanistan from the other instances cited because it alone qualifies as 'counter-intervention.' As a proportionate response to a prior, overt, large-scale foreign intervention it is a beneficial precedent if confined to comparable circumstances." Falk, Book Review, 63 N.Y.U. L. Rev. 1376, 1385 n.7 (1988). *See also,* Reisman, *The Resistance in Afghanistan is Engaged in a War of National Liberation,* 81 A.J.I.L. 906 (1987).
47. For background on the missile crisis see Facts on File 1962; M. Whiteman, Digest of United States Practice in International Law, Department of State, vol. 4, 523–28, 676–77 (1965); vol. 5, 443–49, 1054–57 (1965); vol. 10, 10–18, 874 (1968); Sorensen, Kennedy (1965); A. Schlesinger, A Thousand Days (1965). On the decision-making process see, G. Allison, Essence of Decision (1971); I. Janis, Groupthink (2d ed. 1982).
48. N. Khrushchev, Khrushchev Remembers 493–94 (1970).

49. R. Medvedev, Khrushchev, 186–87 (1982).

50. On October 3, 1962, a joint resolution was passed (86 to 1 and 384 to 7) expressing the determination of Congress "(a) to prevent by whatever means may be necessary, including the use of arms, the Marxist-Leninist regime in Cuba from extending its aggressive or subversive activities to any part of the hemisphere; (b) to prevent in Cuba the creation or use of an externally supported military capability endangering the Security of the United States . . . " S.J. Res. 230, P.L. 87–733, 76 Stat. 697 (1962). Also see, Whiteman, *supra* note 47, vol. 5 at 440–42, 1053–54.

51. For an excellent discussion of the methods of intelligence gathering used during the Cuban Missile Crisis as well as an analysis of the organizational dynamics behind the timing of this particular U-2 flight, see G. Allison, Essence of Decision: Explaining the Cuban Missile Crisis, 118–23 (1971).

52. For the complete text, see Pub. Papers, John F. Kennedy, 806 (Oct. 22, 1962). Kennedy briefed nineteen congressional leaders from both parties prior to the address. On October 24 closed briefings were offered to all members of Congress in five separate cities in order to accommodate congressional members who were campaigning. Facts on File 1962, at 365.

53. Whiteman, *supra* note 47, vol. 5, at 447. Record of the Security Council discussions is contained in S/PV.1022, Oct. 23, 1962; S/PV.1023, Oct. 24, 1962; S/PV.1024, Oct. 24, 1962; S/PV.1025, Oct. 25, 1962; S/5182, S/5187, S/5190.

54. Whiteman, *supra* note 47, vol. 5, at 445. Uruguay, which was awaiting instructions from its government did not record its vote until October 24. Facts on File 1962, at 362.

55. Argentina, Costa Rica, the Dominican Republic, Panama, Nicaragua, and Guatemala. Facts on File 1962, at 364. On October 25, Haiti pledged its support.

56. Whiteman, *supra* note 47, vol. 4, at 525 (quoting Cristol and Davis, *Maritime Quarantine: The Naval Interdiction of Offensive Weapons and Associated Material in Cuba, 1962*, 57 Am. J. Int'l L. 525 (1963).

57. Facts on File 1962, at 364.

58. Interdiction of the Delivery of Offensive Weapons to Cuba, Presidential Proclamation 3504, Oct. 23, 1962, 3 C.F.R. 232 (1959–63 Comp.). The list of prohibited material included "surface-surface missiles; bomber aircraft; bombs; air-to-surface rockets and guided missiles; warheads for any of the above weapons; mechanical or electronic equipment to support or operate the above items; and any other classes of material hereafter designated" by the secretary of defense. During the quarantine the United States Navy regularly broadcast warnings advising incoming vessels that certain channels might be dangerous. In addition, the Department of Defense announced that the navy would drop harmless explosive sound devices into the water that may be accompanied by the international code for "rise to the surface" in order to induce submarines to surface within the quarantine zone.

59. On November 14, the Defense Department disclosed that forty-nine Communist and non-Communist vessels, including an East German passenger liner, had been allowed to pass through the blockade since October 24. Facts on File 1962, at 398.

60. On October 26, Khrushchev sent two letters to Kennedy, the second proposed that the United States withdraw its jupiter missiles from Turkey in exchange for withdrawing Soviet missiles from Cuba. Kennedy chose to respond only to the first note and on October 27 demanded the unconditional withdrawal of missiles from Cuba. On October 28, Khrushchev broadcast his acceptance of Kennedy's request over Moscow radio. See Whiteman, *supra* note 47, vol. 5, at 447; Facts on File 1962, at 374, 375.

61. There were no subsequent reports of medium-range ballistic missile sightings. On December 6, the United States announced that 42 IL-28 bombers had been observed on Soviet freighters leaving Cuba and that this was believed to represent all the IL-28s shipped to Cuba. Facts on File 1962, at 439.

62. *See generally,* 57 Am. J. Int'l L. (1963) and *Panel: Cuban Quarantine: Implications for the Future,* 57 Am. Soc. Int'l L. 1 (1963).

63. Dean Acheson, who served on President Kennedy's Executive Committee during the crisis, for example, remarked

    I must conclude that the propriety of the Cuban quarantine is not a legal issue. The power, position and prestige of the United States had been challenged by another state, and law simply does not deal with such questions of ultimate power— power that comes close to the sources of sovereignty. I cannot believe that there are principles of law that say we must accept destruction of our way of life. One would be surprised if practical men, trained in legal history and thought, had devised and brought to a state of general acceptance a principle condemnatory of an action so essential to the continuation of pre-eminent power as that taken by the United States last October. Such a principle would be as harmful to the development of restraining procedures as it would be futile. No law can destroy the state creating the law. The survival of states is not a matter of law.

    Acheson, however, went on to acknowledge that

    . . . in the action taken in the Cuban quarantine, one can see the influence of accepted legal principles. These principles are procedural devices designed to reduce the severity of a possible clash. Those devices cause wise delay before drastic action, create a cooling off period, permit the consideration of others' views . . . [*Panel: Cuban Quarantine: Implications for the Future,* Remarks by the Honorable Dean Acheson, 57 Proc. Am. Soc. Int'l L. 14 (Apr. 1963)].

    The Soviets, for example, at one point refused to accept United States notices regarding the quarantine through the bilateral diplomatic process, but nevertheless remained apprised of United States positions at the United Nations. Facts on File 1962, at 347.

    International law also helped define the authoritative basis of United States decision. Thus the deputy legal adviser of the State Department was careful to argue that the naval operation was neither a pacific blockade nor a belligerent blockade but rather a quarantine. Whiteman, *supra* note 47, vol. 10, at 874. Moreover, in contrast to the Bay of Pigs, President Kennedy integrated the Organization of

American States and United Nations with the United States quarantine operation, albeit after Kennedy had already announced that the U.S. would impose a quarantine, but before promulgation of the Quarantine Proclamation and its implementation.

Abraham Chayes, who served as legal adviser for the State Department during the crisis, found that law was a "significant but not determinative" factor during the crisis. Although recognizing the "blunt fact" that the quarantine "involved the use of naval force to interfere with shipping on the high seas," the quarantine, Chayes argued, was a lawful use of force by a regional organization to preserve the peace.

[T]he overriding object of international law is not to regulate the conduct of war, but to keep and defend the peace. . . . If non-alignment continues to be a goal for some countries, non-involvement has become a luxury beyond price. A threat to the peace of any nation is a threat to the peace of all nations, and maintenance of peace has therefore become a collective responsibility. [*Panel: Cuban Quarantine: Implications for the Future,* Remarks by A. Chayes, 57 Proc. Am. Soc. Int'l L. 14 (Apr. 1963)].

64. The deputy legal adviser of the State Department explained, "Because it had this purpose of interdiction and because naval vessels would be used to carry it out, the press and other commentators were quick to analogize the quarantine to the concept of 'blockade' in international law. To the extent the traditional 'blockade' implies and requires a state of belligerency or war, the United States did not seek to justify the quarantine as a blockade." Meeker, *Defensive Quarantine and the Law,* 57 Am. J. Int'l L. 515 (1963). Under the doctrine of "pacific blockade," on the other hand, vessels of third party states are generally not subject to search or seizure.

65. Sorensen, *supra* note 47, at 707–8.

66. *But see* Wright, *The Cuban Quarantine,* 57 Am. J. Int'l L. 546, 549 (1963) (arguing that the Soviet Union did not violate any obligation of international law by shipping missiles to Cuba as "under general international law, states are free to engage in trade in any articles whatever in time of peace.")

67. Skubiszwski, *Use of Force by States, Collective Security, Law of War and Neutrality,* in Manual of Public International Law, 755 (Sorensen ed., 1968).

68. When, for example, a Soviet captain allowed only part of his vessel to be searched, the vessel was allowed to proceed without interference. Facts on File 1962, at 397.

69. McDougal, *The Soviet-Cuban Quarantine and Self-Defense,* 57 Am. J. Int'l L. 597 (1963).

70. Mallison, *Limited Naval Blockade or Quarantine-Interdiction: National and Collective Defense Claims Valid Under International Law,* 31 Geo. L.J. 335, 345 (1962) (quoted in Whiteman, *supra* note 47, vol. 4, at 528.

71. W. Reisman, Nullity and Revision, 842 (1971).

72. Efforts to legitimize the Grenada operation on the basis of the quarantine precedent (e.g., Rostow, "Law Is Not a Suicide Pact," N.Y. Times, Nov. 15, 1983, at A35) received little favorable commentary. Nor, we would argue, was the test of necessity still operable when the United States continued to justify overflights of Cuban

airspace in April 1964 on the basis of the Oct. 23, 1962, OAS Resolution. Whiteman, *supra* note 47, vol. 5, at 448.

73. *Panel: Cuban Quarantine: Implications for the Future,* Remarks by the Honorable Dean Acheson, 57 Proc. Am. Soc. Int'l L. 14 (Apr. 1963).

74. 7:00 P.M., Apr. 14, Eastern Standard Time.

75. See discussion of political assassination in chapter 3, "Factors Conditioning Elite Response," and chapter 6, "Conduct."

76. Keesing's Contemporary Archives 1986, at 34263.

77. The Lebanese Shi'a Moslem leader Imam Moussa Sadr had disappeared while visiting Libya in 1978. Many in the Shi'a Moslem community linked Qaddafi to the Imam's disappearance.

78. L.A. Times, Apr. 16, 1986, at 1, col. 6.

79. G.A. Res. 41/38, Declaration of the Assembly of Heads of State and Government of the Organization of African Unity on the Aerial and Naval Military Attack against the Socialist People's Libyan Arab Jamahiriya by the Present United States Administration in April 1986, 41 U.N. GAOR (Supp. 51) at 34, U.N. Doc. A/41/51 (1986).

80. Arsanjani, Survey of State Practice and Doctrine on Counter-Measures, 116 (1989) (unpublished paper prepared for the United Nations Secretariat, Codification Division, on file with the authors.)

81. Zoller, *supra* note 1, at 40–41.

82. Notable among these other incidents was the Libyan supported attack by the Abu Nidal group at the Rome and Vienna airports, attacks on Libyan expatriates abroad, disclosure of a United States effort to enlist Egyptian help in a covert military operation to topple Qaddafi, United States support to Chad in its war against Libya, United States naval operations in the Gulf of Sidra, and the aerial bombing of a TWA airliner just three days before the Berlin bombing.

83. Facts on File 1987, at 685.

84. Senator Moynihan argued that "[e]ven if no 'armed attack' occurred, Sir Claude Humphrey Meredith Waldock, after serving as counsel to the government of the United Kingdom in the Corfu Channel case, wrote that the court's opinion in that case authorized a State to use force to prevent the coercive denial of the rights of that State by another." 133 Cong. Rec. S13,547–50 (daily ed. Oct. 6, 1987) (Amendment No. 862 to the Foreign Relations Authorization Act, FY 1988, S. 1394).

85. Air Transport Agreement, July 19, 1972, United States-Poland, 23 U.S.T. 4269, T.I.A.S. No. 7535.

86. Malamut, *Aviation: Suspension of Landing Rights of Polish Airlines in the United States,* 24 H. Int'l L. J. 190 (1983); Van Houtte, *Treaty Protection against Economic Sanctions,* 18 Belgian R. Int'l L. 34, 48–49 (1984–1985).

87. G. Levitt, Democracies against Terror 48–55 (1988).

88. See 1949 I.C.J. 4; Zoller, *supra* note 1, at 70.

89. Convention on Offenses and Certain Other Acts Committed on Board Aircraft, Sept. 14, 1963, 20 U.S.T. 2941, T.I.A.S. No. 6768, 704 U.N.T.S. 219 (Tokyo

Convention); Convention for Suppression of Unlawful Seizure of Aircraft (Hague Convention); Convention for Suppression of Unlawful Acts against the Safety of Civil Aviation (Montreal Convention).

90. See Report to the President by the President's Commission on Aviation Security and Terrorism, May 15, 1990, at i ("the United States must work to isolate politically, diplomatically and militarily the handful of outlaw nations sponsoring terrorism. These more vigorous policies should include training for preemptive or retaliatory military strikes against known terrorist enclaves in nations that harbor them. Where such direct strikes are inappropriate, the Commission recommends a lesser option, including covert operations, to prevent, disrupt or respond to terrorism.").

### CHAPTER 6: UNITED STATES
### INTERNAL PROCEDURES

1. For further detail on United States statutory law, case law, and executive orders applicable to U.S. special activities, see Suggested Readings, "Statutory Law."
2. Report on the Covert Activities of the Central Intelligence Agency, Sept. 30, 1954.
3. *See, e.g.,* E.O. 11,905, Feb. 18, 1976 (President Ford's executive order on the conduct of intelligence activities); Rules of the House of Representatives, Rule XLVIII (1977) (establishing the House Permanent Select Committee on Intelligence) and S. Res. 400, Rep. Nos. 675 and 770, 94th Cong., 2d Sess. (1976) (Senate Select Committee on Intelligence); Section 662 of the Foreign Assistance Act of 1961, 22 U.S.C. 2422 ("the Hughes-Ryan Amendment" re: requirement for a presidential finding prior to expenditure of funds for CIA covert activities in foreign countries); P.L. 95–370, the Intelligence and Intelligence Related Activities Authorization Act for FY 1979 (Sept. 17, 1978) (the first annual authorization bill subjecting the intelligence agencies to the congressional budget process of authorization and appropriation); Foreign Intelligence Surveillance Act of 1978, 50 U.S.C. sec. 1801–1811 (1982).
4. Youngstown Sheet & Tube Co. v. Sawyer, 343 U.S. 579, 635 n.1 (1952) (Jackson, J., concurring).
5. United States v. Curtiss-Wright Export Corp., 299 U.S. 304, 319 (1936). Critics of the "sole organ" power note that Justice Sutherland was quoting John Marshall in the House of Representatives who was speaking within the limited context of a debate on interpretation of an extradition treaty. Justice Sutherland's dictum, however, has been adapted and expanded in subsequent cases, *see, e.g.,* United States v. Pink, 315 U.S. 203, 229 (1942).
6. U.S. Const., art. II, sec. 2, cl. 2.
7. U.S. Const., art. II, sec. 3. This power has been interpreted by presidents since Jefferson to include the authority to grant and withhold recognition to foreign states and governments, as well as establishing the executive's sole control over diplomatic communications. The Court has endorsed this view in United States v.

Curtiss-Wright Export Corp., 299 U.S. 304 (1936), United States v. Belmont, 301 U.S. 758 (1932), and United States v. Pink, 315 U.S. 203 (1942).

8. The Federalist No. 70, at 423 (A. Hamilton) (C. Rossiter ed. 1961); Curtiss-Wright, 299 U.S. at 319; The War Powers Resolution sec. 2(C)(3), 50 U.S.C. sec. 1541–48 (1982).

9. U.S. Const., art. II, sec. 2, cl. 1. *See,* Totten, Administrator v. United States, 92 U.S. 105 (1875) (the President "undoubtedly authorized during the war, as commander-in-chief of the armies of the United States, to employ secret agents . . . and contracts to compensate such agents are so far binding upon the government as to render it lawful for the President to direct payment of the amount stipulated out of the contingent fund under his control.")

10. U.S. Const., art. II, sec. 3.

11. U.S. Const., art. II, sec. 1, cl. 1. Article I refers to "All legislative Powers herein granted . . . " the argument continues. The "executive Power," however, is not textually limited to what follows in Article II. *See* Pacificus No. 1, (A. Hamilton), The Papers of Alexander Hamilton vol. 15, 33 (H. Syrett ed. 1969) (excerpted in part in National Security Law 760 (J. Moore, F. Tipson, and R. Turner, eds. 1990)). *See* E. Corwin, The President: Office and Powers, 1787–1984 (5th ed. 1984).

12. Dames & Moore v. Regan, 453 U.S. 654, 686 (1981) (quoting Youngstown, 343 U.S. at 610–11 (Frankfurter, J. concurring)).

13. A. Sofaer, War, Foreign Affairs and Constitutional Power 129 (1976); S. Knott, Historical and Legal Foundation of American Intelligence Activities (1990) (dissertation in progress, on file with the authors).

14. U.S. Const. art. I, sec. 8, cl. 11, 14. *See* Lobel, *Covert War and Congressional Authority: Hidden War and Forgotten Power,* 134 U. Pa. L. Rev. 1035 (1986). Lobel argues that the "covert use of paramilitary force to conduct American foreign policy abroad is the modern day analogy to the private wars for which letters of marque and reprisal were historically required." At 1051. Thus because "the marque and reprisal clause grants Congress sole authority to authorize private individuals to use force against another country or its citizens, whether in peacetime or during declared war . . . " (at 1040), Congress alone has the constitutional power to authorize covert action employing the use of military force by nongovernmental surrogates.

15. U.S. Const. art. I, sec. 9, cl. 7. "No Money shall be drawn from the Treasury, but in Consequence of Appropriations made by Law; and a regular Statement and Account of the Receipts and Expenditures of all public Money shall be published from time to time."

16. U.S. Const., art. I, sec. 8, cl. 18.

17. *See, e.g.,* The Pacificus (Hamilton)–Helvidius (Madison) exchange re: President Washington's so-called neutrality proclamation of 1793, The Papers of Alexander Hamilton (H. Syrett 1969) and The Writings of James Madison (G. Hunt ed. 1906) (excerpted in part in Sofaer, *supra* note 13, at 112–15 and National Security Law

759–65 (J. Moore, F. Tipson, and R. Turner, eds. 1990). House Select Comm. to Investigate Covert Arms Transactions with Iran and Senate Select Comm. on Secret Military Assistance to Iran and the Nicaraguan Opposition, Report of the Congressional Comms. Investigating the Iran-Contra Affair, S. Rep. No. 216, H.R. No. 433, 100th Cong., 1st Sess. 387–93, 411–21, 457–79 (1987) [hereinafter Iran-Contra Report]; *Legal and Policy Issues in the Iran-Contra Affair: Intelligence Oversight in a Democracy,* 11 Hous. J. Int'l L. (1988).

18. National Security Act of 1947, 50 U.S.C. sec. 403 (1982); *See also* National Security Council Directive 5412/2, Dec. 28, 1955, on Covert Operations (reproduced in The Central Intelligence Agency 146–49 (W. Leary ed. 1984).

19. One dissenter was Admiral Roscoe H. Hillenkoetter (Director of Central Intelligence, May 1947–Oct. 1950). During executive branch debate over an early covert action proposal regarding psychological operations, Hillenkoetter argued that such operations were military rather than intelligence functions and that they required prior congressional authorization. *See* Karalekas, *History of the Central Intelligence Agency* in The Central Intelligence Agency 37–43 (W. Leary ed. 1984); *see also Alleged Assassination Plots Involving Foreign Leaders,* An Interim Report of the Select Committee to Study Governmental Operations with Respect to Intelligence Activities 9 (1976); Hearings Before the Select Committee to Study Governmental Operations with Respect to Intelligence Activities (Dec. 4–5, 1975), vol. 7, Covert Action (1976), Statement of Clark M. Clifford: "It was under this clause that, early in the operation of the 1947 Act, covert activities were authorized . . . covert activities undertaken under the Act were to be carefully limited and controlled" (at 51).

20. "Whenever it is made known to the President that any citizen of the United States has been unjustly deprived of his liberty by or under the authority of any foreign government, . . . the President shall use such means, not amounting to acts of war, as he may think necessary and proper to obtain or effectuate the release . . . " Rev. Stat. Sec. 2001, 22 U.S.C. Sec. 1732. *See* Dames & Moore, 453 U.S. at 675–79; American Int'l Group, Inc. v. Islamic Republic of Iran, 657 F.2d 430, 452–53 (1981) (Mikva, J. separate statement; arguing inter alia that "the floor debates demonstrate that the major stimuli behind the congressional sense of urgency were the involuntary repatriation of naturalized American citizens visiting Europe;" the statute carries an implied statute of limitations; the act was not intended to apply to domestic actions; but, in the words of the author of the Act's language, Senator Williams, "cases may arise where it would be the duty of the Executive . . . without any delay to wrest an American citizen from the clutches of a despot in a foreign country.") *See also* Reisman, "Should We Just Write Off Hostages?" N.Y. Times, Dec. 3, 1986, at A31.

21. The Foreign Assistance Act of 1961 sec. 662, 22 U.S.C. 2422 (1988).

22. Title V of the National Security Act of 1947, 50 U.S.C. 413 (1982).

23. National Security Council Directive 10/2, June 18, 1948, on Office of Special

Projects (excerpted in The Central Intelligence Agency 131–33 (W. Leary ed. 1984)).

24. Karalekas, *supra* note 19, at 36–50.

25. Exec. Order No. 12,333 sec. 1.8(e) (Dec. 4, 1981, 46 F.R. 59941).

26. Exec. Order 12,333, 1.11(c) itself provides that the secretary of defense shall "(c) Conduct programs and missions necessary to fulfill national, departmental and tactical foreign intelligence requirements".

27. National Security Decision Directive 286 (Oct. 15, 1987) provides inter alia that the "National Security Advisor and the NSC staff . . . shall not undertake the conduct of special activities." Quoted in Bruemmer and Silverberg, *The Impact of the Iran-Contra Matter on Congressional Oversight of the CIA*, 11 Hous. J. Int'l L. 219, 235 (1988).

28. *See, e.g.*, Iran-Contra Report at 416 (DEA hostage rescue operation); United States v. Yunis, 681 F. Supp. 909 (D.D.C. 1988) (FBI seizure of fugitive).

29. S. Emerson, Secret Warriors: Inside the Covert Military Operations of the Reagan Era (1988).

30. Arms Export Control Act, 22 U.S.C. secs. 2751–96c (1988); Foreign Assistance Act of 1961, 22 U.S.C. secs. 2301–49aa-b (1988); Export Administration Act of 1979, 50 U.S.C. secs. 2401–20 (1988); Exec. Order No. 12,163, 49 F.R. 56673, 3 C.F.R. 435 (1979); Exec. Order No. 11,958, 42 F.R. 4311, 3 C.F.R. 79 (1979); D. Scheffer provides an excellent overview in *U.S. Law and the Iran-Contra Affair*, 81 A.J.I.L. 696 (1987).

31. *E.g.*, G. Treverton, Covert Action: The Limits of Intervention in the Postwar World 211 (1987).

32. The Hughes-Ryan Amendment to the Foreign Assistance Act of 1961 (1974) applied only to the Central Intelligence Agency. NSDD 286, however, provides that no special activity may take place without a presidential finding. Bruemmer and Silverberg, *supra* note 27, at 235. Moreover, the Intelligence Authorization Act for FY 1991, which repealed the Hughes-Ryan amendment, requires a presidential finding prior to conduct of a covert action "by departments, agencies, or entities of the United States Government." Each finding shall be in writing unless immediate action is required in which case the president's decision shall be reduced to writs within 48 hours. For text of Act and comment see 137 Cong. Rec. H5898-H5907 (daily ed. July 25, 1991) and 137 Cong. Rec. H6160-6167 (daily ed. July 31, 1991). *See also*, Sec. 654 of the Foreign Assistance Act of 1961, 22 U.S.C. 2414 (1988) (findings and determinations pursuant to the Foreign Assistance Act of 1961, the Foreign Military Sales Act, or the Foreign Assistance and related appropriations act for each fiscal year shall be reduced to writing and signed by the president prior to any action being taken) and Letter from President Reagan to David L. Boren, Chairman of the Senate Select Committee on Intelligence, N.Y. Times, Aug. 8, 1987, in which the president "express[es] . . . support for the following key concepts" including:

3. If the President directs any agency or persons outside of the CIA or traditional

intelligence agencies to conduct a special activity, all applicable procedures for approval of a finding and notification to Congress shall apply to such agency or persons.

33. Intelligence Authorization Act for FY 1991 (supersedes 22 U.S.C. 2422 [1988]); NSDD 286 (Oct. 15, 1987).

34. For example, the function performed by President Reagan's National Security Planning Group was performed during the Carter administration by the Special Coordination Committee (SCC) which was directed by Executive Order 12,063 "to consider and submit to the President a policy recommendation, including dissents, on each special activity." Membership on this functional committee has also varied. The SCC, for example, in addition to the members of the NSPG, included by presidential order the attorney general, the director of the Office of Management and Budget, and the chairman of the Joint Chiefs of Staff (JCS).

35. W. Webster, Remarks before the Yale Political Union (Nov. 16, 1988). Richelson refers to this group as the Covert Action Planning Group (CAPG). J. Richelson, The U.S. Intelligence Community 407 (2d ed. 1989).

36. President Reagan, for example, included the White House chief of staff, deputy chief of staff, and presidential counsel.

37. *See* Title V of the National Security Act of 1947, 50 U.S.C. 413 (Accountability for Intelligence Activities). *See also* 50 U.S.C. sec. 414, "Funding of intelligence activities," (1982 & Supp. V 1987) (Intelligence Authorization Act of 1986, Pub. L. No. 99–169, sec. 502(a), 99 Stat. 1004 (Dec. 4, 1985) ("Appropriated funds . . . may be obligated or expended for an intelligence or intelligence-related activity only if - (1) those funds were specifically authorized by the Congress for use for such activities; or (2) in the case of funds from the Reserve for Contingencies of the Central Intelligence Agency and consistent with the provisions of section 413 . . . the Director of Central Intelligence has notified the appropriate congressional committees . . . ").

38. Title V of the National Security Act of 1947, as amended, Accountability for Intelligence Activities, 50 U.S.C. 413 provides inter alia: "If the President determines that it is essential to limit access to the finding to meet extraordinary circumstances affecting vital interests of the United States, the finding may be reported to the chairmen and ranking minority members of the intelligence committees, the Speaker and minority leader of the House of Representatives, the majority and minority leaders of the Senate, and such other member or members of the Congressional leadership as may be included by the President."

39. *Id.* Former Director of Central Intelligence Stansfield Turner cites three instances regarding the Iranian hostage rescue mission in which Congress was not informed of covert activities until after the operations were over. "Covert Common Sense: Don't Throw the CIA out with the Ayatollah," Wash. Post, Nov. 23, 1986.

40. President Bush described how his administration would address congressional concerns about such notice in a letter to Senators Cohen and Boren dated October 30, 1989. The letter states in relevant part: "The statute requires prior notice or,

when no prior notice is given, timely notice. I anticipate that in almost all instances, prior notice will be possible. In those rare instances where prior notice is not provided, I anticipate that notice will be provided within a few days. Any withholding beyond this period would be based upon my assertion of the authorities granted this office by the Constitution." Quoted in Statement on Signing the Intelligence Authorization Act, Fiscal Year 1990, 25 Weekly Comp. Pres. Doc. 1851 (Nov. 30, 1989). *See also,* Letter from George Bush to Anthony Beilenson, Chairman of the HPSCI, Aug. 20, 1990 (reprinted in Conference Report, to accompany the Intelligence Authorization Act for Fiscal Year 1991, (initial version) 101 Cong., 2d Sess. 56 of initial SSCI issue Oct. 23, 1990.)

41. Opinion of the Office of Legal Counsel, Dec. 17, 1986. The Office of Legal Counsel, Department of Justice, has "responsibility for preparing the formal opinions of the Attorney General, rendering informal opinions to the various federal agencies, assisting the Attorney General in the performance of his function as legal adviser to the President, and rendering opinions to the Attorney General and the heads of the various organizational units of the Department of Justice." 6 op. O.L.C. at v. These opinions are intended to guide executive branch activities, but do not have the standing of statutory law, case law, or executive orders. Selected opinions are published in Opinions of the Office of Legal Counsel.

42. *See* Hamilton, *The Role of Intelligence in the Foreign Policy Process,* 6–7 (Essays on Strategy and Diplomacy No. 9, the Keck Center for International Strategic Studies, 1987).

43. Sen. Eagleton sought to apply the resolution "to all war making alternatives" by amending the resolution so as to deem "[a]ny person employed by, under contract to, or under the direction of any department or agency of the United States government . . . " a member of the armed forces for the purposes of the act. The amendment was defeated by a vote of 34–53 with 13 senators not voting. The floor managers, Senators Muskie and Javits, found the amendment too inclusive and tactically unsound for the purposes of achieving passage and overcoming an expected presidential veto. 119 Cong. Rec. 25,079–25,092 (1973).

44. *See e.g.,* Excerpts from Statement by Rep. Lee Hamilton, July 15, 1987. ("During my six years on the Intelligence Committee, over 90 percent of the covert actions that were recommended to us by the president were supported and approved. And only the large-scale paramilitary operations, which really could not be kept secret, were challenged . . . ") *See also* Letter from Barry Goldwater to William Casey (Apr. 9, 1984) (re: mining of Nicaraguan harbors—"This is an act violating international law.")

45. Report of the Senate Select Committee on Intelligence, United States Senate, Jan. 1, 1981 to Dec. 31, 1982, S. Rep. No. 10, 98th Cong., 1st Sess. 2 (1983); Report to the Senate of the Select Committee on Intelligence, United States Senate, Covering the Period Jan.1, 1979 to Dec. 31, 1980, together with Additional Views, S. Rep. No. 193, 97th Cong., 1st Sess. 20 (1981); S. Engelberg, "Bush Aide and Senator Clash on Coup Attempt in Panama," N.Y. Times, Oct. 9, 1989, at 1, col. 1; N.Y. Times, Oct. 4, 1989, at A11, col. 1.

46. Report of the Select Committee on Intelligence, United States Senate, Jan. 1, 1987 to Dec. 31, 1988, S. Rep. No. 219, 101st Cong., 1st Sess. 17–18 (1990).
47. For a complete list of the criteria see, Report of the Senate Select Committee on Intelligence, United States Senate, Jan. 1, 1985 to Dec. 31, 1986, S. Rep. No. 236, 101st Cong., 2d Sess. 8–9 (1990). *See* Halperin, *American Military Intervention: Is It Ever Justified?* 228 The Nation 668 (1979) (Halperin argues that U.S. decisions to intervene should be consistent with "a reasonable interpretation of the United Nations Charter, of international law and of any bilateral agreements which we may have negotiated." Intervention decisions should also be made in a manner consistent with American constitutional process.)
48. S. Rep. No. 101–219, 101st Cong., 1st Sess. 18–19.
49. With the exception of Canada, very little has been written about legislative oversight of intelligence outside the United States. The United States system of legislative oversight would, however, appear unique among democracies. Legislative oversight within the parliamentary systems, where it exists, is apparently conducted by the same committees that oversee operations.

    Canada's Security Intelligence Review Committee is the closest approximation to the U.S. system. The review committee was established in July 1984 by an Act of Parliament. As of 1987, the committee consisted of five members and a staff of thirteen. The committee oversees the intelligence operations of the Royal Canadian Mounted Police and the Canadian Security Intelligence Service and is required to submit an annual report to the solicitor general of Canada for submission to parliament. Book Reviews, 5 Intelligence and National Security 224 (1988) (review of Canada, House of Commons, Security Intelligence Review Committee, Annual Reports (1984–1985, 1985–1986, 1986–1987) by R. H. Roy, University of Victoria). Significantly, the committee has "authority, which it has exercised, to conduct surprise, random audits of intelligence files." Johnson, *Controlling the CIA: A Critique of Current Safeguards,* 12 H. J. L & Pub. Pol. 371, 388 n.11 (1989). *See also,* Gill, *Symbolic or Real? The Impact of the Canadian Security Intelligence Review Committee, 1984–1988,* 4 Intelligence and National Security 550 (1989); Blais, *The Political Accountability of Intelligence Agencies—Canada, Id.* at 108.

    In Australia, a joint parliamentary committee did not begin oversight of the Australian Security Intelligence Organisation (ASIO) until 1987. The same year, the post of inspector general of intelligence and security was created as an "independent watchdog." Andrew, *The Growth of the Australian Intelligence Community and the Anglo-American Connection,* 4 Intelligence and National Security 213 (1989).

    Italy's Law No. 801, passed in October 1977, assigns to the prime minister responsibility for intelligence and security policy. The law empowers the prime minister to issue directives to the intelligence services and requires that the prime minister report in writing to the Parliament on intelligence and security policy every six months. A parliamentary committee comprised of four senators and four deputies is empowered to request information on intelligence policy and make recommendations, subject to the prime minister's state security privilege over information. J. Richelson, Foreign Intelligence Organizations, 116–17 (1988).

The Basic Law, the constitution of the Federal Republic of Germany, restricts certain domestic intelligence activities. Article 10 declares that the privacy of the posts and telecommunications shall be inviolable and may be restricted only pursuant to law. Article 13 prohibits searches of homes except by order of a judge or pursuant to a law. A. Blaustein and G. Flanz, ed., Constitutions of the Countries of the World, vol. 5, (1985). Oversight in the Bundestag is rudimentary. However, German unification and revelations about the former East German Ministry for State Security, or Stasi, will likely result in enhanced legislative oversight of German intelligence activities.

Perestroika, we are told, has also brought manifestations of legislative oversight to the Soviet Union. In July 1989, Soviet legislators were allowed for the first time to ask questions of KGB Director Vladimir Kryuchkov during confirmation hearings held 9 months after Kryuchkov assumed his post. N.Y. Times, July 15, 1989. at A3, col. 1. However, there have been no reports of a repeat performance and such displays appear to have more to do with public relations than legislative oversight. *See also,* Keller, "Ex-K.G.B. Officer, Speaking Out, Asserts Spy Agency Is Unchanged," N.Y. Times, June 17, 1990, at A12, col. 5 (press reports indicate that retired MGen. Kalugin continued to speak out during his 1990 campaign for a seat in the Soviet parliament.)

50. Exec. Order 12,334 (Dec. 4, 1981, 46 F.R. 59955).

51. In 1985 the IOB's counsel was asked to investigate allegations that the NSC staff was circumventing a congressional ban on aid to the Contras. The counsel's investigation was, at best, cursory, apparently consisting of two interviews and a superficial document search. The Majority Iran Contra Report questioned the counsel's professional qualifications, experience, and conclusions. Iran-Contra Report, *supra* note 17, at 400.

52. Executive Order No. 12,537 of President's Foreign Intelligence Advisory Board (Oct. 28, 1985, 50 F.R. 45083). Whether covert operations are considered "other intelligence activities" for the purposes of the board is not made clear in the executive order.

53. Bush administration panel members include: Admiral Bobby Ray Inman, vice chairman, formerly deputy director of central intelligence and director of the National Security Agency; Lew Allen, vice president of the California Institute of Technology and former director of the National Security Agency; Dr. William J. Perry, former director of research and engineering at the Pentagon; John M. Deutch, former provost of the Massachusetts Institute of Technology; and, William G. Hyland, editor of Foreign Affairs. Senator John Tower was appointed chairman. At the time of this writing President Bush had yet to appoint a new chairman following Tower's death in a 1991 plane crash. Wines, "Bush Scraps Intelligence Board, Appointing a New Panel of 6," N.Y. Times, July 17, 1990, at A6, col. 3.

54. The National Security Act of 1947, sec. 102(d)(3)("the Director of Central Intelli-

gence shall be responsible for protecting intelligence sources and methods from unauthorized disclosure."), for example, may create a countervailing duty.

55. 22 U.S.C. 2422 (repealed).

No funds appropriated under the authority of this or any other Act may be expended by or on behalf of the Central Intelligence Agency for operations in foreign countries, other than activities intended solely for obtaining necessary intelligence, unless and until the President finds that each such operation is important to the national security of the United States. Each such operation shall be considered a significant anticipated intelligence activity for the purpose of Section 501 of the National Security Act of 1947.

56. S. Rep. No. 101–358, 101st Cong., 2d Sess. 52 (1990) (report to accompany S. 2834, the Intelligence Authorization Act for FY 1991, Senate bill).

57. Paramilitary operations are military operations conducted by irregular or civilian personnel.

58. *E.g.,* director of central intelligence directives.

59. Specifically the Office of Intelligence Policy and Review.

60. S. Rep. No. 174, (to accompany S. 1324 the Intelligence Authorization Bill for FY 1990 and 1991) 101 Cong., 1st Sess. 29 (1989); American Bar Association, Standing Committee on Law and National Security, Oversight and Accountability of the U.S. Intelligence Agencies: An Evaluation 40 (1985) (citing response to a questionnaire).

61. Treverton, *supra* note 31, at 211 (Afghanistan); Engelberg, "U.S. Grant to 2 Czech Parties Is Called Unfair Interference," N.Y. Times, June 6, 1990, at A8. *See also,* P.L. 101–193, 103 Stat. 1701, The Intelligence Authorization Act for FY 1990, sec. 104 (prohibiting expenditure of funds, including the CIA's Reserve for Contingencies, for covert assistance to opposition parties or candidates in the Feb. 1990 elections in Nicaragua.)

62. See, JCS Pub. 1, Department of Defense Dictionary of Military and Associated Terms (1987).

63. See R. Holt, Radio Free Europe (1958); S. Mickelson, America's Other Voice: The Story of Radio Free Europe and Radio Liberty (1983); J. Tyson, International Broadcasting and National Security (1983). *See generally,* 22 U.S.C. Chap. 43 (international broadcasting) secs. 2871–83 (1988); 22 U.S.C. Chap. 18 (United States Information and Educational Exchange Programs) in particular Subchapter V, secs. 1462 (policies governing information activities), 1463 (Voice of America principles governing communications) and Subchapter V-A (radio broadcasting to Cuba).

64. N.Y. Times, Feb. 16, 1990, at A11, col. 1.

65. Report by the Advisory Board for Radio Broadcasting to Cuba, G.P.O. (1989); *see also* Statement for Cuba (no. 69) and Statement for the United States (no. 111), Final Protocol to the International Telecommunication Convention (Nairobi, 1982), United States Senate Treaty Doc. 99-6, 99th Cong., 1st Sess. (1985).

66. Kamm, "'Free' Europe Embraces That Radio and Its Mate," N.Y. Times, May 6, 1990, at A20.

67. The original executive prohibition on assassination was adopted by President Ford in 1976 in the wake of congressional hearings on assassination. Exec. Order 11,905, "United States Foreign Intelligence Activities," (Feb. 18, 1976). Richard Helms issued the first CIA directive against assassination in 1972. *Alleged Assassination Plots, supra* note 19, at 273.

68. Engelberg, "C.I.A. Seeks Looser Rules on Killings during Coups," N.Y. Times, Oct. 17, 1989, at 1, col. 3 (quoting Director Webster.)

69. Wash. Post, Sept. 16, 1990, at A1, col. 1.

70. One result of this review was reportedly a decision by the Bush administration to forego an earlier policy that required the United States to warn foreign political leaders in the event the United States learned of an assassination plot. Engelberg, "Justice Department Studying U.S. Role in Coups," N.Y. Times, Nov. 5, 1989, at A11.

71. This list is adapted from NSC 10/2 (1948). Unusually candid press reports on aid to the noncommunist resistance in Cambodia offer a window onto implementation of at least one insurgent support program. That aid was channeled through an entity known as the Cambodian Working Group composed of representatives from Thailand, Malaysia, Singapore, the CIA, and the resistance groups, Steven Erlanger reports. This covert aid, which up until 1990 amounted to approximately $24 million per year, was spent on uniforms; vehicles; rice; canned fish; political offices in Bangkok, Tokyo, Bonn, and Paris; and two radio stations broadcasting to Cambodia. In addition, the Thais and Malaysians were reimbursed for the costs of training the resistance in "nonlethal" skills. To avoid graft, United States officials purchased supplies directly and then turned them over to Thai officials for distribution to the rebels. S. Erlanger, "Aid to Cambodia Non-Communists Is Detailed," N.Y. Times, Nov. 16, 1989, at A16, col. 1. According to other reports, the Working Group also "reviews battle plans, approves specific weapons, disburses direct cash payments, and reimburses resistance leaders." J. Stone, "No More U.S. Money for Cambodia's War," Wash. Post (Op-ed), Feb. 19, 1990. Secretary of State Baker suspended U.S. aid to the Cambodian resistance in July 1990.

72. See, Turner, *supra* note 181, chap. 4.

73. *See* B. Berkowitz and A. Goodman, Strategic Intelligence for American National Security 143–47 (1989). For a graphic representation of covert action as a percentage of CIA annual budget see L. Johnson, America's Secret Power 101–4 (1989) (depicting 1986 at 20%). *But see* Webster, *The Role of Intelligence in a Free Society,* 43 U. Miami L. Rev. 155, 158 (1988) ("covert action traditionally claims only a small part of the CIA's budget, less than three percent"); Gates, *The CIA and American Foreign Policy,* 66 For. Aff. 215, 216 (1987/88) ("over 95 percent of the national intelligence budget is devoted to the collection and analysis of information. Only about three percent of the CIA's people are involved in covert action.")

74. N.Y. Times, Oct. 14, 1989, at 6, col. 4. Congress has passed a number of laws granting extraterritorial jurisdiction to United States courts over acts of violence against U.S. citizens overseas. See, e.g., 18 U.S.C. 2331 (terrorist acts abroad against U.S. nationals); 18 U.S.C. 351(i) (Congressional, cabinet, and Supreme

Court assassination, kidnapping, and assault). But Congress does not appear to have considered that these extraterritorial extensions of judicial jurisdiction necessarily import certain executive responsibilities, some of which, by their nature, may have to be accomplished covertly.

75. *See* United States v. Yunis, 681 F. Supp. 909 (D.D.C. 1988). 4B. O.L.C. 543, 551 (Mar. 31, 1980).

76. Although unclassified, the 1989 O.L.C. opinion (June 21, 1989) is considered "confidential" and has not been released to the public. The opinion, however, has been the subject of public commentary by among others William P. Barr and former Department of State Legal Adviser Abraham D. Sofaer. See Statement of Assistant Attorney General William P. Barr, Office of Legal Counsel, On the Legality as a Matter of Domestic Law of Extraterritorial Law Enforcement Activities That Depart from International Law, Subcommittee on Civil and Constitutional Rights of the Committee on the Judiciary, U.S. House of Representatives, Nov. 8, 1989; Statement of Abraham D. Sofaer, the Legal Adviser, Department of State, on The International Law and Foreign Policy Implications of Nonconsensual Extraterritorial Law Enforcement Activities, Subcommittee on Civil and Constitutional Rights of the Committee on the Judiciary, U.S. House of Representatives, Nov. 8, 1989. The O.L.C. opinions draw on *The Paquette Habana, Brown v. United States, The Schooner Exchange v. M'Faddon,* and *In Re Neagle.* For a summaries of these and other cases, see the Suggested Readings. See also, N.Y. Times, Oct. 14, 1989, at A6, col. 4.

77. United States v. Toscanino, 500 F.2d 277–78 (1974).

78. The Ker-Frisbie doctrine stands for the proposition that "forcible abduction neither offends due process nor requires dismissal of an indictment." United States v. Yunis, 681 F. Supp. 909, 918 (D.D.C. 1988). Ker is the overseas arm of the doctrine. In Ker v. Illinois, 119 U.S. 436, 7 S. Ct. 225, 30 L. Ed. 421 (1886), the Court declined to revise a decision of the Supreme Court of Illinois upholding the conviction of a man abducted by a Pinkerton agent in Peru to stand trial in Illinois. In fact, the agent was carrying extradition papers, for larceny, but chose to kidnap Ker instead. Ker was convicted of embezzlement, but did not benefit from the doctrine of specialty either because an extradition treaty was not used to obtain his custody.

79. Toscanino, at 267, 273 (quoting Rochin v. California, 342 U.S. 165 (1952)); Ex rel. Lujan v. Gengler, 510 F.2d 62 *cert. denied,* 421 U.S. 1001 (1975). *See also* Leich, Digest of United States Practice in International Law 1980 234 (1986) (irregular apprehension).

80. Toscanino, at 275.

81. Toscanino alleged that he was abducted in Uruguay and taken to Brazil at gun point where he was interrogated and brutally tortured. He also asserted that the U.S. government and U.S. attorney for the eastern district of New York were aware of the interrogation and that a U.S. law enforcement agent participated in some of the interrogation.

On remand, the district court declined to hold an evidentiary hearing and denied a motion to vacate the judgment and dismiss the indictment on jurisdictional grounds. Chief Judge Mishler wrote,

Assuming all the allegations of the affidavit to be true, there is no claim of participation by United States officials in the abduction and torture of the defendant. The defendant has not submitted any credible evidence which would indicate any participation on the part of United States officials prior to the time the defendant arrived in this country. Nor is there any evidence which shows that the abduction was carried out at the direction of United States officials. [United States v. Toscanino, 398 F. Supp. 916 (1975).]

82. Matta-Ballesteros v. Henman, 896 F.2d 255, 261 (7th Cir. 1990); United States v. Yunis, 681 F. Supp. 909, 919 (D.D.C. 1988). Moreover, the doctrine, or one like it, has been rejected by the Fifth, Ninth, Tenth, and Eleventh Circuits. Matta-Ballesteros v. ex. rel. Stolar v. Henman, 697 F. Supp. 1040 (S.D. Ill. 1988) (citing United States v. Postal, 589 F.2d 862 (5th Cir), *cert. denied,* 444 U.S. 832 (1979); United States v. Winter, 509 F.2d 975 (5th Cir.), *cert. denied,* 423 U.S. 825 (1975); United States v. Cotten, 471 F.2d 744 (9th Cir.), *cert. denied,* 411 U.S. 936 (1973); Hobson v. Crouse, 332 F.2d 561 (10th Cir. 1964); United States v. Rosenthal, 793 F.2d 1214 (11th Cir. 1986), *cert. denied,* 480 U.S. 919 (1987).

83. United States v. Verdugo-Urquidez, No. 88-5462 (9th Cir., filed July 22, 1991).

84. United States v. Alvarez-Machain, et al., ——F. Supp.—— (C.D. Cal. Aug. 10, 1990). See also Matta-Ballesteros ex rel. Stolar v. Henman, 697 F. Supp. 1040 (S.D. Ill. 1988), aff'd, 896 F.2d 255 (7th Cir. 1990) (joint abduction by U.S. and Honduran agents in Honduras); *but see* United States v. Verdugo-Urquidez, *supra* note 83.

A review of related citations, however, indicates that covert extradition, abduction, and forcible deportation are not methods reserved for just high profile cases like the Camarena murder. Indeed, one could argue that such methods were "traditional" law enforcement activities." See, e.g., United States v. Reed, 639 F.2d 896 (2d Cir. 1981) (complaint that defendant was unilaterally abducted by CIA from Bimini in the Bahamas. No standing to raise absent protest or objection by offended sovereign.); United States v. Yunis, 681 F. Supp. 909, 916 (D.D.C. 1988) (Lebanese citizen lacks standing to challenge abduction as violation of extradition treaty in absence of objections by governments of Cyprus or Lebanon); United States v. Valot, 625 F.2d 308, 310 (9th Cir. 1980) (defendant abducted in Thailand; failure to comply with extradition treaty did not bar prosecution); United States v. Cordero, 668 F.2d 32, 38 (1st Cir. 1981); United States ex rel Lujan v. Gengler, 510 F.2d 62, 67–78 (2d Cir. 1975) *cert. denied,* 421 U.S. 1001 (1975) (Bolivian abducted by U.S. officials lacks standing to assert violation of extradition treaty.); Lovato, 520 F.2d 1270, 1272, *cert. denied,* 423 U.S. 985, 96 S.Ct. 392, 46 L.Ed.2d. 302 (1975); Stevenson, v. United States, 381 F.2d 142, 144 (9th Cir. 1967); United States v. Herrera, 504 F.2d 859 (5th Cir. 1974); United States v. Sobell, 244 F.2d 520 (2d Cir.), *cert. denied,* 355 U.S. 873 (1957); Myers v. Rhay, 577 F.2d 504, 510 (9th Cir.), *cert. denied,* 439 U.S. 968, 99 S.Ct. 459, 58 L.Ed.2d

427 (1978). See United States v. Cotten, 471 F.2d 744, 748 (9th Cir.), *cert. denied,* 411 U.S. 936, 93 S.Ct. 1913, 36 L.Ed.2d 396 (1973); United States v. Hamilton, 460 F.2d 1279 (9th Cir. 1972); Wentz v. United States, 244 F.2d 172, 176 (9th Cir.) *cert. denied,* 355 U.S. 806, 78 S.Ct. 49, 2 L.Ed.2d 50 (1957).

85. The court found Dr. Machain's allegation of mistreatment "not worthy of belief." Moreover, the court could find no case in which an indictment was dismissed under the Toscanino, or a similar exception, to the Ker-Frisbie doctrine.

86. The Court did note, however, "that while the United States' participation in the abduction of Dr. Machain would appear to violate these international instruments the weight of authority indicates that these international instruments are not self-executing and therefore are not enforceable in federal courts absent implementing legislation."

87. The 9th Circuit Court of Appeals subsequently ordered a stay of the order. Judge Rafeedie has denied bail pending the appeal.

88. United States v. Verdugo-Urquidez, 494 U.S. 259, 108 L.Ed. 222, 110 S.Ct. 1056 (1990).

89. See, e.g., H. Koh, The National Security Constitution: Sharing Power After the Iran-Contra Affair (1990).

90. See Intelligence Authorization Act for FY 1990, Pub. L. No. 101–93, sec. 801, 103 Stat. 1701, 1711 (1989); Statement on Signing the Intelligence Authorization Act, Fiscal Year 1990, Nov. 30, 1989, Weekly Compilation of Presidential Documents, vol. 25, 1851–53.

91. See S. Rep. No. 174, 101st Cong., 1st Sess. 22–23 (1989).

92. Memorandum of Disapproval for the Intelligence Authorization Act, Fiscal Year 1991, 26 Weekly Comp. Pres. Doc. 1958 (Nov. 30, 1990). Sec. 602 of the act provided that a "request by any department, agency, or entity of the United States shall be deemed to be a covert action." As we go to press, the president is expected to sign into law a revised authorization bill for FY 1991 passed by Congress in July 1991.

The act's provisions will likely continue to define the debate over legislative oversight of covert action, as they have since the Iran-Contra Affair. Therefore, we note a few of the act's provisions. The act requires that a finding must be in writing, "unless immediate action by the United States is required;" retroactive findings are prohibited; and the intelligence committees must receive notification of significant changes in previously approved covert actions. Further, the act assigns direct responsibility to the president for keeping the intelligence committees "fully and currently" informed of intelligence activities, which as defined, "includes, but is not limited to, covert actions . . . " And with an eye towards legal specificity verging on evasion, this provision covers "the intelligence activities of the *United States*" as opposed to "activities engaged in by . . . any department, agency, or entity of the United States." Moreover, the president must determine that a covert action "is necessary to support *identifiable* foreign policy objectives of the United States and is important to the national security of the United States, which determination shall be set forth in a finding."

Title V of the National Security Act, however, will retain many of the earlier oversight provisions which left questions of constitutional authority unresolved. "To meet extraordinary circumstances affecting vital interests of the United States," for example, the president may still limit notification to eight designated members of Congress, although he might also inform "such other Member or Members of the joint congressional leadership as may be included by the President." In addition, *"on rare occasions,"* the president may initiate covert actions before reporting such actions, and "nothing contained in this title shall be construed as requiring the approval of the intelligence committees as a condition precedent to the initiation of such activities."

93. In the language of the Explanatory Statement, the new definition is meant to clarify the understanding of intelligence activities that require presidential approval and reports to Congress, not to relax or go beyond previous understandings. 137 Cong. Rec. H5905 (daily ed. July 25, 1991).

But,

Whether or not activities undertaken well in advance of a possible or eventual U.S. military operation constitute "covert action" will depend in most cases upon whether they constitute "routine support" to such an operation . . .

If hostage and prisoner-of-war rescue is a "traditional military activity," as legislative reports, military doctrine, and history suggest, this new definition appears to grant the president more discretion than Congress intended. The legislation allows future interpreters to bring together missions with as diverse tactical and political contexts as Son Tay, Mayaguez, and Iran under the permissive rubric of "traditional military activities," which, under the act, could remain outside the scope of the finding and notification process. Only Son Tay, however, clearly occurred during an existing period of conflict.

The act also appears to give the president latitude to prepare for covert military operations. Indeed, the original Senate report language appears to specifically address Admiral Turner's concern that disclosure of covert operations conducted in advance, and in support, of other covert actions might jeopardize the broader mission, e.g., the rescue of the hostages in Iran. "It is also clear," the Senate report concludes, "that activities undertaken to collect intelligence to support traditional military operations are themselves not covert actions, . . . and do not require presidential findings." It is only when support operations "include covert U.S. attempts to recruit, influence, or train foreign nationals" that "such support is not 'routine.'" In the Iranian case, however, the exposure of covert action taken in support of the military operation might well have shaped the direction of United States relations with Iran and led to the death of the hostages. All told, the act appeared to leave the door to legislative interpretation open and may presage an eventual increase in the use of military forces to undertake traditional covert actions which may be acknowledged after the fact.

94. See, ABA Report, *supra* note 60, at 40, concluding that "the oversight relationship with the Congress, . . . in any event is dependent on political relationships between

the executive and legislative branches and cannot readily be defined in statute. . . .
The resulting language, which represents a compromise between the positions of
the two branches of government, in fact appears to play little or no effective role in
determining what the oversight relationship will be."

95. Mill, *A Few Words on Non-Intervention,* Fraser's Magazine (Dec. 1859). Republished among other places in *The Vietnam War and International Law* (Falk ed.
1968).

96. See Suggested Readings, section 1.

97. S. Rep. No. 101–358, 101st Cong., 1st Sess. 55.

98. Letter from Sen. Barry Goldwater to William Casey (Apr. 9, 1984) (asserting that
the 1984 mining of Nicaraguan harbors "is an act violating international law.")

### CHAPTER 7: COVERT OPERATIONS IN THE FUTURE

1. A. Taheri, Holy Terror: Inside the World of Islamic Terrorism (1987); see also, for
the complex dynamics leading to such actions, M. H .A. Reisman, "Islamic Fundamentalism and Its Impact on International Law and Politics," in The Influence of
Religion on the Development of International Law 107 (Janis ed. 1991).

2. W. Weyrauch, Gestapo V-Leute: Tatsachen und Theories des Geheimdienstes Untersuchungen zur Geheimen Staatspolizei waehrend der nationalsozialistischen
Herrschaft (1989).

3. W. Reisman, Folded Lies 98–117 (1979).

4. E.g., Psychological Operations in Guerrilla Warfare by Tayacan, reprinted by
Random House (1985) (see esp. p. 57 discussing the "neutralization" of selective
targets for propaganda purposes). The Tayacan manual was a CIA revision of a 1968
army manual on psychological operations that was provided by the CIA to the
Nicaraguan Contras. Existence of the manual was publicly disclosed in October
1984.

5. I. Janis, Victims of Groupthink: A Psychological Study of Foreign Policy Decisions
and Fiascos (1972); *idem.,* Groupthink in Two Small Groups and Social Interaction
(Blunberg, Hare, Kent, and Davies, eds. 1983).

# Suggested Readings

The study of covert action presents special research challenges. There is both a scarcity of primary source material and a dearth of operational accounts and leaks of varying credibility. Thus, although *U.S. News and World Report* noted in July 1987 that over fifty covert operations were presented to the Congress during the first seven years of the Reagan administration, the authors are aware of only one Presidential Finding that has appeared in public print verbatim (Iran January 17, 1986). More often, covert operations are disclosed in fragments, if at all, or they simply become apparent during the course of events. Clearly, even less is known about covert actions undertaken by states other than the United States and by private actors.

This bibliography is intended to guide the reader to some of the sources on intelligence and covert action we found useful. It is divided into seven sections. Because our work focuses on covert operations in international law, Section 1 offers a more extensive bibliography for the reader looking for background on United States law. This section includes subsections dealing with statutory law, executive documents, case law, and government documents. A case summary or statute description follows most entries. These summaries focus on those aspects of statutory or case law relevant to the study of covert operations and thus should not be equated with standard legal case briefs.

Section 1 is not a comprehensive digest of United States law, but rather a guide to some of the more important laws and cases. Other authors, for example, adequately explain the quasi-constitutional standing of *Goldwater v. Carter* in the District of Columbia Circuit. Moreover, some of the legislative authorities and executive orders cited below have been repealed, superseded, or amended just as some cases may have been distinguished or overruled, but they remain part of the fabric of U.S. law in the area of national security. These materials should put the reader on the trail of applicable case

law. Those unfamiliar with the U.S. system of legal citation should consult their li-
brarian on the use of *Sheperd's United States Citations* or one of the computer citation
services.

Section 2 offers a brief selection of materials on comparative intelligence oversight.
However, there has been surprisingly little written on the subject; a comprehensive
treatment is overdue.

Section 3 is a list of United Nations documents cited in the text. This section, like the
others, only covers a fraction of potential source material. but it provides a starting point
for anyone interested in further study. For some, the task of sorting through United
Nations documents is as mysterious as any covert operation, although one not intentionally clouded by secrecy. We recommend an official United Nations depository, such
as the Mudd Library at Yale, whose excellent staff can guide even the novice along.

Section 4 provides citations to many of the treaties, conventions, and charters that
form the textual basis of international law, but as we argue, only a part of the larger fabric
of international law. Relevant international "case law" is provided in Section 5, although
the reader should note that the common law doctrine of *stare decisis* is not an international legal doctrine. Decisions by the International Court of Justice, for example, are
not viewed as binding precedents on future litigants, although these decisions often
provide evidence of expectations and are indicative of potential outcomes.

Sections 6 and 7 provide a general review of the literature in the field of intelligence
operations and covert operations. Separate sections are provided for books and articles.
This is a select bibliography. Newspaper citations and references to the weekly compilation of presidential documents, for example, appear in the notes but not in the bibliography. In addition, some sources for our incident studies are provided in the notes accompanying each report but are not found in the bibliography.

## 1. UNITED STATES LAW

### Statutory Law

*General Authorities*

National Security Act of 1947, 50 U.S.C. sec. 403 (1988). Provides basic authorities
and structure of post–World War national security establishment. Section 101 establishes the National Security Council for, among other things, "the purpose of more
effectively coordinating the policies and functions of the departments and agencies of
the Government relating to the national security . . . " Section 102 establishes a
Central Intelligence Agency and provides for a director of central intelligence (DCI)
and deputy director of central intelligence. The act further provides that the DCI shall
be responsible for protecting intelligence sources and methods from unauthorized
disclosure and that it shall be the duty of the agency "to perform such other functions
and duties related to intelligence affecting the national security as the National
Security Council may from time to time direct." The act, as amended by Title V,
provides for congressional oversight of intelligence activities.

Central Intelligence Agency Act of 1949, 50 U.S.C. 403a (1988). Provides for the
administration of the Central Intelligence Agency, e.g., procurement, travel, al-
lowances. Section 7, 50 U.S.C. 403h, under the agency's "General Authorities,"

provides for a national security exception to applicable immigration laws and regulations permitting the DCI, attorney general, and commissioner of immigration to grant permanent resident status to aliens in the interest of national security or in furtherance of the national intelligence mission. Use of this authority is not to exceed one hundred persons in any fiscal year.

Central Intelligence Agency Retirement Act of 1964 for Certain Employees, 50 U.S.C. 403 note. Establishes retirement and disability system for limited number of employees whose duties are "(i) in support of Agency activities abroad hazardous to life or health or (ii) so specialized because of security requirements as to be clearly distinguishable from normal government employment . . . "

*Specific Authorities*

3 Stat. 472 (enacted 1811). Relating to the occupation of the Floridas by the United States—"and he [the President] may, for the purposes of taking possession and occupying the territory aforesaid, and in order to maintain therein the authority of the United States, employ any part of the army and navy of the United States which he may deem necessary."

The Hostage Act of 1868, Rev. Stat. sec. 2001, 22 U.S.C. sec. 1732 (1988). "Whenever it is made known to the President that any citizen of the United States has been unjustly deprived of his liberty by or under the authority of any foreign government, . . . the President shall use such means, not amounting to acts of war, as he may think necessary and proper to obtain or effectuate the release . . . "

Foreign Intelligence Surveillance Act of 1978, 50 U.S.C. secs. 1801–11 (1982). Authorizes the attorney general or deputy attorney general to approve warrants for electronic surveillance within the United States for the purposes of foreign intelligence. Applications must include "a statement whether physical entry is required to effect the surveillance." The attorney general may authorize surveillance without a court order when the surveillance is solely directed at "communications used exclusively between or among foreign powers." Applications are heard by one of seven district judges publicly designated by the chief justice to serve on the Foreign Intelligence Surveillance Court. Each judge serves for one term not to exceed seven years. The act further provides for a Court of Review comprised of three federal judges to hear government appeals of adverse decisions. The attorney general is required to submit an annual report to Congress specifying the number of applications made for orders, or extensions of orders, and the number of applications granted, modified, or denied. The act has spawned little case law and less commentary. See, e.g., *In Matter of Kevork,* 788 F.2d 566 (9th Cir. 1986); also, FISA Act of 1978: The First Five Years, S. Rep. 98–660, 98th Cong., 2d Sess. (1984).

Foreign Assistance Act of 1961, sec. 614, 22 U.S.C. 2318. Special presidential authorities to waive provisions of act.

22 U.S.C. 3970. Compensation for certain imprisoned CIA-related foreign nationals.

10 U.S.C. 192. DIA and National Security Agency combat support role.

*Intelligence Agency Exemptions*

12 U.S.C. 3414(a) .Providing intelligence agency exemption to the Right to Financial Privacy Act of 1978. Exemption applies to "a Government authority authorized to

conduct foreign counter—or foreign positive—intelligence activities for purposes of conducting such activities." The attorney general must report all requests made pursuant to this exemption on a semi-annual basis to the congressional intelligence committees.

10 U.S.C. 192. Defense Intelligence Agency and National Security Agency exemption from statute providing for oversight by the secretary of defense over defense agencies and Department of Defense field activities.

18 U.S.C. 1028(e). Intelligence exemption from false identification statute for "lawfully authorized investigative, protective, or intelligence activity of . . . any intelligence agency of the United States." For the purposes of statute, "identification document" includes inter alia a document made or issued by or under the authority of the United States government, a state, a foreign government, an international governmental or international quasi-governmental organization.

18 U.S.C. 1029(f). Intelligence exemption from credit card protection statute for "any lawfully authorized . . . intelligence activity of . . . any intelligence agency of the United States." Applies to cards, plates, codes, account numbers, or other means of account access.

18 U.S.C. 1030(f). Intelligence exemption from computer fraud statute for "any lawfully authorized . . . intelligence activity of . . . any intelligence agency of the United States." Statute applies to persons who knowingly access a computer or exceed authorized access without authorization, to United States government restricted data, classified data, financial records of a financial institution, or federal interest computer.

18 U.S.C. 1367(b). Intelligence exemption from satellite interference statute.

18 U.S.C. 1546. Exemption for "any lawfully authorized . . . intelligence activity . . . of any intelligence agency of the United States" from false visa statute. Applicable to visas, permits, or other documents required for entry into the United States.

Intelligence Authorization Act, FY 1986, Title VI Facilitating Naturalization of Certain Foreign Intelligence Sources (amends 8 U.S.C. 1427). Whenever the DCI, attorney general and commissioner of immigration determine that a petitioner otherwise eligible for naturalization has made an extraordinary contribution to the national security or to the conduct of U.S. intelligence activities the petitioner may be naturalized without regard to the residence and physical requirements. Petitioner, however, must have resided within the United States for at least one year prior to naturalization. Authority limited to no more than five aliens per fiscal year.

*Funding*

31 U.S.C. secs. 1341, 1342, 1350–51. The "Anti-Deficiency Act" and related provisions:

1341. Limitations on expending and obligating amounts
    (a)(1) An officer or employee of the United States Government or of the District of Columbia government may not—
    (A) make or authorize an expenditure or obligation exceeding an amount available in an appropriation or fund for the expenditure or obligation; or

(B) involve either government in a contract or obligation for the payment of money before an appropriation is made unless authorized by law.

1342. Limitation on voluntary services

An officer or employee of the United States Government . . . may not accept voluntary services for either government or employ personal services exceeding that authorized by law except for emergencies involving the safety of human life or the protection of property. . . .

The law further provides that any employee who knowingly and willfully violates these sections shall be subject to a fine of up to $5,000 and/or imprisoned for not more than 2 years.

Recurring language Department of Defense Appropriations Acts, on Transfer and Reprogramming contingent on Congressional committee notification, e.g., P.L. 99–591, The Resolution Making Continuing Appropriations for FY 1987, Oct. 30, 1986:

Sec. 9037. None of the funds appropriated in this Act may be made available through transfer, reprogramming, or other means for any intelligence or special activity different from that previously justified to the Congress unless the Director of Central Intelligence or the Secretary of Defense has notified the House and Senate Appropriations Committees of the intent to make such funds available for such activity.

Foreign Assistance Act of 1961, secs. 109, 610, 614, codified at 22 U.S.C. sec. 2151g (transfer of funds); 22 U.S.C. 2360 (transfer between accounts); 22 U.S.C. 2364 (special authorities). Authorizes president to furnish assistance under the act without regard to other provisions of act, the Arms Export Control Act, any law relating to receipts and credits accruing to the United States, and any act authorizing or appropriating funds for use under the Arms Export Control Act, in the security interest of the country and for other reasons. Section includes funding ceilings and is contingent on provisions for congressional notification or certification.

31 U.S.C. 1535, 1536. Provides for agency agreements and crediting of payments from purchases between executive agencies.

31 U.S.C. 3524(c). Provides comptroller general with authority to audit expenditures approved or authorized by the president or an official of an executive agency without vouchers. Sec. (c) authorizes president to exempt a financial transaction about sensitive foreign intelligence activities. Sec. (e) permits information about exempt transactions to be reviewed by the congressional intelligence committees.

50 U.S.C. 403j(b). CIA exemption for certain laws governing expenditure of appropriated funds. "The sums made available to the Agency may be expended without regard to the provisions of law and regulations relating to the expenditure of Government funds; and for objects of a confidential, extraordinary, or emergency nature, such expenditures to be accounted for solely on the certificate of the Director . . . "

50 U.S.C. sec. 414, Funding of Intelligence Activities.

(a) Appropriated funds available to an intelligence agency may be obligated or expended for an intelligence or intelligence-related activity only if—

(1) those funds were specifically authorized by the Congress for use for such activities; or

(2) in the case of funds from the Reserve for Contingencies of the Central Intelligence Agency . . . the Director of Central Intelligence has notified the appropriate congressional committees of the intent to make such funds available for such activity; or

(3) in the case of funds specifically authorized by the Congress for a different activity—

    (A) the act to be funded is a higher priority . . .

    (B) the need for funds . . . is based on unforseen requirements . . .

    (C) the Director of Central Intelligence, the Secretary of Defense or the Attorney General, as appropriate, has notified the appropriate congressional committees . . .

(b) Funds available to an intelligence agency may not be made available for any activity . . . for which funds were denied by the Congress.

(c) As used in this section—

(1) the term "intelligence agency" means any department, agency, or other entity of the United States involved in intelligence or intelligence related activities; . . .

Recurring language Department of Defense Appropriations Acts, on Reserve for Contingencies of the Central Intelligence Agency, e.g., Continuing Resolution, FY 1987:

Sec. 9128. None of the funds provided by this Act may be used to pay the salaries of any person or persons who authorize the transfer of unobligated and deobligated appropriations into the Reserve for Contingencies of the Central Intelligence Agency.

*Protection of Intelligence Sources and Methods*

Central Intelligence Information Act, 50 U.S.C. 431 (1988). Provides Freedom of Information Act (FOIA) exemption for certain operational files. *See also,* H. Rep. 98–726 Part I, noting that for the purposes of the act "foreign intelligence operations consist both of collection of information . . . and of special activities (also called covert actions) conducted in support of United States foreign policy objectives in which the role of the United States Government is not apparent or acknowledged publicly."

Classified Information Procedures Act (CIPA), 18 U.S.C. App. Provides for procedures in cases involving classified information. Addresses the issue of "greymail" whereby a defendant could threaten to discover and expose at trial relevant classified information and thereby pressure the government to drop the case before trial. Under CIPA the judge may review classified material *in camera* for relevance. If the judge finds the material relevant, the government may move to substitute a statement admitting relevant facts that the specific classified information would tend to prove, or move to substitute a summary of the classified information. The court shall grant such a motion if it finds that the statement or summary will provide the defendant "with substantially the same ability to make his defense as would disclosure of the specific classified information." If the court denies the motion, the attorney general may file an affidavit with the court objecting to disclosure of the material, in which case the court will order defendant not to disclose. The court, however, shall then also dismiss the indictment, dismiss specific counts of the indictment, find against the United States on any related issue or strike or preclude the testimony of a witness.

Intelligence Identities Protection Act of 1982, 50 U.S.C. 421 (Title VI of the National Security Act of 1947). Provides for fines and/or imprisonment for "whoever, having or having had authorized access to classified information that identifies a covert agent, intentionally discloses any information identifying such covert agent . . . knowing that . . . the United States is taking affirmative measures to conceal such covert agent's intelligence relationship to the United States." The act further provides for penalties for persons convicted of engaging in a "pattern of activities" intended to identify and expose covert agents. The act provides for extraterritorial jurisdiction over U.S. citizens and permanent resident aliens for offenses committed outside the United States. For background on the origin of the act see *Haig v. Agee,* 453 U.S. 280 (1981).

National Security Act of 1947, sec. 102(d) (3), 50 U.S.C. 403. "And provided further, that the Director of Central Intelligence shall be responsible for protecting sources and methods from unauthorized disclosure."

18 U.S.C. sec. 1114. Assault on intelligence officers.

*Executive Oversight*

Inspector General Act of 1978, Oct. 12, 1978, P.L. 95–452, 82 Stat. 1101 (Sec. 8(b). Provides secretary of defense power to suspend inspector general from initiating, carrying out, or completing any audit of investigations requiring access to information concerning sensitive operational plans, intelligence matters, counterintelligence matters, ongoing criminal investigations by other administrative agencies of the Department of Defense related to national security, or other matters whose disclosure would constitute a serious threat to national security. Congressional reporting of exemptions is required.

Intelligence Authorization Act, FY 1990, Pub. L. No. 101–93, sec. 801, 103 Stat. 1701, 1711 (1989). Title VIII of the act creates the post of statutory inspector general (IG) of the CIA. The statutory IG reports directly to the DCI. Congress has a right of access to IG inspection, audit, and investigation reports on demand. The act further provides criteria for the appointment of the IG who shall be appointed with the advice and consent of the Senate. If the IG is removed, the president is required to communicate in writing the reasons for such removal. Finally, the DCI may prohibit the IG from initiating, carrying out, or completing any audit, inspection, or investigation to protect vital national security interests.

10 U.S.C. secs. 3013(c)(7); 5013(c)(7); 8013(c)(7). Service secretaries supervision and control of departmental intelligence activities.

*Congressional Oversight*

S. Res. 21, 94th Cong., 1st Sess. (1975). "[T]o establish a Select Committee of the Senate to conduct an investigation and study with respect to intelligence activities carried out by or on behalf of the Federal Government . . . with respect to the following matters or questions: (14) The extent and necessity of overt and covert intelligence activities in the United States and abroad."

S. Res. 400, Rep. Nos. 675 and 770, 94th Cong., 2d Sess. (1976). Establishes Senate Select Committee on Intelligence.

Rules of the House of Representatives, Rule XLVIII (1977). Establishes the House Permanent Select Committee on Intelligence.

Intelligence Oversight Act of 1980, adopted as part of the Intelligence Authorization Act for FY 1981, as amended by the Intelligence Authorization Act for FY 1991, codified at Title V of the National Security Act, 50 U.S.C. 413. Accountability for intelligence activities requires, among other things, that the DCI and the heads of all departments, agencies, and other entities of the United States involved in a covert action keep the Congressional intelligence committees "fully and currently informed" of all intelligence activities and covert actions except that (A) the provision shall not require approval of the intelligence committees as a condition precedent to the initiation of any significant anticipated intelligence activity, and (B) if the President determines it is essential to limit prior notice, in the form of a finding, to meet extraordinary circumstances affecting vital interests of the United States, such notice shall be limited to the chairman and ranking minority members of the intelligence committees, the Speaker and minority leader of the House of Representatives, and the majority and minority leaders of the Senate and such other members of the congressional leadership as may be included by the president. The act further provides that the President shall fully inform the intelligence committees in a timely fashion where prior notice of a finding is not given and shall provide a statement of the reasons for not giving prior notice.

### Congressional Investigative Authorities

Sections 102, 103, 104 of the Revised Statutes of the United States, 2 U.S.C. 192. Congressional investigative authority to hold witnesses in contempt for refusing to answer "any question pertinent to the question under inquiry" or for failing to produce papers.

5 U.S.C. 7211, Employees' right to petition Congress. "The right of employees, individually or collectively, to petition Congress or a Member of Congress, or to furnish information to either House of Congress, or to a committee or Member thereof, may not be interfered with or denied."

18 U.S.C. secs. 6002, 6005. Testimonial immunity: Sec. 6002 provides use immunity for a witness who asserts his privilege against self-incrimination before a court or grand jury, an agency of the United States, or before either House of Congress, a joint committee or committee or subcommittee of either house; "witness may not refuse to comply with order on basis of privilege against self-incrimination; but no testimony or other information compelled under the order (or any information directly or indirectly derived from such testimony or other information) may be used against the witness in any criminal case, except a prosecution for perjury, giving a false statement, or otherwise failing to comply with the order." Sec. 6005 defines conditions

under which U.S. district courts shall issue order to compel use immunity testimony before congressional proceedings.

*Constraints on Intelligence Activities*

Arms Export Control Act, 22 U.S.C. secs. 2751–96c (1988).

Export Administration Act of 1979, 50 U.S.C. secs. 2401–20 (1988). Provides for export regulation, including national security controls (2404), foreign policy controls (2405), and export license procedures (2409).

Recurring language on Authority for the Conduct of Intelligence Activities, e.g., Intelligence Authorization Act, FYs 1979–1991:

The Authorization of appropriations by this Act shall not be deemed to constitute authority for the conduct of any intelligence activity which is not otherwise authorized by the Constitution or laws of the United States.

Section 654 of the Foreign Assistance Act of 1961, 22 U.S.C. 2414 (1988). Findings and determinations pursuant to the Foreign Assistance Act of 1961, the Foreign Military Sales Act, or the foreign assistance or related appropriations act for each fiscal year shall be reduced to writing and signed by the President prior to any action being taken. Such findings and determinations shall be published in the Federal Register unless the President concludes that publication would harm the national security in which case only a statement that a determination or finding has been made shall be published.

Section 662 of the Foreign Assistance Act of 1961, 22 U.S.C. sec. 2422 (1988) (the "Hughes-Ryan Amendment"). Presidential finding required prior to expenditure of funds for CIA covert activities in foreign countries. Superseded by the Intelligence Authorization Act for FY 1991, which requires presidential finding prior to covert actions by departments, agencies, or entities of the U.S. government.

10 U.S.C. 167(g). Special operations forces authority contained in sec. 167 establishing a unified special operations command "does not constitute authority to conduct any activity which, if carried out as an intelligence activity by the Department of Defense, would require" a finding under sec. 662 of the Foreign Assistance Act or a notice to the congressional intelligence committees pursuant to section 501(a)(1) of the National Security Act of 1947.

Section 620A of the Foreign Assistance Act of 1961, 22 U.S.C. 2371. Prohibits furnishing foreign assistance to countries that grant sanctuary to international terrorists.

Section 660 of the Foreign Assistance Act of 1961, 22 U.S.C. 2420(a). Prohibits using the funds made available to carry out the act, as well as any of the local currencies generated by the act, for police, prisons, or other law enforcement for any foreign government or any program of internal intelligence or surveillance. Exceptions and qualifications are provided in secs. 2420(b)(c)(d).

"Neutrality Acts," prohibitions on private activities with respect to foreign countries, 18 U.S.C. secs 956 (conspiracy to injure property of foreign government); 9570 (possession of property in aid of foreign government); 958 (commission to serve against friendly nation); 959 (enlistment in foreign service); 960 (expedition against friendly nation); 961 (strengthening armed vessel of foreign nation).

50 U.S.C. 415, Sec. 503 of the National Security Act of 1947. Concerns reporting of covert arms transfers. Applicable to the transfer, or the anticipated transfer, in any fiscal year of any aggregation of defense articles or defense services exceeding $1,000,000 in value.

*Examples of Country Specific Restrictions*
*Angola*

Tunney-Clark Amendment to the Arms Export Control Act, June 1976, Sec. 404, P.L. 94–329, 94 Stat. 1421 ("Clark Amendment"). Prohibiting covert assistance for military or paramilitary activities in Angola.

Intelligence Authorization Act for FY 1991, text in Classified Annex to Joint Explanatory Statement. Summarized in Conf. Rep. to Accompany S.2834, 101st Cong., 2d Sess. [Note: This version of the act was vetoed but is cited here for purposes of illustration.]: "The conferees further agree that half of any lethal assistance to UNITA which may be authorized shall be placed in a restricted account and its release subject to the approval of the intelligence committees. The conferees further agree that any lethal assistance to UNITA shall be suspended if the President certifies: [inter alia] that the Government of Angola has expressed a willingness to accept a reasonable ceasefire and political settlement and proposes a reasonable and specific timetable for internationally supervised free and fair multiparty elections in which UNITA would be free to participate." This version of the act provided further that "if the President has not certified by March 31, 1991 that the conditions required for suspension of lethal aid to UNITA have been met, he shall submit to the intelligence committees a report setting forth the reason or reasons why."

*Nicaragua*

Sec. 793 of the Defense Appropriations Act, FY 1983, Pub. L. 97–377, 96 Stat. 1865 (Boland I).

Sections 108 and 109 of the Intelligence Authorization Act for FY 1984, Pub. L. 98–215, 97 Stat. 1475; Sec. 775 of the Department of Defense Appropriations Act, 1984, Pub. L. 98–212, 97 Stat. 1452.

Intelligence Authorization Act, FY 1984. Sec. 108 "Limitation on Covert Assistance for Military Operations in Nicaragua"; Sec. 109 Congressional Findings [Relating to the Situation in Central America] including "(2) by providing military support (including arms, training, and logistical, command and control, and communications facilities) to groups seeking to overthrow the Government of El Salvador and other Central American governments, the Government of National Reconstruction of Nicaragua has violated article 18 of the Charter of the Organization of American States . . . "

Sec. 106(c) of the Continuing Appropriations, Temporary, 1985, Pub. L. 98–441, 98 Stat. 1700.

Sec. 8066 of the Department of Defense Appropriations Act 1985, as enacted in Further Continuing Appropriations Act, 1985, Pub. L. 98–473, 98 Stat. 1935 (Boland II); Sec. 801 of the Intelligence Authorization Act for FY 1985, Pub. L. 98–618, 98 Stat. 3304.

Sec. 722 of the International Security and Development Cooperation Act of 1985, Pub. L. 99–83, 99 Stat. 149; Secs. 101–06 of the Supplemental Appropriations Act, FY 1985, Pub. L. 99–88, 99 Stat. 324.

Sec. 105 of the Intelligence Authorization Act for FY 1986, Pub. L. 99–169, 99 Stat. 1003 (Boland III).

Sec. 8050 of Further Continuing Appropriations, 1985, Pub. L. 99–190, 99 Stat. 1211 (Boland III).

Continuing Resolution for FY 1987, Pub. L. 99–591 (1986).

Sec. 104, Intelligence Authorization Act, FY 1990, as reported in Conference Report, H. Rep. 101–367, 101st Cong., 1st Sess. 20 [to accompany H.R. 2748]

. . . the conference report does not authorize any funds for covert assistance to opposition parties or candidates in the February, 1990 Nicaraguan elections. Further the Classified Schedule of Authorizations prohibits use of the CIA's Reserve for Contingencies for such purpose, thus leaving a reprogramming request, which must be approved by the intelligence and appropriations committees of each House, as the only FY 1990 funding vehicle for covert assistance to the Nicaraguan electoral opposition if the Administration should change its mind and decide to provide such assistance.

### South Africa

Sec. 107, Intelligence Authorization Act for FY 1987, Pub. L. 99–569. Restriction on intelligence agency cooperation with South Africa. Bars "any form of cooperation, direct or indirect, . . . except activities which are reasonably designed to facilitate the collection of necessary intelligence." Section states that it is U.S. policy that no agency or entity of the United States involved in intelligence activities may provide any intelligence to the Government of South Africa which pertains to a South African internal opposition group, movement, organization, or individual. Any change in policy to be considered a significant anticipated intelligence activity which requires a presidential finding and notification.

Sec. 322, Anti-Apartheid Act of 1986, Pub. L. 99–440. Prohibition on cooperation with the armed forces of South Africa.

### Cambodia

Intelligence Authorization Act for FY 1991, text in Classified Annex to Joint Explanatory Statement. Summarized in Conference Report to accompany S.2834, 101st Cong., 2d Sess. [Note: This version of the act was vetoed by the president, but is included here for purposes of illustration.]:"The conferees agree that any program of non-lethal assistance to the Cambodian non-communist resistance should be structured in such a way as to promote a Cambodian peace settlement. The conferees also agree that any non-lethal assistance being provided the non-communist resistance should transition to an overt, acknowledged program of U.S. assistance. . . . Finally, the conferees agree that no assistance shall be provided under this provision to any Cambodian resistance organization that the President determines is engaged in tactical or strategic cooperative activities with the Khmer Rouge in their military operations."

*Afghanistan*

22 U.S.C. 2374, the Foreign Assistance Act of 1961, as amended. Prohibits assistance to Afghanistan from funds authorized and appropriated pursuant to the Foreign Assistance Act until the president certifies that "(1) the Government of Afghanistan has apologized officially and assumes reponsibility for the death of Ambassador Adolph Dubs; and (2) the Government of Afghanistan agrees to provide adequate protection for all personnel of the United States Government in Afghanistan . . . The provisions of subsection (a) of this section shall not apply if the President determines that such assistance is in the national interest of the United States because of substantially changed circumstances in Afghanistan."

*Conduct of Diplomacy*

Act for the Prevention and Punishment of Crimes against Internationally Protected Persons, P.L. 94–467, Oct. 8, 1976, 90 Stat. 1997, 18 U.S.C. secs. 1116, 112, 878, 1201 (1988). Implements the Convention on Prevention and Punishment of Crimes against Internationally Protected Persons, Including Diplomatic Agents.

1 U.S.C. sec. 112b (United States International Agreements). The "Case-Zablocki Act" requires (1) Secretary of State to transmit to Congress the text of any international agreement, oral or written, other than a treaty, to which the U.S. is a party as soon as practicable but in no event later than sixty days thereafter. (2) Where President determines public disclosure would be prejudicial to national security agreements shall be transmitted to Foreign Relations Committee and Foreign Affairs Committee only under injunction of secrecy. (3) Any department or agency of the USG which enters into an international agreement shall transmit the text to the Secretary of State within twenty days. (4) An international agreement may not be concluded on behalf of the U.S. without prior consultation with the Secretary of State. Consultation may constitute a class of agreements rather than a particular agreement.

Foreign Agents Registration Act (FARA), 22 U.S.C. 611–621 (chap. 11). Requires inter alia registration of foreign propagandists not otherwise exempted by Sec. 612; the conspicuous identification of propaganda material transported through foreign or interstate commerce; the filing of "political propaganda" with the attorney general. A statutory definition of "political propaganda" is contained in sec. 11(j):

The term "political propaganda" includes any oral, visual, graphic, written, pictorial, or other communication or expression by any person (1) which is reasonably adapted to, or which the person disseminating the same believes will, or which he intends to, prevail upon, indoctrinate, convert, induce, or in any other way influence a recipient or any section of the public within the United States with reference to the political or public interests, policies, or relations of a government of a foreign country or a foreign political party or with reference to the foreign policies of the United States or promote in the United States racial, religious, or social dissensions, or (2) which advocates, advises, instigates, or promotes any racial, social, political, or religious disorder, civil riot, or other conflict involving the use of force or violence in any other American republic or the overthrow of any government of political subdivision of any other American republic by any means involving the use of force or violence.

18 U.S.C. 951. Agents of foreign governments. Notification to attorney general required.

Act of Aug. 1, 1956, 50 U.S.C. 851–58. Registration of certain persons trained in foreign espionage systems.

Foreign Corrupt Practices Act as amended, 15 U.S.C. secs. 78dd-1, 78dd-2, 78ff (1982).

Foreign Missions Act, 22 U.S.C. 4301. Provides for the review and control of the operations of foreign missions in the United States, including the provision of benefits, e.g., any type of good or service.

22 U.S.C. 3927, Foreign Service Act of 1980, Sec. 207. Duties and authority of chiefs of U.S. diplomatic missions abroad:

(a) Duties . . .

Under the direction of the President, the chief of mission to a foreign country—

(1) shall have full responsibility for the direction, coordination, and supervision of all Government executive branch employees in that country except for employees under the command of a United States area military commander; and

(2) shall keep fully and currently informed with respect to activities and operations of the Government within that country . . .

(b) Duties of agencies with employees in foreign countries

Any executive branch agency having employees in a foreign country shall keep the chief of mission to that country fully and currently informed with respect to all activities and operations of its employees in that country, and shall ensure that all of its employees within that country (except for employees under the command of a United States area military commander) comply fully with all applicable directives of the chief of mission.

International Organizations Immunities Act, 59 Stat. 669 (1945) codified at 22 U.S.C.A. sec. 288 et seq. (1976).

18 U.S.C. 953, "the Logan Act." Provides criminal penalties for "[a]ny citizen of the United States, . . . who without authority of the United States, directly or indirectly commences or carries on any correspondence . . . with any foreign government or any officer or agent thereof, in relation to any disputes or controversies with the United States . . . "

The War Powers Resolution, 50 U.S.C. secs. 1541–48 (1982). See discussion in chapter 6 on accountability.

22 U.S.C. Chap. 43, secs. 2871–83 (1988). International broadcasting.

22 U.S.C. Chap. 18, secs. 1462 (VOA principles governing communications), 1463 (radio broadcasting to Cuba)(1988).

### Executive Documents (Chronological)

Coordinator of Information, the White House, July 11, 1941, Franklin Delano Roosevelt, 3 C.F.R. 1324. Establishing position of coordinator of information and appointing William J. Donovan to the post.

Military Order of June 13, 1942, 3 C.F.R. 1308, the White House, June 13, 1942. Coordinator of information hereinafter designated the Office of Strategic Services (OSS) which "shall perform the following duties: . . . 2.b. plan and operate such special services as may be directed by the United States Joint Chiefs of Staff."

Exec. Order No. 9,621, Sept. 20, 1945, Termination of the Office of Strategic Services and Disposition of Its Functions. Transferring functions of OSS to the Department of State and Department of War (authority repealed by Pub. L. 89–554 (80 Stat. 651, 50 U.S.C. 601).

Presidential Directive, Coordinator of Federal Foreign Intelligence Activities, Jan. 22, 1946, F.R. Vol. II, No. 25, Feb. 5, 1946. Establishing a National Intelligence Authority comprised of the secretary of state, secretary of war, secretary of the navy, and a director of central intelligence to be appointed by the president; establishing the Central Intelligence Group (CIG)); and, providing inter alia that

3. Subject to existing law, and to the direction and control of the National Intelligence Authority, the Director of Central Intelligence shall:
d. Perform such other functions and duties related to intelligence affecting the national security as the President and National Intelligence Authority may from time to time direct.

Exec. Order No. 9,698. Designating public international organizations entitled to enjoy certain privileges, exemptions, and immunities, Feb. 19, 1946, 3 C.F.R. 508 (1943–1948) (supplemented by Exec. Orders 9,751, 9,823, 9,863, 9,887, 9,911, 9,972, 10,025, amended by Exec. Orders Nos. 10,083, 10,533).

National Security Council Directive 10/2, June 18, 1948, Office of Special Projects.

Exec. Order No. 10,206. Providing for support of United Nations' activities directed to the peaceful settlement of disputes, Jan. 19, 1951, 3 C.F.R. 388 (1949–1953) (nullified by Exec. Order 10,214).

Exec. Order No. 10,290, 3 C.F.R. 789 (1953) First executive order governing security classifications, subsequently revoked.

Exec. Order No. 10,483, Sept. 2, 1953. Establishing the Operations Coordination Board, comprised of the under secretary of state who shall serve as chairman, the deputy secretary of defense, the director of the Foreign Operations Administration, the director of central intelligence, and a representative of the president to be designated by the president; and providing for the integrated implementation of national security policies by the several agencies; such board to report to the National Security Council; and abolishing the Psychological Strategy Board)(amended by Exec. Order 10,598; superseded by Exec. Order 10,700.)

National Security Council Directive 5412/2, Dec. 28, 1955, on Covert Operations.

Reorganization of the U.S. Intelligence Community, Announcement Outlining Management Steps for Improving the Effectiveness of the Intelligence Community, Nov. 5, 1971, Weekly Compilation of Presidential Documents, Nov. 8, 1971.

Exec. Order No. 11,905, Feb. 18, 1976, 41 F.R. 7703. President Ford's order on "United States Foreign Intelligence Activities," including the first executive prohibition on assassination (amended by Exec. Orders 11,985, 11,994, 12,038; superseded by Exec. Order 12,036).

Exec. Order No. 11,958. Administration of arms export controls, Jan. 18, 1977, 3 C.F.R. 79 (1977), 42 F.R. 4311.

Exec. Order 12,036. United States Foreign Intelligence Activities, Jan. 24, 1978, 43 F.R. 3674 (revoked by Exec. Order 12,333).

Exec. Order No. 12,139. Exercise of Certain Authority Respecting Electronic Surveillance, May 23, 1979, 3 C.F.R. 397 (1979). Includes designation of authority to make certifications in support of applications to, among others, the secretary of state, secretary of defense, director of central intelligence (amended by Exec. Order 12,333).

Exec. Order No. 12,163. Administration of foreign assistance and related functions, Sept. 29, 1979, 3 C.F.R. 435 (1979), 44 F.R. 56673 (amended by Exec. Orders 12,226, 12,292, 12,321, 12,356, 12,365, 12,423, 12,458, 12,500, 12,560, 12,608, 12,620, 12,639).

Exec. Order No. 12,333. United States Intelligence Activities, Dec. 4, 1981, 3 C.F.R. 200 (1981), 46 F.R. 59941.

Exec. Order No. 12,334. President's Intelligence Oversight Board, Dec. 4, 1981, 3 C.F.R. 216 (1981), 46 F.R. 59955 (amended by Exec. Order 12,701, Feb. 14, 1990, 55 F.R. 5953).

Exec. Order No. 12,356. National Security Information, Apr. 2, 1982, 3 C.F.R. 166 (1982). Classification and declassification authority for United States government.

Exec. Order No. 12,530. Nicaraguan Humanitarian Assistance Office (temporary).

Exec. Order No. 12,537. President's Foreign Intelligence Advisory Board, Oct. 28, 1985, 3 C.F.R. 394 (1985), 50 F.R. 45083 (amended by Exec. Order 12,624).

National Security Council Directive 286, Oct.o15, 1987. Establishing post–Iran-Contra covert operations review process; a classified document, excerpted in 11 Hous. J. Int'l L. 235 (1988).

Exec. Order No. 12,654. Delegating authority to provide assistance for the Nicaraguan resistance, Oct. 7, 1988, 3 C.F.R. 583 (1988).

### U.S. Case Law

*Alvarez-Machain, et al., United States v.* 745 F. Supp. 599 (C.D. Cal. Aug. 10, 1990). See discussion in chapter 6.

*American Int'l Group, Inc. v. Islamic Republic of Iran,* 657 F.2d 430 (U.S. App. D.C. 1981). Legislative history and argument over applicability of the so-called Hostage Act in context of Iranian hostage crisis.

*AT&T, United States v.* 567 F. 2d 121 (D.C. Cir. 1977). Justice Department challenge to subpoena issued to AT&T by Congressional subcommittee investigating warrantless "national security" wiretaps. Political question doctrine does not preclude judicial resolution; Speech and Debate Clause does not immunize congressional investigations from judicial review; executive does not have absolute discretion in area of national security. The court ordered implementation of judicial procedures for incorporating *in camera* review and limited committee access.

*Avery v. United States,* 434 F. Supp. 937 (1977). Federal Torts Claims Act (FTCA) suit against U.S. government seeking monetary damages for injuries allegedly sustained as a result of wrongful acts by government intelligence agents during CIA covert mail opening and reading operation known as HTLINGUAL. Defendant's motion to dismiss denied. The court ruled that Congress had consented to suits under FTCA of this type as the suit did not fall within four FTCA exceptions: (1) "There was no apparent personal or nongovernmental motivation behind the CIA's conduct, as is characteristically the case where employees act outside the scope of their employment. Hence the scope of employment limitation . . . is not a bar to plaintiff's action . . . " (2) Although "the decision to engage HTLINGUAL seems clearly to have been made at a high enough policy level so as to ordinarily come within ambit of sec. 2680(a) [discretionary function exception], . . . 'it is, of course a tautology that a federal official cannot have discretion to behave unconstitutionally or outside the scope of his delegated authority.'" (3) ". . . Plaintiff's letters were neither lost, miscarried, nor negligently transmitted; they were intentionally taken out of the mail . . . " thus "postal matter" exception does not apply. (4) "Plaintiff's legal claim, which basically sounds in the constitutional tort of invasion of privacy, is not among the specific intentional torts excepted by [FTCA]." See also, *Cruikshank v. United States,* 431 F. Supp. 1355 (1977).

*Bas v. Tingy,* 4 U.S. (4 Dall.) 37, 1 L. Ed. 731 (1800). Judicial discussion of distinction between "perfect" and "imperfect" war in the context of undeclared naval war fought with France in 1798–1800. A United States private armed ship commanded by Tingy captured a French privateer, formerly the commercial vessel *Eliza,* of which John Bas was master. At issue was the amount of salvage to be allowed Tingy and his crew. The decision turns upon interpretation of two statutes, one referring directly to France, the other to "the enemy." Washington, Justice: "The decision of this question must depend upon . . . whether . . . there subsisted a state of war between the two nations? . . . Congress is empowered to declare a general war, or congress may wage a limited war; limited in place, in objects, and in time. If a general war is declared, its extent and operations are only restricted and regulated by the *jus belli,* forming a part of the law of nations; but if a partial war is waged, its extent and operation depend on our municipal laws." Paterson, Justice: "As far as congress tolerated and authorised the war on our part, so far may we proceed in hostile operations."

*Belmont, United States v.* 301 U.S. 758 (1932). Settlement of Soviet claims ("Litinov Assignment") stemming from Soviet nationalization decrees. Valid exercise of the president's recognition power and supersedes New York State law. *See also United States v. Pink.*

*Berk v. Laird,* 429 F.2d 302 (2d Cir. 1970). Suit by army private first class seeking declaratory relief and permanent injunction forbidding specified government officials from sending him to Vietnam or Cambodia on grounds that "executive officials of the United States Government have exceeded their constitutional authority by commanding him to participate in military activity not properly authorized by Congress." Denial of preliminary injunction affirmed; remanded to district court. "The political question doctrine itself requires that a court decline to adjudicate an issue involving 'a lack of judicially discoverable and manageable standards for resolving it,' . . . If the executive branch engaged the nation in prolonged foreign military activities without any significant congressional authorization, a court might be able to determine that this extreme step violated a discoverable standard calling for *some* mutual participation by Congress in accordance with Article I, section 8."

The district court's subsequent decision in *Berke* is summarized in *Holtzman v. Schlesinger.* "This court . . . found that Congress in appropriations bills from 1965 through 1969 had shown 'its continued support of the Vietnam action' and that Congress' choice of appropriations bills rather than a formal declaration of war to effectuate its intent involved a political question which did not prevent the finding that the fighting in Vietnam was authorized by Congress and that such fighting was not a usurpation of power by either of the Presidents who had been in office after 1964."

*Chicago and Southern Air Lines, Inc. v. Waterman Steamship Corp.,* 333 U.S. 103 (1948). Statement of the Supreme Court's reluctance to decide cases involving issues of foreign policy—political question doctrine in foreign affairs. Expansive reading of the president's sole-organ power and role as commander-in-chief, particularly in relation to the intelligence services and state secrets privilege. The Civil Aeronautics Board (CAB), with the express approval of the president, granted an overseas air route to the Chicago and Southern Air Lines while denying the route to the rival Waterman Steamship Corporation. Waterman challenged the CAB's decision. The Court found that the CAB had acted pursuant to both congressionally delegated authority over foreign commerce and inherent presidential powers.

Such decisions are wholly confided by our Constitution to the political departments of government, Executive and Legislative. They are delicate, complex, and involve large elements of prophecy. They are and should be undertaken only by those directly responsible to the people whose welfare they advance or imperil. They are decisions of a kind for which the Judiciary has neither aptitude, facilities nor responsibility and have long been held to belong in the domain of political power not subject to judicial intrusion or inquiry.

The President, both as Commander-in-Chief and as the Nation's organ for foreign affairs, has available intelligence services whose reports are not and ought not to be published to the world. It would be intolerable that courts, without the relevant information, should review and perhaps nullify actions of the Executive taken on information properly held secret.

*Curtiss-Wright Export Corp., United States v.* 299 U.S. 304 (1936). Congress passed a joint resolution providing inter alia that "if the President finds that the prohibition of the sale of arms and munitions of war in the United States to those countries now engaged in armed conflict in the Chaco may contribute to the reestablishment of peace . . . it shall be unlawful to sell, except under such limitations and exceptions as the President prescribes, any arms or munitions of war in any place in the United States to the countries now engaged in that armed conflict . . . " The president issued two such proclamations. Defendants, charged with selling fifteen machine guns to Bolivia, challenged the joint resolution as an unconstitutional delegation of legislative powers. Held: the joint resolution was not an unconstitutional delegation of legislative powers; in international relations the president is the sole organ of the federal government.

Justice Sutherland's theory of sovereignty:

As a result of the separation from Great Britain by the colonies, acting as a unit, the powers of external sovereignty passed from the Crown not to the colonies severally, but to the colonies in their collective and corporate capacity as the United States of America. . . . It results that the investment of the federal government with the powers of external sovereignty did not depend upon the affirmative grants of the Constitution.

The Sole Organ power:

[T]he President alone has the power to speak or listen as a representative of the nation. . . . As Marshall said in his great argument of March 7, 1800, in the House of Representatives, "The President is the sole organ of the nation in its external relations, and its sole representative with foreign nations." . . . It is important to bear in mind that we are here dealing not alone with an authority vested in the President by an exertion of legislative power, but with such an authority plus the very delicate, plenary and exclusive power of the President as the sole organ of the federal government in the field of international relations—a power which does not require as a basis for its exercise an act of Congress, but which, of course, like every other governmental power, must be exercised in subordination to the applicable provisions of the Constitution.

On secrecy and agents:

Moreover, he, not Congress, has the better opportunity of knowing the conditions which prevail in foreign countries, and especially is this true in time of war. He has his confidential sources of information. He has his agents in the form of diplomatic, consular and other officials. Secrecy in respect of information gathered by them may be highly necessary, and the premature disclosure of it productive of harmful results.

*Dames & Moore v. Regan,* 453 U.S. 654 (1981). Challenge to the president's authority to nullify various attachments and liens on Iranian property in the United States pursuant to the Algiers Accords, an executive agreement between the United States and Iran ending the Iranian hostage crisis. Held:

[W]here, as here, the settlement of claims has been determined to be a necessary incident to the resolution of a major foreign policy dispute between our country and another, and where, as here, we can conclude that Congress acquiesced in the

President's action, we are not prepared to say that the President lacks the power to settle such claims.

Whether such a settlement violates the Fifth Amendment takings clause not ripe for decision. The Court, Justice Rehnquist writing, declined to conclude that IEEPA or the Hostage Act directly authorized the president's suspension of claims, but found presidential authority in the general tenor of Congress' legislation in this area, congressional acquiescence, and prior case law (e.g., *Pink*).

Such failure of Congress specifically to delegate authority does not, "especially . . . in the areas of foreign policy and national security," imply "congressional disapproval" of action taken by the Executive. . . . At least this is so where there is no contrary indication of legislative intent and when, as here, there is a history of congressional acquiescence in conduct of the sort engaged in by the President.

*Diggs v. Shultz,* 470 F.2d 461 (D.C. Cir. 1972), *cert. denied* 411 U.S. 931, 93 S.Ct. 1897, 36 L.Ed. 2d 390 ("Last in time doctrine"). Plaintiffs sought injunctive and declaratory relief to stop importation of chromite from Rhodesia. Issue arose from asserted conflict between (1) official authorization of such importation by the United States (the 1971 "Byrd Amendment" to the Strategic and Critical Materials Stock Piling Act), and (2) the treaty obligations of the United States under the U.N. Charter (i.e., Security Council Res. 232 (1966 expanded in 1968) directing that all states impose a trade embargo with Southern Rhodesia. Held: Although plaintiffs had standing to assert claim, case dismissed for failure to state a claim upon which relief could be granted.

No amount of statutory interpretation now can make the Byrd Amendment other than what it was as presented to the Congress, namely, a measure which would make— and was intended to make—the United States a certain treaty violator. Under our constitutional scheme Congress can denounce treaties if it sees fit to do so, and there is nothing the other branches can do about it.

*Durand v. Hollins,* 8 Fed. Cas. 111 (No. 4,186)(U.S. Ct. of App., S.D.N.Y. 1860). In response to a bottle being thrown at an American diplomat, defendant, the commander of a U.S. naval vessel, ordered the bombardment of the Nicaraguan town of Greytown. Durand, an American citizen, sued Hollins for trespass to recover damages to his property in Greytown. Hollins defended on grounds that he was following the lawful orders of the president and secretary of the navy and that "community of Greytown had forcibly usurped the possession of the place, and erected an independent government, not recognized by the United States, and had perpetrated acts of violence against the citizens of the United States and their property." The court ruled in favor of defendant Hollins.

The question whether it was the duty of the president to interpose for the protection of the citizens of Greytown against an irresponsible and marauding community that had established itself there, was a public political question, in which the government, as well as the citizens whose interests were involved, was concerned, and which belonged to the executive to determine. . . . Now, as it respects the interposition of the executive abroad, for the protection of the lives or property of the citizen, the duty must, of necessity, rest in the discretion of the president. Acts of lawless violence, or of threatened violence to the citizen or his property, cannot be anticipated and provided for; and the protection, to be effectual or of any avail, may, not unfrequently, require the most prompt and decided action. Under our system of government, the citizen abroad is as much entitled to protection as the citizen at home. The great object and duty of government is the protection of the lives, liberty, and property of the people composing it, whether abroad or at home; and any government failing in the accomplishment of the object, or the performance of the duty, is not worth preserving.

*Edwards v. Carter,* 580 F.2d 1055 (D.C. Cir. 1978). *cert. denied,* 436 U.S. 907 (1978). Challenge to Panama Canal Treaty as violation of property clause which grants Congress authority to dispose of the territory or other property belonging to the United States. Held: Article IV, sec. 3, cl. 2 is not the exclusive method contemplated by the Constitution for disposing of federal property; "we hold that the United States is not prohibited from employing an alternative means constitutionally authorized." Dicta: Treaty power must be read with, and is limited by, the appropriations power.

There are certain grants of authority to Congress which are, by their very terms, exclusive. In these areas, the treaty-making power and the power of Congress are not concurrent; rather, the only department of the federal government authorized to take actions is the Congress. For instance, the Constitution expressly provides only one method—congressional enactment—for the appropriation of money: "No Money shall be drawn from the Treasury, but in Consequence of Appropriations made by Law." Art. I, sec. 9, cl. 7. Thus, the expenditure of funds by the United States cannot be accomplished by self-executing treaty; implementing legislation appropriating such funds is indispensable.

*Fernandez, United States (by the Attorney General) v.* 887 F.2d 465 (4th Cir. 1989); *United States v. Fernandez,* No. 89–5819, Slip. op. (4th Cir. Sept. 6, 1990). CIPA case involving former CIA station chief charged by the independent counsel with lying under oath about activities taken in support of the Nicaraguan Contras. Charges dismissed following CIPA 6(e) filing by attorney general determining national security equities in disclosure outweighed law enforcement equities.

*Filartiga v. Pena-Irala,* 630 F.2d 876 (2d Cir. 1980). Held: deliberate torture perpetrated under color of official authority violates universally accepted norms of the international law of human rights, regardless of the nationality of the parties. Thus, whenever an alleged torturer is found and served with process by an alien within U.S. borders, 28 U.S.C. sec. 1350 provides federal jurisdiction.

*Fitzgibbon v. Central Intelligence Agency,* 578 F. Supp. 704 (1983). Upholding government's claim of FOIA act exemption concerning former CIA station locations, sources, and methods, but denying deletions relating to the installation in Ciudad Trujillo through May 1961. "The fact that a CIA station existed in the Dominican Republic until 1961 is publicly known within the meaning of Afshar v. Department of State."

*Frisbie v. Collins,* 342 U.S. 519 (1952). Case involving the forcible abduction of a murder suspect in Illinois to stand trial in Michigan in apparent violation of the federal Kidnapping Act. Held: Court does not lack jurisdiction over defendant's person because his presence was obtained by forcible abduction.

This Court has never departed from the rule announced in *Ker v. Illinois,* 119 U.S. 436, 444, that the power of a court to try a person for a crime is not impaired by the fact that he had been brought within the court's jurisdiction by reason of "forcible abduction." No persuasive reasons are now presented to justify overruling this line of cases. They rest on the sound basis that due process of law is satisfied when one present in court is convicted of crime after having been fairly apprized of the charges against him and after a fair trial in accordance with constitutional procedural safeguards. There is nothing in the Constitution that requires a court to permit a guilty person rightfully convicted to escape justice because he was brought to trial against his will.

*Frolova v. Union of Socialist Soviet Republics,* 761 F.2d 370 (7th Cir. 1985). Decision based in part on ruling that the United Nations Charter is not self-executing. Articles 55 and 56 are declarations of principles, not a code of legal rights, and thus do not create rights enforceable by private litigants in American courts.

*Garcia-Mir v. Meese,* 788 F.2d 1446 (11th Cir. 1986) *cert. denied,* 479 U.S. 889, 107 S.Ct. 289 (1986). Undocumented aliens detained in the Atlanta penitentiary, two classes of Mariel Cuban refugees, sought court ordered plan to provide for individual parole revocation hearings. Plaintiffs argued inter alia that attorney general's decision to terminate status review plan and incarcerate indefinitely pending efforts to deport, violated nonconstitutionally based due process liberty interest and general public international law principle against prolonged arbitrary detention. Held: "[T]he executive acts here evident constitute a sufficient basis for affirming the trial court's finding that international law does not control"; "[T]he appellees have stated no basis for relief under international law because any rights there extant have been extinguished by controlling acts of the executive and judicial branches."

To the extent possible, courts must construe American law so as to avoid violating principles of public international law. [Citations omitted]. But public international law is controlling only "where there is no treaty and no controlling executive or legislative act or judicial decision . . . "

. . . the *Paquette Habana* does not support the proposition that the acts of cabinet officers cannot constitute controlling executive acts. At best it suggests that lower level officials cannot by their acts render international law inapplicable.

*Goland v. Central Intelligence Agency,* 607 F.2d 339 (D.C. Cir. 1978). FOIA request exploring legislative history of the National Security Act of 1947. (A week after issuance of the court's opinion, denying the FOIA request, "hundreds" of relevant documents were found by the CIA "which had been stored in cardboard boxes and had not been organized in any fashion.") Petition for rehearing denied on grounds that an appellate court has no fact-finding function. "The proper procedure for dealing with newly discovered evidence is for the party to move for relief from the judgment in the district court."

*Goldwater v. Carter,* 617 F.2d 697 (D.C. Cir. 1979). Challenge to the president's authority to terminate Mutual Defense Treaty with the Republic of China absent Senate or Congressional participation.

"The Curtiss-Wright opinion . . . declares in oft-repeated language that the President is the sole organ of the federal government in the field of international relations." That status is not confined to the service of the President as a channel of communication, as the District Court suggested, but embraces an active policy determination as to the conduct of the United States in regard to a treaty in response to numerous problems and circumstances as they arise.

All we decide today is that two-thirds Senate consent or majority consent in both houses is not necessary to terminate this treaty in the circumstance before us now.

The Supreme Court vacated the judgment of the Court of Appeals and remanded to the District Court with orders to dismiss on the ground that the case was nonjusticiable, although the Court was divided on whether the proper ground for that decision was ripeness or the political question doctrine. 444 U.S. 997 (1979).

*Halperin v. Central Intelligence Agency,* 629 F.2d 144 (D.C. Cir. 1980). Plaintiff alleged that sections 403(d)(3) and 403g of Title 50 (the Central Intelligence Agency Act providing FOIA exemption to intelligence sources and methods) violated the Statement and Account Clause. Plaintiff had requested information on, among other things, legal fees paid to any attorneys or law firms retained by CIA. The CIA withheld documents related to legal services connected with covert or classified activities. Held: As evidenced by the intent of the framers and evidence of government practices, e.g., "the contingent fund" established in 1789, Congress and the president have discretion, not reviewable by the courts, to require secrecy for CIA expenditures.

*Holtzman v. Schlesinger,* 361 F. Supp. 553, *reversed* 484 F.2d 1307 (2d Cir. 1973), *cert. denied,* 416 U.S. 936 (1974). Challenge to president's authority to order 1973 bombing of Cambodia as outside congressional authorization. The District Court ruled that "[t]he bombing of Cambodia in July 1973 is 'not the sort of tactical decision traditionally confided to the Commander-in-Chief in the conduct of armed conflict,'" and found "that there is no Congressional authorization to fight in Cambodia after the withdrawal of American troops and the release of American prisoners of war." Summary judgment granted declaratory and equitable relief to halt bombing pending application for stay before Court of Appeals. Court of Appeals reversed on grounds that, whether or not a basic change in the war had occurred, or the Cambodian bombing constituted a "new war" presented nonjusticiable political question.

*I.N.S. v. Chadha,* 462 U.S. 919 (1983). Challenge to one House legislative veto. Pursuant to section 244(c)(2) of the Immigration and Nationality Act, House passed .resolution overriding decision of immigration judge and attorney general to suspend deportation of Chadha. Resolution was not submitted to the Senate or presented to the president for his action. Held: Section 244(c)(2) violates presentment clauses and bicameral requirement of the Constitution in that the action taken by the House was "essentially legislative in purpose and effect."

In purporting to exercise power defined in Art. I, sec. 8, cl. 4, to "establish an uniform Rule of Naturalization," the House took action that had the purpose and effect of altering the legal rights, duties, and relations of persons, including the Attorney General, Executive Branch officials and Chadha, all outside the Legislative Branch.

Justice White, Dissenting:

[T]he Court would have been well advised to decide the cases, if possible, on the narrower grounds of separation of powers. . . . Over the quarter century following World War II, Presidents continued to accept legislative vetoes by one or both Houses as constitutional, while regularly denouncing provisions by which congressional Committees reviewed Executive activity. . . . The legislative veto is an important if not indispensable political invention which allows the President and Congress to resolve major constitutional and policy differences, assures the accountability of independent regulatory agencies, and preserves Congress' control over lawmaking.

White appended to his opinion a list of fifty-five statutes containing provisions for legislative review, including twelve "Foreign Affairs and National Security" statutes.

*Ker v. Illinois,* 119 U.S. 436 (1886). Foreign application of the "Ker-Frisbie" doctrine. Personal jurisdiction challenge to state conviction of U.S. citizen abducted by Pinkerton agent in Peru to stand trial in Illinois. The Pinkerton agent was carrying extradition papers for Ker, but chose not to use them. At the time, Peru was under occupation by Chile.

The "due process of law" here guaranteed is complied with when the party is regularly indicted by the proper grand jury in the state court, has a trial according to the forms and modes prescribed for such trials, and when, in that trial and proceedings, he is deprived of no rights to which he is lawfully entitled. . . . [B]ut for mere irregularities in the manner in which he may be brought into the custody of the law, we do not think he is entitled to say that he should not be tried at all for the crime with which he is charged in a regular indictment.

So here, when found within the jurisdiction of the state of Illinois, and liable to answer for a crime against the laws of that state, unless there was some positive provision of the constitution or of the laws of this country violated in bringing him into court, it is not easy to see how he can say that he is there "without due process of law," within the meaning of the constitutional provision.

In fact, that [extradition] treaty was not called into operation . . . the facts show that it was a clear case of kidnapping within the dominions of Peru, without any pretense of authority under the treaty or from the government of the United States.

. . . this view of the subject does not leave the prisoner, or the government of Peru, without remedy for his unauthorized seizure within its territory. Even this treaty with that country provides for the extradition of persons charged with kidnapping, and, on demand from Peru, Julian, the party who is guilty of it, could be surrendered, and tried . . .

*Letelier v. Republic of Chile*, 488 F. Supp. 665 (1980). Tort claim against the government of Chile stemming from 1976 assassination of former Chilean Foreign Minister Orlando Letelier and aide Ronni Moffitt in Washington. Held: Court has subject matter jurisdiction over action; Chile can not claim sovereign immunity under Foreign Sovereign Immunities Act nor excuse itself from jurisdiction of court on basis of act of state doctrine when "the actions of its alleged agents resulted in tortious injury in this country."

While it seems apparent that a decision calculated to result in injury or death to a particular individual or individuals, made for whatever reason, would be one most assuredly involving policy judgment and decision and thus exempt as a discretionary act under section 1605(a)(5)(A)[of the FSIA], that exception is not applicable to bar this suit. . . . Whatever policy options may exist for a foreign country, it has no "discretion" to perpetrate conduct designed to result in the assassination of an individual or individuals, action that is clearly contrary to the precepts of humanity as recognized in both national and international law.

*Little v. Barreme*, 6 U.S. (2 Cranch) 170 (1804). Captain of U.S. frigate answerable to owners of neutral vessel for damages stemming from seizure on high seas during undeclared naval war with France. An act of Congress, the non-intercourse law, provided that "no ship or vessel owned, hired or employed, wholly or in part, by any person resident within the United States, and which shall depart therefrom, shall be allowed to proceed directly, or from any intermediate port or place, to any port or place within the territory of the French Republic, or to any place in the West Indies . . . " Executive instructions to the commanders of U.S. ships, however, ordered commanders "to be vigilant that vessels or cargoes really American but covered by Danish or other foreign papers, and bound to and from French ports, do not escape you." Pursuant to these instructions Captain Little of the frigate *Boston* captured the *Flying Fish* en route from Jeremie to St. Thomas (i.e., not to France) with Danish and neutral property on board. While admitting a bias that "though the instructions of the executive could not give a right, they might yet excuse from damages," Justice Marshall for the Court, ruled against Captain Little. "That implicit obedience which military men usually pay to the orders of their superiors, which indeed is indispensably necessary to every military system, appeared to me strongly to imply the principle, that those orders, if not to perform a prohibited act, ought to justify the person whose general duty it is to obey them, and who is placed by the laws of his country in a situation which, in general, requires that he should obey them. I was strongly inclined to think, that where, in consequence of orders from the legitimate authority, a vessel is seized, with pure intention, the claim of the injured party for damages would be against that government from which the orders proceeded, and would be a proper subject for negotiation. But . . . I have receded from this first opinion. I acquiesce in that of my brethren, which is, that the instructions cannot change the nature of the transaction, nor legalize an act which, without those instructions, would have been a plain trespass . . . since had she been an American, the seizure would have been unlawful [in that she was not bound to a French port but from a French port]."

*Lowry, et al. v. Reagan,* 676 F. Supp. 333 (D.D.C. 1987). Suit by 115 members of Congress for declaratory judgment and injunctive relief in form of a court order compelling the president to submit a report to Congress pursuant to sec. 4(a)(1) of the War Powers Resolution. Suit arose in context of the commitment of U.S. forces to the Persian Gulf to escort reflagged Kuwaiti oil tankers. Section 4(a)(1) of the resolution provides that in the absence of a declaration of war in any case in which U.S. armed forces are introduced into hostilities or situations where imminent involvement in hostilities is clearly indicated by the circumstances; the president shall submit within forty-eight hours a report in writing. The congressional members alleged that absent such a submission by the president, or a court finding that a report was required to be submitted, plaintiffs were disenfranchised from voting pursuant to sec. 5(b) of the resolution which provides that "within sixty days after a report is submitted or required to be submitted the President shall terminate any use of U.S. armed forces for which the report was submitted unless Congress (1) declares war or enacts specific authorization . . . " The district court declined to exercise jurisdiction and dismissed case on basis of political question doctrine and considerations of equitable discretion. "This Court declines to accept jurisdiction to render a decision that, regardless of its substance, would impose a consensus on Congress. . . . Judicial review of the constitutionality of the War Powers Resolution is not, however, pre-cluded by this decision. A true confrontation between the Executive and a unified Congress, as evidenced by its passage of legislation to enforce the Resolution, would pose a question ripe for judicial review." Appeal dismissed: As to U.S. forces then currently involved in the Persian Gulf—appeal dismissed as a nonjusticiable politi-cal question; as to hostilities "present" or "imminent" in the past—the claim is moot. Order, United States Court of Appeals, District of Columbia Circuit, Oct. 17, 1988.

*Lujan v. Gengler,* 510 F.2d 62 *cert. denied,* 421 U.S. 1001 (1975). Second Circuit applying and narrowing *Toscanino:* only where the defendant proves "government conduct of a most shocking and outrageous kind" will due process be violated and the Toscanino exception to Ker-Frisbie apply. "Lujan, a licensed pilot, was hired in Argentina by one Duran to fly him to Bolivia. Duran had been hired by American agents to lure Lujan to Bolivia. Once in Bolivia Lujan was taken into custody by Bolivian police who were not acting at the direction of their own superiors or government, but as paid agents of the United States. Lujan was not permitted to communicate with the Argentine embassy, an attorney, or any member of his family . . . " Five days later, Bolivian police, acting together with American agents, placed Lujan on a plane bound for New York. The court ruled against Lujan. "In sum, but for the charge that the law was violated during the process of transporting him to the United States, Lujan charges no deprivation greater than that which he would have endured through lawful extradition. . . . [W]e recognized in *Toscanino* that abduction from another country violates international law only when the offended state objects to the conduct."

*Matta-Ballesteros ex rel. Stolar v. Henman,* 697 F. Supp. 1040 (S.D. Ill. 1988), *aff'd,* 896 F.2d 255 (7th Cir. 1990). Defendant, a Honduran citizen, sought habeas corpus alleging that he was illegally abducted from his home in Honduras and tortured by Honduran special troops and United States marshals before being transported to United States to face narcotics charges. Specifically, Matta-Ballesteros asserted that his arrest violated the Honduran Constitution and two extradition treaties that bar the extradition of Honduran nationals and violated his Fourth and Fifth Amendment due process rights. Held: Defendant was not entitled to evidentiary hearing on allegations. Notwithstanding alleged popular protests before the American embassy and introduction of a bill in Honduran legislature objecting to abduction (which was never voted on), "Without an official protest, we cannot conclude that Honduras has objected to Matta's arrest. . . . It is well established that individuals have no standing to challenge violations of international treaties in the absence of a protest by the sovereigns involved."

*Meese v. Keene,* 481 U.S. 465 (1987). Suit to enjoin application of Foreign Registration Act on basis of First Amendment. California State Senator sought to show three Canadian films (*If You Love this Planet, Acid Rain: Requiem or Recovery, Acid Rain from Heaven*) deemed "political propaganda" by the chief of the registration unit of the Internal Security Section, Criminal Division, Department of Justice. Held: Plaintiff had standing to challenge act, but the term *propaganda* is neutral and therefore constitutionally permissible. "[D]espite the absence of any direct abridgment of speech, the District Court in this case assumed that the reactions of the public to the label 'political propaganda' would be such that the label would interfere with freedom of speech. . . . We should presume that the people who have a sufficient understanding of the law to know that the term 'political propaganda' is used to describe the regulated category also know that the definition is a broad, neutral one rather than a pejorative one."

*Mitchell v. Laird,* 488 F.2d 611 (D.C. Cir. 1973). Challenge to constitutionality of war in Vietnam absent Congressional Declaration of War.

We are unanimously agreed that it is constitutionally permissible for Congress to use another means than a formal declaration of war to give its approval to a war such as is involved in the protracted and substantial hostilities in Indo-China. . . . [W]e deem it a political question, or to phrase it more accurately, a discretionary matter for Congress to decide in which form, if any, it will give its consent to the continuation of a war already begun by a President acting alone.

*Neagle, In re* 135 U.S. 1 (1890). Neagle, a deputy U.S. marshal, while assigned to protect Supreme Court Justice Stephen J. Field, riding as circuit justice, shot and killed a would-be assailant. Neagle was subsequently charged with murder and held by Sheriff Cunningham. On petition for release, the state of California argued that no statute authorized Neagle's action. The Court, however, found that Neagle's actions were within both the scope of the president's duty to take care that the laws be faithfully executed and consistent with positive statutory law granting U.S. marshals the same powers as local sheriffs in executing the laws of the United States.
In dicta, the Court sought to define the scope of the president's duty to take care that the laws be faithfully executed. "Is this duty limited to the enforcement of acts of congress or of treaties of the United States according to their express terms; or does it include the rights, duties, and obligations growing out of the constitution itself, our international relations, and all the protection implied by the nature of the government under the constitution?" The Court answered by way of illustration with the case of Martin Koszta, a native of Hungary who was seized by the Austrian Consul-General in Smyrna while in possession of his U.S. naturalization papers. Kostza was released to the French consul pending diplomatic negotiations after an American warship entered the harbor and trained its guns on the Austrian vessel. The captain of the U.S. vessel subsequently received a congressional gold medal. The Court asked rhetorically: "Upon what act of congress then existing can any one lay his finger in support of the action of our government in this matter?"

*Palestine Liberation Organization, United States v.* 695 F. Supp. 1456, 1464–65 (S.D.N.Y. 1988).

Congress has the power to enact statutes abrogating prior treaties or international obligations entered into by the United States. [Citations omitted]. However, unless this power is unequivocally exercised, this court is under a duty to interpret statutes in a manner consonant with existing treaty obligations. . . .

Only where a treaty is irreconcilable with a later enacted statute and Congress has clearly evinced an intent to supersede a treaty by enacting a statute does the later enacted treaty take precedence.

*Paquette Habana,* 175 U.S. 677 (1900). U.S. Navy gunboats seized two Cuban fishing vessels in Cuban coastal waters as prizes of war during the Spanish American War. The Court held that the vessels were not subject to capture under customary international law.

International law is part of our law, and must be ascertained and administered by the courts of justice of appropriate jurisdiction, as often as questions of right depending upon it are duly presented for their determination. For this purpose, where there is no treaty, and no controlling executive or legislative act or judicial decision, resort must be had to the customs and usages of civilized nations; . . . by the general consent of the civilized nations of the world, and independent of any express treaty or other public act, it is an established rule of international law, . . . that coast fishing vessels,

. . . unarmed and honestly pursuing their peaceful calling . . . are exempt from capture as prize of war.

*Pink, United States v.* 315 U.S. 203 (1942). As a condition precedent to U.S. recognition, the Soviet government in 1933 assigned to the U.S. government its claims against certain assets in the United States held by businesses that earlier had been nationalized by the Soviet government. Held: Power over external affairs is not shared by the States; it is vested in the national government exclusively.

Power to remove such obstacles to full recognition as settlement of claims of our nationals certainly is a modest implied power of the President who is the "sole organ of the federal government in the field of international relations."

*The Prize Cases,* 67 U.S. (2 Black) 635 (1862). At the outset of the Civil War, President Lincoln imposed a blockade of Southern coastal states. No statute authorized a president to do so. The prize cases were cases of condemnation by district attorneys for the vessels seized. Claimants took appeal from condemnation. The Court upheld the president's actions (5–4) Justice Grier:

Whether the President in fulfilling his duties, as Commander in chief, in suppressing an insurrection, has met with such armed hostile resistance, and a civil war of such alarming proportions as will compel him to accord to them the character of belligerents, is a question to be decided *by him,* and this Court must be governed by the decisions and acts of the political department of the Government to which this power was entrusted. "He must determine what degree of force the crisis demands." The proclamation of blockade is itself official and conclusive evidence to the Court that a state of war existed which demanded and authorized a recourse to such a measure, under the circumstances peculiar to the case.

And finally, in 1861, we find Congress *"ex majore cautela"* and in anticipation of such astute objections, passing an act approving, legalizing, and making valid all the acts, proclamations, and orders of the President, etc., as if they had been *issued and done under the previous express authority* and direction of the Congress of the United States.

*Reynolds, United States v.* 345 U.S. 1 (1952). Upholding state military secrets privilege, pre-CIPA, in context of civil discovery request by survivors of personnel killed in a military aircraft crash where aircraft was on a flight to test secret equipment. "The Court itself must determine whether the circumstances are appropriate for the claim of privilege, and yet to do so without forcing a disclosure of the very thing the privilege is designed to protect." See also, *Nixon v. Sirica,* 487 F.2d 700, 762–81 (D.C. Cir. 1973). (It is for the court to determine applicability of executive privilege to material subpoenaed by grand jury.)

*Rochin v. California,* 342 U.S. 165 (1952). When law enforcement officers entered defendant's bedroom, defendant swallowed capsules. In ensuing struggle, officers tried to open Rochin's mouth and remove what was there. An emetic was later forced into defendant's stomach to produce swallowed evidence. Evidence inadmissible; actions violated due process clause of the Fourteenth Amendment.

These standards of justice are not authoritatively formulated anywhere as though they were specifics. Due process of law is a summarized constitutional guarantee of respect for those personal immunities which . . . are "so rooted in the traditions and conscience of our people as to be ranked as fundamental," or are "implicit in the concept of ordered liberty."

This is conduct that shocks the conscience. Illegally breaking into the privacy of the petitioner, the struggle to open his mouth and remove what was there, the forcible extraction of his stomach's contents—this course of proceeding by agents of the government to obtain evidence is bound to offend even hardened sensibilities.

*The Schooner Exchange v. McFaddon,* 11 U.S. 116 (7 Cranch) (1812). In 1809, an American schooner, the *Exchange,* was seized by a French warship while en route to Spain. Two years later, the same vessel, now sailing as the French armed vessel *Balaou,* was forced by weather into Philadelphia. The original owners of the vessel including McFaddon brought process to assert title over the vessel. The U.S. government petitioned to quash the decree of allotment. Held: Chief Justice Marshall for the Court, "[N]ational ships of war, entering the port of a friendly power, open for their reception, are to be considered as exempted by the consent of that power from its jurisdiction."

The preceding reasoning, has maintained the propositions that all exemptions from territorial jurisdiction, must be derived from the consent of the sovereign of the territory; that this consent may be implied or expressed; and that when implied, its extent must be regulated by the nature of the case, and the views under which the parties requiring and conceding it must be supposed to act.

*Senate Select Committee on Presidential Campaign Activities v. Nixon,* 498 F.2d 725 (D.C. Cir. 1974). Committee sought declaratory judgment that president had duty to comply with subpoena for documents ("original electronic tapes").

We must, however, consider the nature of its need when we are called upon, in the first such case in our history, to exercise the equity power of a court at the request of a congressional committee, in the form of a judgment that the President must disclose to the Committee records of conversations between himself and his principal aides. We conclude that the need demonstrated by the Select Committee in the peculiar circumstances of this case, including the subsequent and on-going investigation of the House Judiciary Committee, is too attenuated and too tangential to its functions to permit a judicial judgment that the President is required to comply with the Committee's subpoena.

*Toscanino, United States v.* 500 F.2d 267 (2d Cir. 1974). See discussion in chapter 6. *United States v. Toscanino,* 398 F. Supp. 916 (1975). On remand Toscanino's motion to dismiss denied.

*ιotten Administrator v. United States,* 92 U.S. 105 (1875). President "undoubtedly authorized during the war [Civil War], as commander-in-chief of the armies of the United States, to employ secret agents . . . and contracts to compensate such agents are so far binding upon the government as to render it lawful for the President to direct payment of the amount stipulated out of the contingent fund under his control."

*Verdugo-Urquidez, United States v.* 494 U.S. 259, 110 S.Ct. 1056 (1990). Defendant was arrested in Mexico by Mexican police officers who delivered Verdugo-Urquidez to U.S. agents at the border. Defendant moved for suppression of evidence obtained during search of his residence in Mexico by Drug Enforcement Agency (DEA) investigators. Held: The Fourth Amendment does not apply to the search and seizure of property that is owned by a nonresident alien and located in a foreign country.

*Whitney v. Robertson,* 124 U.S. 190 (1888). Last in Time Doctrine: "When the two [treaty and statute] relate to the same subject, the courts will always endeavor to construe them so as to give effect to both, if that can be done without violating the language of either; but, if the two are inconsistent, the one last in date will control the other; provided, always, the treaty on the subject is self-executing."

*Winter v. United States,* 509 F.2d 975 (5th Cir. 1975), *cert. denied* Sub. nom. *Parks v. United States,* 423 U.S. 825. Challenge to court's jurisdiction by Jamaican and Bahamian nationals seized by Coast Guard 35 miles off the Florida coast and within 11.9 miles of the Bahamas on basis that resort to self-help violated treaty of extradition. Held: Court has jurisdiction because Ker-Frisbie doctrine applies to nonresident aliens as well.

*Youngstown Sheet & Tube Co. v. Sawyer,* 343 U.S. 579 (1952). During the Korean War a collective bargaining dispute arose between the steel companies and their employees. Mediation having failed, in April1952 the United Steelworkers of America gave notice of a nationwide strike. Hours before the strike was to begin, President Truman ordered the secretary of commerce to take possession of most of the steel mills and keep them running. The Court ruled that authority for presidential actions must come either from statute or from the constitution. The president was not acting pursuant to an express or implied statutory authorization to take possession of property as done. Nor was the president acting within his executive power, or constitutional authority as commander-in-chief or to take care that the laws be faithfully executed. Hence, the president was exercising a law-amking function, i.e., a legislative function in violation of the constitutional separation of powers.

In commentary and case law, Justice Jackson's concurrence has, in effect, assumed the stature of the Court's holding, see e.g., *Dames and Moore* at 674 and H. Koh, The National Security Constitution at 105–13. Jackson formulated three relative categories of presidential power "depending upon their disjunction or conjunction with those of Congress."

1. When the President acts pursuant to an express or implied authorization of Congress, his authority is at its maximum, for it includes all that he possesses in his own right plus all that Congress can delegate . . .

2. When the President acts in absence of either a congressional grant or denial of authority, he can only rely on his own independent powers, but there is a zone of

twilight in which he and Congress may have concurrent authority, or in which distribution is uncertain . . .

3. When the President takes measures incompatible with the expressed or implied will of Congress, his power is at its lowest ebb, for then he can only rely on his own powers minus any constitutional powers of Congress over the matter . . .

Jackson found that the president's acts fell into category three, and could not be sustained on the president's independent constitutional authority as chief executive officer or commander-in-chief. Jackson noted, however, that his analysis might have been different "were the case not one of domestic focus."

I should indulge the widest latitude of interpretation to sustain his exclusive function to command the instruments of national force, at least when turned against the outside world for the security of our society. But, when it is turned inward, not because of rebellion but because of a lawful economic struggle between industry and labor, it should have no such indulgence.

Justice Frankfurter, concurring, highlighted the principle that

a systematic, unbroken, executive practice, long pursued to the knowledge of the Congress and never before questioned, engaged in by Presidents who have also sworn to uphold the Constitution, making as it were such exercise of power part of the structure of our government, may be treated as a gloss on "executive Power" vested in the President by sec. 1 of Art. II.

Frankfurter, however, found the principle of constitutional gloss inapplicable to the president's actions in this case.

*Yunis, United States v.* 681 F. Supp. 896 (D.D.C. 1988). In 1987, Fawaz Yunis, the suspected ringleader of the 1985 hijacking of Royal Jordanian Air flight 402, was lured into international waters off the coast of Cyprus and arrested by Federal Bureau of Investigation agents. After being charged in a multicount indictment in the U.S. district court for the District of Columbia, Yunis filed a variety of motions challenging the jurisdiction of the court, the manner in which he was arrested and his access to classified government information. The court decisions on these motions are briefly summarized below. Jurisdiction under international law. Defendant moved to dismiss indictment on grounds that court lacked subject matter jurisdiction under international law and United States Code for crimes committed in foreign air space and on foreign soil. After reviewing five traditional bases of jurisdiction under international law (territorial, national, protective, universal, passive personal) and principles of domestic jurisdiction, court dismissed three counts and part of a fourth, but denied motion to dismiss on five counts. Dicta:

When another government harbors international terrorists or is unable to enforce international law, it is left to the world community to respond and prosecute the alleged terrorists. As long as governments which step into this enforcement role act within the constraints imposed by international and domestic law, their efforts to combat terrorism should be praised.

*Yunis, United States v.* 681 F. Supp. 909 (D.D.C. 1988). Pretrial motion to dismiss indictment on grounds that seizure in international waters violated extradition treaties with Cyprus and Lebanon and that "outrageous government conduct" in course of the arrest divested court of jurisdiction (*Toscanino* challenge). In addition, defendant challenged the validity of a confession taken after his arrest as violative of his Fifth Amendment Miranda rights and Sixth Amendment right to counsel. The court ruled that "(1) individuals, alone, are not empowered to enforce extradition treaties; (2) the government's actions did not rise to level of 'outrageousness' that 'shocks the conscience;'(3) defendant did not knowingly and voluntarily waive his right against compulsory self-incrimination or right to counsel." But see, *United States v. Yunis,* 859 F.2d 953 (D.C. Cir. 1988). Reversing district court's order suppressing use of confession at trial.

*Yunis, United States v.* 867 F.2d 617 (D.C. Cir. 1989). Application of CIPA. Defendant sought discovery of fourteen transcripts of conversations between defendant and informant. Held: "[T]hat the contents of the transcripts were on the whole not relevant to the defendant's guilt or innocence and the few statements that were even marginally relevant were not sufficiently helpful or beneficial to overcome the classified information privilege. We conclude the District Court abused its discretion in ordering the disclosure . . . "

### Government Documents

*Alleged Assassination Plots Involving Foreign Leaders,* An Interim Report of the Select Committee to Study Governmental Operations with Respect to Intelligence Activities (1976).

Congressional Record, 25066–25076, July 20, 1973 ("a chronological list of 199 U.S. military hostilities abroad without a declaration of war, 1798–1972" submitted by Sen. Barry Goldwater during debate over the War Powers Resolution).

Department of Defense Dictionary of Military and Associated Terms, Joint Chiefs of Staff Publication 1 (1987).

Digest of United States Practice in International Law 1974, Department of State, Office of the Legal Adviser (A. Rovine ed. 1975).

Digest of United States Practice in International Law 1979, Department of State, Office of the Legal Adviser (M. Nash ed. 1983).

Digest of United States Practice in International Law 1980, Department of State, Office of the Legal Adviser (Leich ed. 1986).

Final Report of the Select Committee to Study Governmental Operations with Respect to Intelligence Activities, Apr. 1976, Rep. No. 94–755 (Church Committee Report).

Hearings before the Select Committee to Study Governmental Operations with Respect to Intelligence Activities, vol. 7, Covert Action (1976).

House Select Committee to Investigate Covert Arms Transactions with Iran and Senate Select Committee on Secret Military Assistance to Iran and the Nicaraguan Opposition, Report of the Congressional Committees Investigating the Iran-Contra Affair, S. Rep. No. 216, H. Rep. No. 433 (1987).

Letter from Senator Barry Goldwater to Director of Central Intelligence William Casey, Apr. 9, 1984, re: Mining of Nicaraguan Harbors.

*Meeting the Espionage Challenge,* Report of the Select Committee on Intelligence, United States Senate (1986).

Procedures Governing Reporting to the Senate Select Committee on Intelligence (SSCI) on Covert Action, June 6, 1984; and, June 1986 Addendum to Procedures ("Casey Accords").

Report by the Advisory Board for Radio Broadcasting to Cuba (1989).

Report on the Covert Activities of the Central Intelligence Agency, Sept. 30, 1954 (Doolittle Committee).

Report of the Department of Defense Commission on Beirut International Airport Terrorist Act, Oct. 23, 1983 (Long Commission)(Dec. 20, 1983).

Report to the President by the President's Commission on Aviation Security and Terrorism, May 15, 1990.

Report of the Senate Select Committee on Intelligence, Jan. 1, 1979 to Dec. 31, 1980, S. Rep. No. 193 (1981).

Report of the Senate Select Committee on Intelligence, Jan. 1, 1981 to Dec. 31, 1982, S. Rep. No. 10, (1983).

Report of the Senate Select Committee on Intelligence, Jan. 1, 1985 to Dec. 31, 1986, S. Rep. No. 236 (1990).

Report of the Senate Select Committee on Intelligence, Jan. 1, 1987 to Dec. 31, 1988, S. Rep. No. 219 (1990).

S. Rep. Nos. 101–174, 101st Cong., 1st Sess. (1989) (to accompany S. 1324 the Intelligence Authorization Act for FY 1990 and 1991).

S. Rep. No. 101–358, 101st Cong., 2d Sess. (1990) (to accompany S. 2834, Intelligence Authorization Act for FY 1991).

*Soviet Active Measures,* Hearings before the Permanent Select Committee on Intelligence (1982).

*Soviet Active Measures,* Hearings before the Subcommittee on European Affairs, Committee on Foreign Relations, United States Senate (1985).

M. Whiteman, Digest of United States Practice in International Law, vols. 4 (1965), 5 (1965), 10 (1968), Department of State.

### 2. COMPARATIVE INTELLIGENCE OVERSIGHT

Andrew, *The Growth of the Australian Intelligence Community and the Anglo-American Connection,* 4 Intelligence and National Security 213 (1989).

Bill C-9, 2d Sess., 32d Parliament, 32 Elizabeth II, 1983–84, "The Canadian Security Intelligence Service Act," (sec. 34 establishes the Security Intelligence Review Committee.)

Blais, *The Political Accountability of Intelligence Agencies—Canada,* 4 Intelligence and National Security 108 (1989).

Gill, *Symbolic or Real? The Impact of the Canadian Security Intelligence Review Committee,* 4 Intelligence and National Security 550 (1989).

Richelson, *Foreign Intelligence Organizations* (1988).

Roy, *Canadian Security and Intelligence: A Bibliography* (1986).

Royal Commission on Intelligence and Security, *Report,* Canberra: Australian Government Pub. Service (1977).

Security Intelligence Review Committee, Annual Report, 1985–86.

### 3. UNITED NATIONS DOCUMENTS

G.A. Res. 110 (II) (1949). Measures to be taken against propaganda and the inciters of a new war.

G.A. Res. 1514 (xv), (1960). Special committee to examine application of Declaration on Granting Independence.

G.A. Res. 1654 (xvi), (1961). Special committee.

G.A. Res. 1761 (1962). Sanctions against South Africa.

G.A. Res. 2200A, International Covenant on Civil and Political Rights (1966). Also 999 U.N.T.S. 171, 6 I.L.M. 369 (1967).

G.A. Res. 2625, Declaration on Principles of International Law concerning Friendly Relations and Co-Operation among States in Accordance with the Charter of the United Nations (1970).

G.A. Res. 2734 (xxv), Declaration on the Strengthening of International Security (1970).

G.A. Res. 3281 (xxix), Charter of Economic Rights and Duties of States (1974).

G.A. Res. 3201 (xxix), Declaration on the Establishment of a New International Economic Order (1974).

G.A. Res. 3314, Definition of Aggression (1974).

G.A. Res. 36/103, Declaration on the Inadmissibility of Intervention in the Internal Affairs of States (1981).

G.A. Res. 35/206 (1980). Sanctions against Rhodesia.

G.A. Res. 36/27, (1981). Israeli attack on Iraq nuclear reactor.

G.A. Res. 36/34, The Situation in Afghanistan and Its Implications for International Peace and Security (1981).

G.A. Res. 36/172C, Acts of Aggression by the *Apartheid* Regime against Angola and Other Independent African States (1981).

G.A. Res. 37/92, Principles Governing the Use by States of Artificial Earth Satellites for International Direct Television Broadcasting (1983).

G.A. Res. 41/38, on the aerial and naval military attack against the Socialist People's Libyan Arab Jamahiriya by the present United States Administration (1986).

G.A. Res. 173, Economic Measures as a Means of Political and Economic Coercion against Developing Countries (1987).

G.A. Res. 185, Trade Embargo against Nicaragua (1988).

S.C. Res. 56, (1948). Middle East conflict and reprisals.

S.C. Res. 138, Question Relating to the Case of Adolf Eichmann (1961).

S.C. Res. 188, Harib Incident and Reprisals (1964).

S.C. Res. 228, Military Reprisals by Israel (1966).

S.C. Res. 333 (1973). Sanctions against Rhodesia.

S.C. Res. 457 (1980). Seizure of United States hostages in Teheran.

S.C. Res. 461 (1980). Seizure of United States hostages in Teheran.

S.C. Res. 611, (1988). Assassination of Khalil al-Wazir.

U.N. Doc. A/8340, Draft Convention on Freedom of Information (1971).

U.N. Doc. A/4708 letter to President of the General Assembly from Cuban Minister for External Affairs, Mar. 13, 1961.

20 U.N.E.S.C.O. GCOF, Res. 100, U.N.E.S.C.O. Doc. 20C/Res. 3/3.2/2, Declaration on Fundamental Principles concerning the Contribution of the Mass Media to Strengthening Peace and International Understanding to the Promotion of Human Rights and to Countering War Propaganda, Racialism, Apartheid and Incitement to War (1978).

*Many Voices One World* (Report of the International Commission for the Study of Communication Problems) (MacBride Commission) U.N.E.S.C.O. (1980).

Report of the International Law Commission on the Work of Its Thirty-first Session: State Responsibility, 2 Y.B. Int'l L. Comm'n. (1980).

Report of the Special Committee on the Question of Defining Aggression, Mar. 11 to Apr. 12, 1974, 29 U.N. GAOR, Supp. No. 19.

Sixth Report on the Content, Forms and Degrees of International Responsibility, 2 Y.B. Int'l L. Comm'n (1985).

Seventh Report on State Responsibility by Mr. Willem Riphagen, Special Rapporteur, 2 Y.B. Int'l L. Comm'n (1986).

*Yearbook of the United Nations,* Department of Public Information, United Nations, New York.

### 4. TREATIES AND CONVENTIONS

Agreement relating to the privileges and immunities of all members of the Soviet and American embassies and their families, with agreed minute, 30 U.S.T. 2341, T.I.A.S. 9340 (Dec. 14, 1978).

Charter of the Organization of American States (OAS), 2 U.S.T. 2394, T.I.A.S. 2361, 119 U.N.T.J. 3 (1948)(entered into force for the United States 1951).

Charter of the United Nations, signed at San Francisco June 26, 1945; entered into force Oct. 24, 1945. 59 Stat. 1031, TS 993, 3 Bevans 1153.

Conference on Security and Co-Operation in Europe, Final Act (Helsinki Accords)(Aug. 1975), 14 I.L.M. 1292 (1975).

Convention Concerning the Laws and Customs of War on Land, Hague Convention IV, October 18, 1907, 36 Stat 2277, TS 539

Convention on the International Right of Correction, 435 U.N.T.S. 191 (Aug. 24, 1962).

Convention on Offenses and Certain Other Acts Committed on Board Aircraft, Sept. 14, 1963, 20 U.S.T. 2941, T.I.A.S. 6768, 704 U.N.T.S. 219 (Tokyo Convention).

Convention on the Prevention and Punishment of the Crime of Genocide, Dec. 9, 1948, 78 U.N.T.S. 277 (entered into force for the United States 1989).

Convention on the Prevention and Punishment of Crimes Against Internationally Protected Persons, Including Diplomatic Agents, Dec. 14, 1973, 28 U.S.T. 1975, T.I.A.S. 8352.

Convention on the Privileges and Immunities of the United Nations, 21 U.S.T. 1418, T.I.A.S. 6900, 1 U.N.T.S. 16 (1946).

Convention to Punish Acts of Terrorism Taking the Form of Crimes against Persons and Related Extortion That Are of International Significance (OAS), Feb. 2, 1971, 27 U.S.T. 3949, T.I.A.S. 8413.

Convention for Suppression of Unlawful Acts against the Safety of Civil Aviation (Montreal Convention), Sept. 23, 1971, 24 U.S.T. 565, T.I.A.S. 7570, 974 U.N.T.S. 177.

Convention for Suppression of Unlawful Seizure of Aircraft (Hague Convention), Dec. 16. 1970, 22 U.S.T. 1641, T.I.A.S. 7192, 860 U.N.T.S. 105.

The European Agreement for the Prevention of Broadcasts Transmitted From Stations Outside National Territories, 634 U.N.T.S. 239, 59 A.J.I.L. 715 (1965).

International Convention against the Taking of Hostages, Dec. 17, 1979, 34 U.N. GAOR Supp. (No. 39) at 23, U.N. Doc. A/34/39.

International Convention concerning the Use of Broadcasting in the Cause of Peace, Sept. 23, 1936, U.N.T.S. 29 (1938), 32 Am. J. Int'l. Supp. 113.

The International Telecommunication Convention, Nairobi, 1982, United States Senate Treaty Doc. 99-6, 99th Cong., 1st sess. (1985).

Protocol Additional to the Geneva Conventions of 12 August 1949, and Relating to the Protection of Victims of International Armed Conflicts (Protocol I), 1125 U.N.T.S. 3 (1977).

Protocol Additional to the Geneva Conventions of 12 August 1949, and Relating to the Protection of Victims of Non-International Armed Conflicts (Protocol II), 1125 U.N.T.S. 609 (1977).

United Nations Convention on the Law of the Sea, Dec. 10, 1982, 21 I.L.M. 1261.

Vienna Convention on Consular Relations, April 24, 1963, 21 U.S.T. 77, T.I.A.S. 6820, 596 U.N.T.S. 261.

Vienna Convention on Diplomatic Relations, April 18, 1961, 23 U.S.T. 3227, T.I.A.S. 7502, 500 U.N.T.S. 95.

### 5. INTERNATIONAL CASE LAW

Case concerning the Air Services Agreement of 27 March 1946 between the United States of America and France (U.S. v. France), 18 R. Int'l Arb. Awards 417 (1978).

Case Concerning Right of Passage over Indian Territory (merits)(India v. Portugal), 1960 I.C.J. 6.

Case Concerning United States Diplomatic and Consular Staff in Iran, (U.S. v. Iran), 1980 I.C.J. 3.

The Corfu Channel Case (United Kingdom v. Albania) 1949 I.C.J. 4.

Fisheries Jurisdiction (U.K. v. Ice.), 1974 I.C.J. 3 (Judgment).

Military and Paramilitary Activities in and Against Nicaragua (Nicaragua v. United States), 1986 I.C.J. 1 (merits).

New Zealand v. France, International Arbitration Award of the Tribunal, 30 Apr. 1990.

Nuclear Tests Case (Australia v. France), 1973 I.C.J. 98 (Request for the Indication of Interim Measures Protection).

Nuclear Tests Case (Australia v. France), 1974 I.C.J. 252 (Judgment).

Responsibility of Germany for acts committed subsequent to 31 July 1914 and before Portugal entered into the War ("Cysne" case), 2 R. Int'l Arb. Awards 1035 (1930).

Responsibility of Germany for damage caused in the Portuguese colonies in the South of Africa (Naulilaa Incident), 2 R. Int'l Arb. Awards 1011 (1928).

Tribunal Arbitral Pour La Determination de La Frontiere Maritime (Guinea-Bissau v. Senegal), 1990 Affaire Relative a la Sentence Arbitrale du 31 Juillet 1989, Annexe 23 Aout 1989, [1989] I.C.J.

## 6. SELECT BOOKS ON INTELLIGENCE, COVERT ACTION, AND LAW

P. Agee, *Inside the Company: CIA Diary* (1976).

P. Agee, *On the Run* (1987).

G. Allison, *Essence of Decision: Explaining the Cuban Missile Crisis* (1971).

American Bar Association, Standing Committee on Law and National Security, *Oversight and Accountability of the U.S. Intelligence Agencies: An Evaluation* (1985).

*Armed Conflict and the New Law* (M. Meyer ed. 1989).

*Article 19 World Report 1988* (K. Boyle ed. 1988).

J. Barron, *KGB* (1974).

J. Barron, *KGB Today: The Hidden Hand* (1983).

M. Beck, *Secret Contenders: The Myth of Cold War Counterintelligence* (1984).

C. Beckwith & D. Knox, *Delta Force* (1983).

B. Berkowitz & A. Goodman, *Strategic Intelligence for American National Security* (1989).

L. Bittman, *The KGB and Disinformation: An Insiders View* (1985).

B. Blechman & S. Kaplan, *Force without War: U.S. Armed Forces as a Political Instrument* (1978)(see the Appendix for a list of 215 incidents involving the use of United States armed forces as a political instrument, 1946–1975.)

J. Bloch & P. Fitzgerald, *British Intelligence and Covert Action: Africa, Middle East and Europe since 1945* (1983).

W. Blum, *The CIA, A Forgotten History* (1986).

S. Breckinridge, *The CIA and the U.S. Intelligence System* (1986).

*The Central Intelligence Agency* (W. Leary ed. 1984).

R. Cline, *The CIA under Reagan, Bush, and Casey* (1983).

W. Colby, *Honorable Men: My Life in the CIA* (1978).

E. Corwin, *The President: Office and Powers, 1787–1984* (5th ed. 1984).

N. Davis, *The Last Two Years of Salvador Allende* (1985).

W. Davison, *International Political Communication* (1965).

J. Dinges & S. Landau, *Assassination on Embassy Row* (1980).

S. Emerson, *Secret Warriors: Inside the Covert Military Operations of the Reagan Era* (1988).

*Facts on File* (for the years 1953, 1960, 1961, 1962, 1973, 1974, 1980, 1981, 1982, 1986, 1987.

*The Federalist Papers* (C. Rossiter ed. 1961).

B. Ferencz, *Defining International Aggression* (1975).

K. Follett, *On the Wings of Eagles* (1983).

M. Ganji, *International Protection of Human Rights* (1962).

E. Herman, *Demonstration Elections: U.S. Staged Elections in the Dominican Republic, Vietnam, and El Salvador* (1984).

R. Holt, *Radio Free Europe* (1958).

G. Hufbauer, J. Schott, & K. Elliott, *Economic Sanctions Reconsidered: History and Current Policy* (1985).

*Humanitarian Intervention and the United Nations* (R. Lillich ed. 1973).

*Intelligence Requirements for the 1980s: Covert Action* (R. Godson ed. 1981).

*Intelligence Requirements for the 1990s: Covert Action* (R. Godson ed. 1989).

I. Janis, *Groupthink* (2d ed. 1982).

I. Janis, *Victims of Groupthink: A Psychological Study of Foreign Policy Decisions and Fiascos* (1972).

M. Jensen-Stevenson & W. Stevenson, *Kiss the Boys Goodbye* (1990).

L. Johnson, *America's Secret Power: The CIA in a Democratic Society* (1989).

F. Kalshoven, *Belligerent Reprisals* (1971).

*Keesings Contemporary Archives* (for the years 1959–1960, 1961, 1962, 1986, 1987).

N. Khrushchev, *Khrushchev Remembers* (1970).

S. Knott, Historical and Legal Foundation of American Intelligence Activities (1990) (unpublished dissertation).

H. Koh, *The National Security Constitution* (1990).

*Law and Civil War in the Modern World* (J. Moore ed. 1974).

G. Levitt, *Democracies against Terror* (1988).

G. McClanahan, *Diplomatic Immunity* (1989).

M. McDougal & F. Feliciano, *Law and Minimum World Public Order* (1961).

V. Marchetti & J. Marks, *The CIA and the Cult of Intelligence* (1974).

R. Medvedev, *Khrushchev* (1982).

C. Meyer, *Facing Reality: From World Federalism to the CIA* (1980).

S. Mickelson, *America's Other Voice: The Story of Radio Free Europe and Radio Liberty* (1983).

J. Moore, *Law and the Indo-China War* (1972).

B. Murty, *The International Law of Propaganda* (1989).

S. Neumann, *Permanent Revolution: Totalitarianism in the Age of International Civil War* (2d ed. 1965).

J. Paust & A. Blaustein, *The Arab Oil Weapon* (1977).

J. Persico, *Casey: From the OSS to the CIA* (1990).

D. Phillips, *The Night Watch* (1977).

T. Powers, *The Man Who Kept the Secrets: Richard Helms and the CIA* (1979).

J. Prados, *President's Secret Wars: CIA and Pentagon Covert Operations since World War II* (1986).

J. Ranelagh, *The Agency: The Rise and Decline of the CIA* (1986).

W. Reisman, *Folded Lies: Bribery, Crusades and Reforms* (1979).

W. Reisman & A. Willard, *International Incidents* (1988).

*Restatement (Third) of Foreign Relations Law of the United States* (1987).

J. Richelson, *The U.S. Intelligence Community* (2d ed. 1989).

C. Robbins, *Air America* (1978).

R. Rocca & J. Dziak, *Bibliography on Soviet Intelligence and Security Services* (1985).

A. Roosevelt, *For Lust of Knowing: Memoirs of an Intelligence Officer* (1988).

K. Roosevelt, *Countercoup: The Struggle for the Control of Iran* (1979).

H. Rositzke, *The CIA's Secret Operations* (reprint 1988).

P. Ryan, *The Iranian Hostage Mission* (1985).

A. Schlesinger, *A Thousand Days* (1965).

R. Shultz & R. Godson, *Dezinformatsia: Active Measures in Soviet Strategy* (1984).

G. Sick, *All Fall Down: America's Tragic Encounter with Iran* (1985).

J. Smith, *Portrait of a Cold Warrior* (1976).

F. Snepp, *Decent Interval* (1977).

A. Sofaer, *War, Foreign Affairs and Constitutional Power* (1976).

T. Sorensen, *Kennedy* (1965).

J. Stockwell, *In Search of Enemies: A CIA Story* (1978).

A. Taheri, *Holy Terror: Inside the World of Islamic Terrorism* (1987).

F. Teson, *Humanitarian Intervention: An Inquiry into Law and Morality* (1988).

G. Treverton, *Covert Action: The Limits of Intervention in the Postwar World* (1987).

*The Trial of German Major War Criminals: Proceedings of the International Military Tribunal Sitting at Nuremberg Germany* (1950).

S. Turner, *Secrecy and Democracy: The CIA in Transition* (1985).

J. Tyson, *International Broadcasting and National Security* (1983).

W. Weyrauch, *Gestapo V-Leute: Tatsachen und Theorie des Geheimdienstes Untersuchungen zur Geheimen Staatspolizei waehrend der nationalsozialistischen Herrschaft* (1989).

J. Whitton & A. Larson, *Propaganda: Towards Disarmament in the War of Words* (1963).

B. Woodward, *Veil: The Secret Wars of the CIA 1981–1987* (1987).

P. Wright, *Spycatcher* (1987).

*The Writings of James Madison* (G. Hunt ed. 1969).

P. Wyden, *Bay of Pigs* (1979).

E. Zoller, *Peacetime Unilateral Remedies* (1984).

## 7. SELECT ARTICLES ON INTELLIGENCE, COVERT ACTION, AND LAW

Arsanjani, Survey of State Practice and Doctrine on Counter-Measures, unpublished paper prepared for the United Nations Secretariat, Codification Division (1989).

Bayzelr, *Reexamining the Doctrine of Humanitarian Intervention in Light of the Atrocities in Kampuchea and Ethiopia,* 23 Stan. J. Int'l L. 547 (1987).

Beitz, *Covert Intervention as a Moral Problem,* 3 Ethics and Int'l Aff. 45 (1989).

Bowett, *Reprisals Involving Recourse to Armed Force,* 66 Am. J. Int'l L. 1 (1972).

Bruemmer & Silverberg, *The Impact of the Iran-Contra Matter on Congressional Oversight of the CIA,* 11 Hous. J. Int'l L. 219 (Fall 1988).

Damrosch, *Retaliation or Arbitration—or Both? The 1978 United States–France Aviation Dispute,* 74 Am. J. Int'l L. 785 (1980).

Eisold, The Rainbow Warrior Incident, unpublished student paper (1989).

Falk, *American Intervention in Cuba and the Rule of Law,* 22 Ohio St. L. J. 546 (1961).

Feith, *Law in the Service of Terror: The Strange Case of the Additional Protocol,* National Interest 36 (Fall 1985).

Franck & Rodley, *After Bangladesh: The Law of Humanitarian Intervention by Military Force,* 67 Am. J. Int'l L. 275 (1973)

Gasser, *An Appeal for Ratification by the United States,* 81 Am. J. Int'l L. 910 (1987).

Gates, *The CIA and American Foreign Policy,* 66 For. Aff. 215 (1987/88).

Gorove, *The Geostationary Orbit: Issues of Law and Policy,* 73 Am. J. Int'l L. 444 (1979).

Halperin, *American Military Intervention: Is It Ever Justified,* 228 Nation 668 (1979).

Hamilton, *The Role of Intelligence in the Foreign Policy Process,* Essays on Strategy and Diplomacy No. 9, Keck Center for International Strategic Studies (1987).

Iga & Auurbach, *Political Corruption and Social Structure in Japan,* 17 Asian Survey 556 (1977).

Johnson, *Controlling the CIA: A Critique of Current Safeguards,* 12 H. J. L. & Pub. Pol. 371 (1989).

Johnson, *Making Things Happen,* London Review of Books (Sept. 6–9, 1984).

Kalshoven, Belligerent Reprisals Revisited (1990) (unpublished paper).

*Legal and Policy Issues in the Iran-Contra Affair: Intelligence Oversight in a Democracy,* Symposium, 11 Hous. J. Int'l L. (1988).

Lobel, *Covert War and Congressional Authority: Hidden War and Forgotten Power,* 134 U. Pa. L. Rev. 1035 (1986).

MacDonald, *The Nicaragua Case: New Answers to Old Questions?,* 24 Can. Y.B. Int'l L. 127 (1986).

McDougal, *The Soviet-Cuban Quarantine and Self-Defense,* 57 Am. J. Int'l L. 597 (1963).

McDougal, Lasswell, & Reisman, *The World Constitutive Process of Authoritative Decision,* 19 J. Legal Ed. 253 (1967).

Malamut, *Aviation: Suspension of Landing Rights of Polish Airlines in the United States,* 24 H. Int'l L. J. 190 (1983).

Meeker, *Defensive Quarantine and the Law,* 57 Am. J. Int'l L. 515 (1963).

Mill, *A Few Words on Non-Intervention,* Fraser's Magazine (Dec. 1859)(republished among other places in *The Vietnam War and International Law* (Falk ed. 1968)).

Note, *The Rainbow Warrior Affair: State and Agent Responsibility for Authorized Violations of International Law,* 5 B.U. Int'l L. J. 398 (1987).

*Panel: Cuban Quarantine: Implications for the Future,* 57 Am. Soc. Int'l L. 1 (1963).

Parry, *Defining Economic Coercion in International Law,* 12 Tex. Int'l L. J. 3 (1977).

Paust, *Responding Lawfully to International Terrorism: The Use of Force Abroad*, 8 Whittier L. Rev. 711 (1986).

Paust & Blaustein, *The Arab Oil Weapon—A Threat to International Peace*, 68 Am. J. Int'l L. 410 (1974).

Reisman, *International Law-Making: A Process of Communication*, Lasswell Memorial Lecture, American Society of International Law, Apr. 24, 1981, Proceedings of the A.S.I.L. 101 (1981).

Reisman, *No Man's Land: International Legal Regulation of Coercive Responses to Protracted and Low Level Conflict*, 11 Hous. J. Int'l L. 317 (Spring 1989).

Reisman, *Old Wine in New Bottles: The Reagan and Brezhnev Doctrines in Contemporary International Law and Practice*, 13 Y. J. Int'l L. 171 (1988).

Reisman, *Private Armies in a Global War System: Prologue to Decision*, 14 Va. J. Int'l L. 1 (1973).

Reisman, *The Tormented Conscience: Applying and Appraising Unauthorized Coercion*, 32 Emory L. J. 499 (1983).

Reisman & Freedman, *The Plaintiff's Dilemma: Illegally Obtained Evidence and Admissibility in International Adjudication*, 76 Am. J. Int'l L. 739 (1982).

Reisman, et al., *The Formulation of General International Law*, 2 Am. J. Int'l L. & Pol'y 448 (1987).

Roberts, *The New Rules for Waging War: The Case against Ratification of the Additional Protocol I*, 26 Va. J. Int'l L. 109 (1985).

Schachter, *The Right of States to Use Armed Force*, 82 Mich. L. Rev. 1620 (1984).

Seidl-Hohenveldern, *The United Nations and Economic Coercion*, 18 Belgian Rev. Int'l L. 9 (1984–1985).

Sheffer, *U.S. Law and the Iran-Contra Affair*, 81 Am. J. Int'l L. 696 (1987).

Shihata, *Destination Embargo of Arab Oil: Its Legality under International Law*, 68 Am. J. Int'l L. 591 (1974).

Singer, *Commitments, Capabilities and US Security Policies in the 1980s*, 9 Parameters 27 (No. 2, 1979).

Skubiszwski, *Use of Force by States, Collective Security, Law of War and Neutrality*, in *Manual of Public International Law* 755 (Sorensen ed. 1968).

Suzuki, *Extraconstitutional Change and World Public Order: A Prologue to Decision-Making*, 15 Hous. L. R. 23 (1977).

*Use of Nonviolent Coercion: A Study in Legality under Article 2(4) of the Charter of the United Nations* (Comment), 122 U. Pa. L. Rev. 983 (1974).

Van Houtte, *Treaty Protection against Economic Sanctions*, 18 Belgian R. Int'l L. 34 (1984–1985).

Webster, *The Role of Intelligence in a Free Society*, 43 U. Miami L. Rev. 155 (1988).

Wright, *The Crime of "War-Mongering,"* 42 Am. J. Int'l L. 128 (1948).

Wright, *The Cuban Quarantine*, 57 Am. J. Int'l L. 546 (1963).

Wright, *Intervention and Cuba in 1961*, 55 Am. Soc. Int'l L. Proc. 2 (1961).

# Index

Accountability, 120–23, 187*n*38
*Achille Lauro*, 87
Aeroflot, 112
Afghanistan, 65, 75, 112–13, 128
African National Congress (ANC), 82, 83, 86
Aggression, 40, 79–80, 81–82, 84, 93, 173*n*6. *See also* Armed attack; Self-defense
*Air Services Award*, 91, 93–95, 114, 176–77*nn*25–26
Air Transport Agreement (*1972*), 112
Albania, 92
Algeria, 109
Allende, Salvador, 59, 60, 72
Alliance for Progress, 70
Alvarez-Machain, Humberto, 130, 134
ANC. *See* African National Congress
Anglo-Iranian Oil Company, 49
Angola, 86, 128
Arab League, 109
Argentina, 51–52, 54, 83, 104

Ariana Afghan Airlines, 112–13
Armed attack, 78, 79, 81, 82, 83–85, 97, 101, 114. *See also* Self-defense
Armed bands, 40, 79, 80, 83, 84
Arms sales, 29, 90
Assassination, 57–59, 69–71, 72, 126–27, 141
Australia, 66, 67
Austria, 65
Authority: central, and the use of force, 39–40; of Central Intelligence Agency, 124, 131, 191*n*55; and the constitutive process, 17–18, 19, 21, 23, 25; of United States Congress, 118, 121, 184*n*14; of United States Executive, 117–18, 120, 129, 131–34, 135, 143, 184*n*9
Authority, constitutional, 117–18. *See also* Constitution, United States
Authority, statutory, 118–19. *See also* Congress, United States